REASONS, RESPECT, AND THE LAW

This is a book about law and its impact in our practical reasoning.

Drawing from Bernard Williams, the book argues that our practical engagements with the law are complex and often obscure. It begins with a novel view on practical reason that is called open-minded reasons internalism. This is a view that emphasises how certain considerations can bear on action for concrete agents, and in doing so it is an explanatory account of reasons and actions. The account is receptive to the considerations that makes much of people's lives: the motivations and dispositions they have, the notions of character and identity, and respect.

The book claims that this account helps in making sense of much of the richness seen in real life in how concrete agents engage with the law. It provides the tools to explain when and why an agent identifies herself totally with the law, as Inspector Javert did in *Les Misérables*, but it can also explain the attitude of respect that many law-abiding citizens have, and even the merely prudential considerations of OW Holmes' famous 'bad man'. What emerges from this book is a view on law and practical reason that takes seriously the phenomenology of action.

This book will be of interest to anyone interested in philosophical accounts of how we engage our practical reasoning with complex social practices.

Volume 20 in the series Law and Practical Reason

Law and Practical Reason

The intention of this series is that it should encompass monographs and collections of essays that address the fundamental issues in legal philosophy. The foci are conceptual and normative in character, not empirical. Studies addressing the idea of law as a species of practical reason are especially welcome. Recognising that there is no occasion to sharply distinguish analytic and systematic work in the field from historico-critical research, the editors also welcome studies in the history of legal philosophy. Contributions to the series, inevitably crossing disciplinary lines, will be of interest to students and professionals in moral, political, and legal philosophy.

Recent titles in the series

Volume 8: Private Law and the Value of Choice
Emmanuel Voyiakis

Volume 9: Freedom and Force: Essays on Kant's Legal Philosophy
Edited by Sari Kisilevsky and Martin J Stone

Volume 10: The Nature and Value of Vagueness in the Law
Hrafn Asgeirsson

Volume 11: Law's Humility: Enlarging the Scope of Jurisprudential Disagreement
Triantafyllos Gkouvas

Volume 12: Rightful Relations with Distant Strangers: Kant, the EU, and the Wider World
Aravind Ganesh

Volume 13: The Making of Constitutional Democracy: From Creation to Application of Law
Paolo Sandro

Volume 14: New Essays on the Nature of Legal Reasoning
Edited by Mark McBride and James Penner

Volume 15: New Essays on the Fish-Dworkin Debate
Edited by Thomas Bustamante and Margaret Martin

Volume 16: A Dynamic Approach to Hans Kelsen's General Theory of Norms
Monika Zalewska

Volume 17: Moral Responsibility and Artificial Intelligence
Maximilian Kiener

Volume 18: Bernard Williams on Law and Jurisprudence: From Agency and Responsibility to Methodology
Edited by Daniel Peixoto Murata, Julieta A Rabanos and Veronica Rodriguez-Blanco

Volume 19: The Concept of Legal Personhood: What the Mind Reveals About Law
Claudio Novelli

Volume 20: Reasons, Respect, and the Law: Jurisprudence as Practical Philosophy
Daniel Peixoto Murata

Reasons, Respect, and the Law

Jurisprudence as Practical Philosophy

Daniel Peixoto Murata

•HART•
OXFORD • LONDON • NEW YORK • NEW DELHI • SYDNEY

HART PUBLISHING

Bloomsbury Publishing Plc

Kemp House, Chawley Park, Cumnor Hill, Oxford, OX2 9PH, UK

1385 Broadway, New York, NY 10018, USA

Bloomsbury Publishing Ireland Limited, 29 Earlsfort Terrace, Dublin 2, D02 AY28, Ireland

HART PUBLISHING, the Hart/Stag logo, BLOOMSBURY and the Diana logo are trademarks of Bloomsbury Publishing Plc

First published in Great Britain 2026

A catalogue record for this book is available from the British Library.

A catalogue record for this book is available from the Library of Congress.

ISBN: HB: 978-1-50996-885-5
ePDF: 978-1-50996-887-9
ePub: 978-1-50996-888-6

Typeset by Compuscript Ltd, Shannon

For product safety related questions contact productsafety@bloomsbury.com

To find out more about our authors and books visit www.hartpublishing.co.uk. Here you will find extracts, author information, details of forthcoming events and the option to sign up for our newsletters.

ACKNOWLEDGEMENTS

This book expands and revisits substantially the PhD thesis that I developed at the University of Surrey from 2019 to 2022. It is also more a fruit of good fortune than of anything else. Firstly, I had the good fortune of having an understanding family. Secondly, the good fortune of a loving and supportive partner, Laís, who encouraged me all along. Thirdly, the good fortune of having the best supervisors one could ask for. Stephen Bero and Hrafn Asgeirsson helped me every step of the way, and I am pretty sure that the number of research reports, pre-drafts, drafts, long versions, edited versions, provisional versions, final versions, and final-final versions that I have sent them during the PhD programme amounts to a human rights violation.

I have benefitted greatly from the careful reading of Veronica Rodriguez-Blanco, Kenneth Ehrenberg and Claudio Michelon, who were the original examiners of the thesis and ongoing partners in academic dialogue. I am also immensely grateful for the feedback and advice I received from Alex Sarch, Ambrose Lee, Bebhinn Donnelly-Lazarov, Chris Taggart, Dennis Patterson, Ira Lindsay and Marie Newhouse, all members of the Surrey Centre for Law and Philosophy. George Pavlakos, from Glasgow, and the editor of the *Law and Practical Reason Series*, was an enthusiastic supporter of this project and of my academic career in general. The same is true for Ronaldo Macedo, from the University of São Paulo and my Masters supervisor. Ronaldo taught a course about Bernard Williams in 2016 that was a main source of inspiration for this book. Caio Ribeiro, Gilberto Morbach, Luana Li, Marco Alberto and Natan Carbone read and commented on excerpts of this book. I am grateful to their commentaries.

Parts of the fifth chapter originally appeared in 'Obligations Beyond Morality: A Critique of Ronald Dworkin's View on Legal Normativity' (2022) 16(2) *Revista Direito Mackenzie* 1. I would like to express my gratitude in relation to the original publisher for allowing me to reutilise those materials.

The thesis that was the basis for this book was possible thanks to the funding provided by the Faculty of Arts and Social Sciences of the University of Surrey. This book, in turn, was possible thanks to the support of the São Paulo Research Foundation – FAPESP (proc. n. 2022/11660-0) during my postdoctoral studies at the University of São Paulo. I also greatly benefitted from the generosity of the Faculty of Laws of the University College London (UCL), where I was an Early Career Visiting Fellow in 2026.

CONTENTS

1

Law, Normativity, and Respect: An Overview

I. Antigone's Defiance

KREON
And still you dared to violate the law?
ANTIGONE
I did. It wasn't *Zeus* who issued me
this order. And justice – who lives below –
was not involved. They'd never condone it!
I deny that your edicts – since *you*, a mere man,
Imposed them – have the force to trample on
the god's unwritten and infallible laws.
Their laws are not ephemeral – they weren't
made yesterday. They will rule forever.
No man knows how far back in time they go.
I'd never let any man's arrogance
bully me into breaking the gods' laws.[1]

Legal theorists are drawn to a reading of the above excerpt in the sense that the debate between Kreon, king of Thebes, and Antigone is a prelude to the debate between legal positivism and Natural Law. Antigone's own language invites that reading: she contrasts Kreon's decree against the laws of the gods, a comparison that is supposed to make the king's command devoid of authority. This common view seems to me somewhat misguided. As Robert Bagg points out, Kreon himself also invokes the laws of the gods as a justification for his decree.[2] There are many moments in which this kind of appeal is evident. Kreon claims that he 'will never tolerate giving a bad man more respect than a good one',[3] and that he acts according to the will of Zeus.[4] The most evident invocation of divine

[1] Sophocles, 'Antigone' lines 449–461. I am here using the following edition: *The Complete Plays of Sophocles – A New Translation*, translated by Robert Bagg and James Scully (London, Harper Perennial, 2011).

[2] R Bagg, 'Introduction "From what kind of parents was I born?"' in *The Complete Plays of Sophocles – A New Translation*, translated by R Bagg and J Scully (London, Harper Perennial, 2011) 623–24.

[3] Sophocles, 'Antigone' lines 206–10.

[4] ibid lines 302–09.

law by Kreon occurs, indeed, in his debate with Antigone.[5] Kreon attempts to ground his authority not on positive law, but on the same sources that Antigone mobilises.

Nonetheless, I believe that legal philosophy has much to learn from the exchange between Antigone and Kreon. It nicely illustrates what I take to be one of the most important aspects of law, the idea that law interacts with our reasons to do or not to do something. Antigone claims that she 'ought not to obey the law *because* …' and Kreon retorts that 'she ought to obey the law *because* …', and even though the threat of a sanction is lurking behind the whole discussion and is ultimately carried to its bloody consequences in the play, sanction in itself plays almost no role in their argumentative exchange. Both Kreon and Antigone share the premise that the law – whatever its content – is certainly more than a matter of sanctions and prudential reasons. They agree that the law is the kind of thing that demands respect from those subject to it, and more generally, that the law can give people reasons for action according to it. In more technical jargon, what their exchange illustrates is the *relationship between law and practical reason*, that is, between legal directives and what an agent concludes that she ought to do. Law, like many other social practices, has an influence in our lives, and this influence can be deadly, as it was in Antigone's case. Law affects our balance of reasons. Why this happens, and how, is what is underdetermined. I will refer to the ways in which law can interact with our practical reason as the *reason-giving character of the law* or as the *normativity of law*. This is going to be the general topic of this book.

At this early stage, I believe that a summary of the claims I am going to develop in the book is in order. This summary is very schematic by necessity, but hopefully by the end of this chapter the reader will have a sense of where I am going. The view I am going to present takes as one of its starting points the fact that there can be reasons for action that arise from the attachments, projects, dispositions, and so on of individuals. This first starting point has been developed by Bernard Williams in his famous discussion about 'reasons internalism' and the 'subjective motivational sets' of individuals. Once we recognise that the world of reasons for action is not reducible to moral or prudential reasons, we can better understand what it means for law to be reason-giving. The other starting point, that I am adapting from John Deigh and Joseph Raz, is that it is a characteristic feature of law that it demands *respect* from its subjects. The law, at least as we know it, involves more than just threats and sanctions. Any account of legal normativity must pay attention to this fact if it wants to move beyond very general considerations about normativity in general.

Taken together, those two points mean that any account of the reason-giving character of the law must explain what it means for law to demand respect, and how concrete agents with subjective motivational sets can recognise this demand. Notions of respect in general, identification, and character will all play

[5] ibid lines 446–526.

a role in a thicker explanation of the reason-giving character of the law. The picture that emerges is one in which there are many layers to the reason-giving character of the law that depend on the emotional relationship between the individual and the law. There will be a layer in which respect is understood in what I take to be the thickest possible sense, as identification of the agent with the law; a layer in which there is a sense of respect in which we have at least some reasons to not offend against the respected object (eg, the law); and so on. There are significant advantages in the proposed picture. Firstly, it avoids the distorting dichotomy between moral and prudential reasons in the law. Secondly, it is compatible with influential views on legal normativity, such as Joseph Raz's and David Enoch's, but at the same time is independent of those views. Thirdly, and to my mind more importantly, it makes sense of legal normativity in a way that is more faithful to the first-person standpoint of agents. My purpose is to provide an account of legal normativity that is faithful to the phenomenology of action.

In this chapter, I will try to make the terms of my inquiry a bit clearer. This will be done mostly in the next section. I will start the next section by narrowing down the sense of normativity I am interested in. This will be followed by a presentation of the two main claims underlying this book: the claim that individuals have dispositions, values, motivations, and so on and that those things play an important role in practical deliberation; and the claim that the law, given its role in a broader narrative of political rule, characteristically demands respect from those subject to it. The second sub-section discusses Williams' view on philosophy in general and his idea of 'making sense' of things. This discussion is important because it explains what kind of philosophical project is the one that I am engaging with. This book is, essentially, a Williamsian account of legal normativity. The third and final sub-section tries to locate my arguments in the context of David Enoch's recent and influential discussion of legal normativity and provides some commentary on the possible readings of the book. With all my cards on the table, I will present a rough sketch of the whole book in the last section of this chapter.

II. The Terms of the Inquiry

A. Locating the Relevant Sense of Normativity

What does it mean to say that the law is normative or capable of giving reasons for action? I will begin by explaining what I do *not* mean by those terms so I can put those other senses aside. A first sense in which we can say that law is normative merely means that legal theory is committed to norms of theory-making. One theory is better than another, we might say, if this theory manages to explain the same phenomena using simpler terms, or if it can account for explanatory deficits of rival theories, etc.[6] This sense of normativity can be seen at work when HLA Hart presents his legal theory as a better model than Austin's because of its explanatory power. Hart's theory, it is argued, can explain important features of the law that are overlooked by Austin's. This sense of normativity is quite trivial and shared by all theoretical enquiries.

We can find a second sense in which we talk about normativity in the debates about whether legal theory is a branch of moral or political philosophy or is influenced by it. Those who claim that legal theory is normative in this sense mean that a theory is better than others in case it presents law in more attractive terms morally speaking.[7] The example here is the difference between those that are sometimes called methodological positivists and those called normative positivists.[8] The methodological positivist claims that we can better describe law if we depict it as a matter of social facts, whereas the normative positivist claims that the law understood as a matter of social facts is the best – morally speaking – understanding of law because it fosters democracy or legitimacy or something of that sort.

Those two senses of normativity share a common trait. They relate to the normativity of *theoretical inquiry*. They are about the ways in which we can discuss and evaluate the adequacy of a legal theory. Like any other kind of theory, legal theory is constrained by the norms of theory-making such as consistency and clarity. Differently from what happens with theories of physics or chemistry, however, there is debate as to whether moral considerations can make a legal theory adequate or inadequate.[9] What interests us here for our purposes is that those senses of normativity usually are not reason-giving, that is, they do not provide reasons *for action* for agents. To be more precise, they can only provide reasons for action in a very limited, conditional way. If I am a legal theorist trying to craft a novel account of law, then I ought to abide by those norms. They provide reasons for me in this specific scenario.

The sense in which law is normative or reason-giving that I am interested in is the one behind Sylvie Delacroix's highly quotable remark: 'If law constrains us, if it somehow has a claim on our conduct or judgment, it cannot be out of mere habit or fear of sanctions.'[10] Andrei Marmor emphasises the same point by saying that

[6] See, for instance, J Coleman, *The Practice of Principle* (Oxford, Oxford University Press, 2001) 177–78; J Dickson, *Evaluation and Legal Theory* (Oxford, Hart Publishing, 2001).

[7] Julie Dickson refers to this as the 'beneficial moral consequences thesis'. See Dickson, *Evaluation and Legal Theory* (2001).

[8] See S Perry, 'Interpretation and Methodology in Legal Theory' in A Marmor (ed), *Law and Interpretation* (Oxford, Clarendon Press, 1995). See also the debate between Dickson, *Evaluation and Legal Theory* (2001) chs 5 and 6; and F Schauer, 'Positivism as Pariah' in R George (ed), *The Autonomy of Law* (Oxford, Clarendon Press, 1999); F Schauer, 'The Social Construction of the Concept of Law: A Reply to Julie Dickson' (2005) 25(3) *Oxford Journal of Legal Studies* 493.

[9] Versions of this debate also appear in moral and political philosophy. One can wonder if meta-ethics influences a theory of ethics, or if moral considerations can make a political theory wrong.

[10] S Delacroix, 'Tracing a Genealogy of Legal Normativity: Responsibility, Authorship and Contingency' in S Bertea and G Pavlakos (eds), *New Essays on the Normativity of Law* (Oxford, Hart Publishing, 2011) 310.

the problem of law's normativity is 'the question of how to explain this obligatory or binding element of legal norms'.[11] To put this in my own words, I am interested in how the law affects our practical reasoning, that is, our deliberative processes about what we ought to do.[12] This is done in terms of reasons for action, but what those reasons are, what their power, scope, and origin are – all those matters are radically underdetermined.[13]

Many authors have tried to shed some light on the obscurity just mentioned. Natural lawyers have argued that law is somehow connected or derived from morality, which they usually took to be objective, and thus law was able to provide an agent with moral reasons for its obedience. *Lex iniusta non est lex* was the classic Augustinian formulation of this, an idea that has been further developed in the twentieth century by authors such as Gustav Radbruch[14] (although we should bear in mind that the Augustinian formulation should not be understood too literally). We can see both Antigone and Kreon attempting arguments of this style when they try to track their understanding of the law in the laws of the gods. The Austrian legal theorist Hans Kelsen, sceptical about the objectivity of morals, wanted to make a science out of jurisprudence, and in his attempt to do so he postulated a 'legal point of view' from which legal statements provide valid legal reasons for action.[15] In Kelsen's view, the reasons for action provided by law are conditional, they depend on the acceptance of the legal point of view.[16]

It was HLA Hart – an author that will be the protagonist of much of this book – that provided us with what I take to be the most useful frame for this matter, albeit one that will demand much additional work later. Taking issue with models of law that revolved around sanctions, notably Austin's, Hart tried to explain how law could involve more than prudential considerations to avoid punishment.

[11] A Marmor, *Philosophy of Law* (Princeton, Princeton University Press, 2011) 57.

[12] Michael Giudice offers an excellent reconstruction of the state of the art regarding the philosophy of legal normativity. Giudice proposes a 'pluralistic approach' to legal normativity and distinguishes three different kinds of inquiry related to it, 'conceptual or analytical', 'evaluative', and 'empirical'. To this tripartite distinction he adds that '[t]here are, of course, relations between these categories, but such relations are compatible with their distinctness. Most importantly, collapsing one approach into another is to be avoided; they are each irreducibly basic'. See M Giudice, *The Normativity of Law* (Cambridge, Cambridge University Press, 2024) 3. I am very sympathetic to this form of pluralism regarding legal normativity, but I would resist the stark distinctions between those three kinds of inquiry. The reasons for this will become clearer as the book progresses, but to anticipate, my reasons to be suspicious about any stark distinction are due to my account of practical reason and my own framing of the problem of normativity, which is first-personal.

[13] Brian Bix frames the question in a succinct, useful way: 'Does the law gives us reason for action?'. See B Bix, 'The Nature of Law and Reasons for Action' (2012) 5 *Problema* 399, 402.

[14] Radbruch's famous essay on this is his 'Statutory Lawlessness and Supra-Statutory Law' (2006) 26(1) *Oxford Journal of Legal Studies* 1. Later in the book I will discuss the work of more sophisticated natural lawyers, such as John Finnis and Christopher Tollefsen.

[15] H Kelsen, *Introduction to the Problems of Legal Theory – A Translation of the First Edition of the Reine Rechtslehre or Pure Theory of Law*, trans B Paulson and S Paulson (Oxford, Clarendon Press, 1992).

[16] I am going to say more about the legal point of view in its more contemporary interpretations in the third chapter.

In Hart's terms, the Austinian view ignored a distinctive aspect of law: that the law is a rule-guided practice. In law, we abide by rules, break rules, and criticise ourselves and others for breaking rules. For Hart, the key idea for the understanding of social rules is the 'internal point of view', an attitude of acceptance of those rules as standards for evaluation and criticism of conduct; that is, it is *because* of such acceptance that those standards are *rules*. For those that accept the law from the internal point of view, law is a matter of reasons for action.[17] In a sense, Hart's project was an attempt to reduce legal reason-giving to an attitude from the agents towards the law.[18]

B. Two Central Claims

Hart wanted his method to be 'hermeneutic'. This meant for him a method that was supposed to depict social practices as they appeared to the agents engaged in those practices.[19] It seems fair to claim that Hart was concerned with the phenomenology of the rule-guided nature of law.[20] By bringing in the internal point of view and the role of attitudes in the explanation of it, Hart avoids the need for claims about law's legitimacy or morality. This is one of the reasons why I have claimed that Hart provides us with a satisfactory frame. Hart's account, however, is significantly incomplete. As Andrei Marmor rightly points out:

> Even if Hart is right that legal ought is reducible to facts about people's beliefs and attitudes, one would still have to give an account of what it is that people need to believe in order to make sense of attributing an 'ought' to the content of a legal directive.[21]

In this book, I will try to present an account of those beliefs and attitudes that Marmor demands. My strategy takes as its starting point two claims that I will present in schematic terms in this chapter but that will be further developed throughout the text.

The first claim is a development of Bernard Williams' views on philosophy and on practical reason: agents have dispositions, motivations, values, and so on that are central to their practical deliberations. Practical reason is not an exercise in which an overly abstract agent engages, but an exercise that belongs

[17] HLA Hart, *The Concept of Law*, 2nd edn (Oxford, Oxford University Press, 1994) chs 5 and 6; D Patterson, 'Explicating the Internal Point of View' (1999) 52 *Southern Methodist University Law Review* 67; SJ Shapiro, 'What Is the Internal Point of View' (2006) 75 *Fordham Law Review* 1157.

[18] Marmor, *Philosophy of Law* (2011) ch 2; Shapiro, 'What Is the Internal Point of View'; J Kaplan, 'Attitude and the Normativity of Law' (2017) 36 *Law and Philosophy* 469.

[19] HLA Hart, 'Introduction' in HLA Hart, *Essays in Jurisprudence and Philosophy* (Oxford, Clarendon Press, 1983) 13–14.

[20] For a different interpretation of Hart's project, one that downplays Hart's claims about the hermeneutical method but that emphasises his metaphysical commitments, see A Marmor, *Foundations of Institutional Reality* (Oxford, Oxford University Press, 2023).

[21] Marmor, *Philosophy of Law* (2011) 72. Marmor believes that Raz can address this challenge, and in his text, he goes on to explain why this is so. I will discuss Raz's arguments in the third and fourth chapters.

to contingent agents, with all their idiosyncrasies.[22] Insofar as an account of the reason-giving character of the law presupposes a view on the agent engaged in practical deliberation that does not pay attention to the diversity of dispositions and the like that concrete agents have, this account is bound to distort the phenomenon it purports to explain. This first claim will play an important role in all the chapters of the book but will be fully developed in the second chapter, where I will propose a revised version of reasons internalism that I will call *open-minded reasons internalism*.

The second claim is about a characteristic feature of law. Joseph Raz and John Deigh rightly point out, although in different ways, that the law as we know it demands respect from those subject to it.[23] Recall our brief discussion of Sophocles' *Antigone*. In that discussion, we saw that both Kreon and Antigone saw more in the law than just the threat of punishment. Hart was correct in his criticism of Austin's theory: an account of law centred in the idea of sanction is going to be a poor fit with reality. Nonetheless, Hart's treatment of law as a rule-guided practice is not enough as an account of the reason-giving character of the law as well. Adapting an idea from Deigh's arguments, we can say that it is characteristic of law that it plays a role in a broader narrative or story of political rule. As part of this broader narrative, the law demands respect from those subject to it, a point that, I think, was neatly captured by Raz's work on the topic. To understand how law can provide reasons for agents, we must understand what it means to say that the law demands their respect. This second claim will receive further refinement mostly in chapters three and four.

The combination of those two claims means that an account of the reason-giving character of the law must explain what it means for law to demand respect, and that an understanding of how it can demand respect demands a view on how concrete agents engage in practical reason, that is, it demands a view on the motivations, dispositions, and so on that agents have and that can bear on those matters. One way I find illuminating to think about those issues is to describe them as claims moving in two directions. We have a claim moving from the law towards the agents, the idea that the law characteristically demands respect from its subjects. This claim is supplemented by a claim moving from the agents towards the law that for the law's claim to be recognised, it must connect to what concrete agents care about or value, to their motivations, dispositions, and so on.

In a slightly different context, Veronica Rodriguez-Blanco has claimed that the mainstream views on legal authority have failed to account for the ways in which 'legal authority truly operates upon human beings as rational creatures with specific psychological make-ups' and defended a 'practical turn' in jurisprudence

[22] As examples of texts in which Williams presents this claim, see in general his papers in B Williams, *Moral Luck* (Cambridge, Cambridge University Press, 1981).

[23] J Deigh, 'Emotion and the Authority of Law' in J Deigh, *Emotions, Values and the Law* (Oxford, Oxford University Press, 2008); J Raz, 'Respect for Law' in J Raz, *The Authority of Law* (Oxford, Oxford University Press, 2009).

to put the agent engaged in practical deliberation at the centre of the philosophical investigation.[24] My own argument will be quite congenial to this broad project. Who is the agent that deliberates, and from what materials does she deliberate? These are points that cannot be neglected in our understanding of the law.[25]

Connected to this point, later in the book I will try to provide more concrete content to the 'psychological make-ups' of individuals. The argument will be that there can be different phenomena grouped under the general idea of law's demand for respect. There can be, firstly, a more specific sense of respect as an attitude that entails the recognition of some value or good in a given practice, institution, and so on. This more specific sense of respect provides at least a reason to not act against the object of respect. Secondly, sometimes there can be considerations of character or identification; that is, sometimes the agent identifies herself with a given practice or institution in a way that this practice or institution impinges on her character. When this happens, we are talking about considerations regarding the self-understanding of that agent, and reasons for action derived from those tend to be much stronger than those derived from mere respect. The resulting picture of the reason-giving character of the law is one that is fairly complex, with many items and relations among them. We have the two starting claims, the more specific notions of respect and identification and character, and much more that will be added later.

C. Philosophy as an Attempt to Make Sense of Ourselves

At this point, one might be tempted to ask: why should we want an account that looks as messy as the one I am proposing? Part of the answer lies, I think, in the sort of philosophical view advanced by Williams that I believe to be extremely useful. Williams claims that philosophy for him is 'part of a more general attempt to make the best sense of our life, and so of our intellectual activities, in the situation in which we find ourselves'.[26] Much of the philosophy done during Williams' lifetime was an attempt to identify the essential conditions or nature of a given concept. In legal philosophy, this would generally take the following form: 'something is law if and only if the following conditions apply: X'. Now, there are many uses for this kind of conceptual enquiry, and Williams does not deny that.[27] However, he wants to press the point that if philosophy is about the 'situation in which we find ourselves', it cannot be restrained to the traditional

[24] V Rodriguez-Blanco, *Law and Authority under the Guise of the Good* (Oxford, Hart Publishing, 2014) 9.

[25] In this sense, my project is congenial to John Deigh's explanation of legal authority. According to Deigh, we can only understand the authority of law if we recognise that there is an 'emotional bond' between the law and the subjects. See Deigh, 'Emotion and the Authority of Law'.

[26] B Williams, 'Philosophy as a Humanistic Discipline' in B Williams, *Philosophy as a Humanistic Discipline* (AW Moore ed, Princeton, Princeton University Press, 2006) 182.

[27] ibid 192.

idea of a priori conceptual analysis; after all, clear-cut a priori concepts are not part (or at least not a big part) of our situation. Given that we are beings with a history and with cultural environments, an understanding of our lives demands attention to other areas of knowledge, such as history, arts, literature and so on.[28] If we want to understand many of our value concepts or institutions, we will need more than just minimum and necessary conditions for the application of a concept (that is, if those are even available).[29] Those other resources violate the self-containment of much twentieth-century analytical philosophy,[30] and are the basis for his motto that philosophy should be a 'humanistic discipline'.[31]

This takes us to the very idea of 'making sense' of something. What does it mean to say that something makes sense? In 'Realism and Moralism in Political Theory', Williams says that the idea of making sense is 'a category of historical understanding (…) a hermeneutical category';[32] and in *Shame and Necessity*, Williams claims that Thucydides has a more useful understanding of human agency than Plato because Thucydides' 'aim is to *make sense* of social events, and that involves relating them intelligibly to human motivations, and to the ways in which situations appear to agents'.[33] The whole point about making sense of things, it seems, is to be able to provide intelligible narratives or explanations that connect people's motivations and dispositions to what they do in the world.[34] So, a main question throughout the book will be how to explain why an agent engaged with a particular kind of action. In the fourth chapter, I will present working definitions of the ideas of respect and character, notions that I take to be key in our understanding of how we deliberate. The materials presented, I contend, enable us to present an intelligible narrative of what it means for the law to be reason-giving for concrete agents.

The discussion up to this point is important to locate the claims about something being characteristic or distinctive of law. Throughout the book, I will rely on claims of that sort, for instance, the claim that it is characteristic of law to demand respect from its subjects. Those terms should not be understood as necessary and sufficient conditions of any sort, but as ways of pointing out things that are an important part of our experience, of our engagement with the law. There

[28] For a discussion on Williams and the 'impurity of philosophy' entailed by his view, see R Moran, 'Williams, History, and "the Impurity of Philosophy"' (2016) 24(2) *European Journal of Philosophy* 315.

[29] B Williams, 'What Might Philosophy Become' in B Williams, *Philosophy as a Humanistic Discipline* (AW Moore ed, Princeton, Princeton University Press, 2006) 211.

[30] See, for instance, Williams' complaints about the purity of analytical philosophy in B Williams, 'Political Philosophy and the Analytical Tradition' in B Williams, *Philosophy as a Humanistic Discipline* (AW Moore ed, Princeton, Princeton University Press, 2006); and B Williams, 'The Moral View of Politics' in B Williams, *Essays and Reviews 1959-2002* (Princeton, Princeton University Press, 2014).

[31] This is the overall view he develops in Williams, 'Philosophy as a Humanistic Discipline'.

[32] B Williams, 'Realism and Moralism in Political Theory' in B Williams, *In the Beginning was the Deed* (G Hawthorn ed, Princeton, Princeton University Press, 2005) 11.

[33] B Williams, *Shame and Necessity* (Los Angeles, University of California Press, 1993) 161.

[34] In this, I take Williams to be joining – with a healthy dose of suspicion – authors like Max Weber, GEM Anscombe and Peter Winch. What ties such a distinct group of authors together is their concern with individual action and how it can make sense.

can be no doubt that the search for necessary and sufficient conditions for a given concept (or for the nature of something) has value and also its uses, but if we want to understand how concrete agents practically engage with something, we need to grasp what is characteristic or distinctive of the engagement of *those* agents with *that* something. I will come back to this point in a moment, as this is connected to an important form of criticism that can be made against the sort of Williamsian philosophy that I am interested in.

Some critics might want to argue that all of this is excessively contingent and too unstable to be philosophy. Surely, the critic might think, philosophy should deliver us more stable, general truths? The criticism is not that the considerations I will be discussing, per se, cannot be subject to philosophical analysis, but that philosophy should aim at something deeper or more general than the contingent historical and cultural resources we happen to have. There are two things to be said in reaction to this objection, at least regarding the branches of philosophy that deal with practical reasoning and agency, like moral, political and legal philosophy.

Regarding the first point, we should go back to the discussion about what it means to say that something makes sense. I said that this is a demand for intelligible explanations and that Williams saw the category as a hermeneutical one. Now, *something* makes sense for *someone*. This raises the point of what can count as an intelligible explanation or narrative, and to whom. We can better grasp this if we look at Williams' use of Wittgenstein. In 'Philosophy as a Humanistic Discipline', Williams quotes favourably Wittgenstein's remark that once we get to a bedrock of explanations, we must admit that 'this is the way we go on'.[35] There are many things that 'seem to simply be there',[36] as a matter of necessity for us,[37] because we run out of justifications for them.[38] Once we reach such bedrocks, basic ideas that structure our 'forms of life',[39] to keep with Wittgenstein's jargon, we get the full intelligible explanation that makes sense for us. It is no coincidence, I think, that once we get those explanations, a usual verbal reaction is 'Oh, I see.'[40] That we reach those bedrocks does not mean that the arguments we formulate taking those materials as a basis are not philosophy or of philosophical interest, or that they are not important. This takes us to the second reaction to the criticism.

The second thing to be said about the criticism, according to Williams, is that it erroneously affirms that more general outlooks are better suited to philosophical investigation than the more local ones.[41] Concepts are deployed by groups of

[35] Williams, 'Philosophy as a Humanistic Discipline' 196. Wittgenstein's argument appears originally in L Wittgenstein, *Philosophical Investigations*, 4th edn (PMS Hacker and J Schulte eds, London, Willey-Blackwell, 2009) para 217.

[36] Williams, 'Philosophy as a Humanistic Discipline' 196.

[37] ibid 195–197.

[38] ibid 195.

[39] The term appears in Wittgenstein, *Philosophical Investigations* (2009) paras 19, 23, 241.

[40] It is also noteworthy that when we come to 'see' something, we sometimes add reticence, as in 'I see …'. This usually denotes discomfort or disagreement, but in a way that we do not know what to say about it.

[41] Williams, 'Philosophy as a Humanistic Discipline' 187.

people when they share them. The group that shares a given concept can be wider or narrower, and the wider the group, the less dependent this concept will be on particularities that belong to a more specific group. The concept of 'night', for instance, is less dependent on particularities of a group than the concept of 'chastity'. Now, we can get to a point that the concepts shared are 'minimally dependent on our own or any other creature's peculiar ways of apprehending the world'.[42] This is Williams' idea of an 'absolute conception of the world'.[43]

According to Williams, the absolute conception of the world works as a sort of goal for scientific inquiry.[44] This seems to be the case when we change our scientific explanation of colours from the way we perceive them through our vision to the different wavelengths colours have.[45] Explaining colours through wavelengths does not demand that the addressees of the explanation see colours as we humans see them. Colour-blind aliens could use the wavelength concept of colours in the same way that we do, even though they do not see red as red. When the absolute conception is taken as our goal, we try to elaborate explanations that are more and more independent of the kinds of beings we are. In a sense, it is the ambition of universal explanations. The criticism, we may put it that way, believes that philosophy should attempt to achieve something like the absolute conception of the world as well. The criticism, however, rests on a mistake:

> Even if it were possible to give an account of the world that was minimally perspectival, it would not be particularly serviceable to us for many of our purposes, such as making sense of our intellectual or other activities, or indeed getting on with most of those activities. For those purposes – in particular, in seeking to understand ourselves – we need concepts and explanations which are rooted in our more local practices, our culture, and our history, and these cannot be replaced by concepts which we might share with very different investigators of the world. The slippery word 'we' here means not the inclusive 'we' which brings together as a purely abstract gathering any beings with whom human beings might conceivably communicate about the nature of the world. It means a contrastive 'we', that is to say, humans as contrasted with other possible beings; and, in the case of many human practices, it may of course mean groupings smaller than humanity as a whole.[46]

To put the same point in other words, the farther we get from 'our more local practices, our culture, and our history', the farther we get from explanations that *make sense* for us. The mistake, to put it bluntly, is to believe that any explanation will be necessarily superior because it is more general. Useful explanations might

[42] ibid 185.

[43] The 'absolute conception of the world' is also discussed in B Williams, *Ethics and the Limits of Philosophy* (London, Routledge, 2011) ch 8. In 'Philosophy as a Humanistic Discipline', Williams stresses, against Putnam, that this is not a conception without concepts.

[44] One should notice that Williams is not saying that this is necessarily an attainable goal. See Williams, 'Philosophy as a Humanistic Discipline' 184–85.

[45] The example is from C Korsgaard, *The Sources of Normativity* (Oxford, Oxford University Press, 1996) 68.

[46] Williams, 'Philosophy as a Humanistic Discipline' 186–87.

very well be contingent, but they are so because the important things that must be explained are also contingent. If jurisprudence is committed to the 'absolute conception of the world', it will not be able to successfully account for the relationship between law and practical reasoning or deliberation. The law is part of *our* lives, and this means that any successful account of law must explain how it relates to *us*.[47] The 'absolute conception of the world' erases the 'us' in the explanation and therefore distorts the relationship between *our* deliberation and the law.[48]

D. Positioning the Account within Practical Reason

In this sub-section, there are a couple of things I would like to address, mostly concerning the 'space' that my account occupies. The first point I want to address is actually a bit of contextualisation. David Enoch has recently argued that there is nothing special or peculiar regarding legal normativity. This is an interesting claim, and I want to situate my own claims in relation to it. The second point concerns the possible readings of the arguments of this book.

Let us begin with Enoch. As I interpret him, Enoch presents a scheme for the understanding of legal normativity that is dependent on two sets of distinctions.[49] The first set of distinctions is about the different ways in which reasons for action can be provided to us.[50] There is much ambiguity in claims like 'the law provides reasons' or 'the law generates reasons', and this first set addresses this problem. According to Enoch, we have sometimes what he calls 'purely epistemic' considerations that merely bring into light a reason that we already have, but that we were unable to appreciate for whatever motive. The example Enoch gives of this is a situation in which an agent has a reason to do φ but does not perceive this reason because she is enraged or not paying attention, so a friend of hers advises her on the matter, pointing out that reason. 'Purely epistemic' reason-giving, says Enoch, 'has nothing to do with the reason's existence, and everything to do with my knowing that it is there'.[51] A second way in which reasons are provided to us is through 'triggering'. Sometimes we have a reason that is 'conditional' or 'dormant', that is, we have a reason that might not be called up unless some non-normative circumstances wake it up. Enoch's example is the case of a general reason to save money. This reason will be triggered if, let's say, the grocer increases the price of

[47] See, too, Giudice, *The Normativity of Law* (2024) 56–60. Giudice's emphasis on the evaluative and empirical aspects of legal normativity are also *exempla* of resistance to something like the absolute conception.

[48] One can argue, indeed, that both the legal realists (American and Scandinavian) and Kelsen were under the spell of the 'absolute conception of the world'. This argument is made by Claudio Michelon. See C Michelon Jr., *Aceitação e objetividade: uma comparação entre as teses de Hart e do positivismo precedente sobre a linguagem e o conhecimento do direito* (São Paulo, Revista dos Tribunais, 2004).

[49] A useful summary of Enoch's view is Bix, 'The Nature of Law and Reasons for Action' 412–14.

[50] D Enoch, 'Reason-Giving and the Law' (2011) 1 *Oxford Studies in the Philosophy of Law* 1.

[51] ibid 4.

the milk. Now, there is a reason to buy less milk.[52] There is also a third possibility, 'robust reason-giving'. In this case, there is the generation of a reason for action for the agent that did not exist before.[53] This is much rarer than people think and happens only when two necessary conditions obtain: the listener must recognise the speaker's attempt to give him robust reasons, and 'the attempt must make it the case that a reason to φ really does emerge (in the appropriate way)'.[54] For Enoch, most cases of apparently robust reason-giving are, in fact, merely cases of reasons being triggered by non-normative considerations.

Enoch combines this account of different ways of reason-giving with a second set of distinctions about the senses in which we might claim that the law generates reasons for action. A first sense in which the law provides reasons is that 'necessarily, the law gives *legal* reasons'.[55] Once we adopt some sort of engaged standpoint within a practice, there might be reasons for action generated within the practice. This sense of legal reason-giving is probably true, but according to Enoch, it is also trivial, because it fails to explain how law can engage in our practical deliberation.[56] A second, more contentious, sense in which law can generate reasons for action affirms that 'necessarily, the law gives (real) reasons'.[57] Because this is a thesis about conceptual necessity, it is easily defeated by counterexamples. According to Enoch, for the thesis to be false, it suffices that we present a case in which the law fails to generate real reasons for obedience, and this can be done by situations like wicked or grossly unfair legal systems, or by cases of stupid or immoral laws in reasonably just systems.[58] The third possibility is to read the reason-giving character of the law as 'often, the law gives reasons'.[59] This reading seems true and, according to Enoch, involves nothing mysterious. For Enoch, 'all relevant cases of reason-giving are cases of triggering (…) where the giving of reasons amounts to a manipulation of the non-normative circumstances in a way that triggers a pre-existing conditional reason'.[60] The law often triggers reasons we might have, but this is not a matter of necessity at all. In addition to that, there are many different ways in which the law can trigger those reasons.[61] This is how he summarises this point:

> Had it been a necessary truth about law that it gives reasons, perhaps a uniform account of law's reason-giving force would have been called for. But we already know that the law only sometimes does – and sometimes does not – give reasons, and we know that

[52] ibid 4–5.
[53] ibid 5–6.
[54] ibid 13.
[55] ibid 16.
[56] ibid 16–19.
[57] ibid 19. Enoch's talk about 'real reasons' is quite controversial, but the idea here is that the law *necessarily* generates moral reasons for its obedience. See in general Enoch, 'Reason-Giving and the Law' 19–20.
[58] ibid 20.
[59] ibid 26.
[60] ibid 26.
[61] ibid 28.

> when it does, it does so by triggering reasons. So it's quite possible – indeed, quite expectable – that the reasons triggered by the law will be many and varied.[62]

So, given that Enoch has presented this scheme for the understanding of legal normativity, the question that emerges is what is gained with the arguments I intend to develop in this book. I believe we can grant all of Enoch's points, but if we want to understand *how* law can provide reasons for action, we still need an account of the typical ways in which the law interacts with the practical reasoning of concrete agents. The considerations of respect, character, and the like that I will provide later in the book are some of those ways. Recall the two central claims made earlier: that agents have dispositions, motivations, and so on that inform their practical reasoning; and that the law characteristically demands respect from its subjects given its role in a narrative of political rule. To make good on those claims, we must provide thicker resources that go beyond the scheme presented by Enoch, even if that scheme is (and I think it is) correct.

There is the additional question of whether those resources I will be adding would consist of cases of triggering or cases of robust reason-giving. I do not think that this question is important because at the end of the day any reasons that the agent recognises as reasons *for action* for her will be dependent on her subjective motivational set, a point that I will develop at length in the second chapter. I will explain what it means for a reason to be a reason for action for concrete agents, but for now we can rest content with the fact that there is no a priori incompatibility between Enoch's scheme and the claims I will develop.

Before concluding this sub-section, I would like to sketch some remarks that are important for the understanding of this book and of what the gains are of the view that I defend on it. Roughly speaking, there can be two different ways to understand the claims I am making. The first, more modest, reading treats my arguments as one more piece in the puzzle of legal normativity. In this first reading, my arguments are understood as casting light into bits of legal normativity that have been overlooked by the literature. The second reading is more ambitious. In the second reading, it is not that I am only pointing out overlooked features of legal normativity, but I am also making a claim in the sense that an account that does not pay attention to the resources I am mobilising (the notions of character, identification and respect, and their relationship with law's characteristic claim to respect) is too restrictive and fails to capture much that is going on in our practical engagements with the law.

I am in favour of the second, more ambitious reading. The reasons underlying my endorsement of the second reading will become apparent as we progress through the book. At this stage, however, what really matters is that a recurrent claim throughout the book is that people have relationships with the law that cannot be explained in moral terms, and that those relationships are central to our understanding of people's practical engagement with the law. There is more to the reason-giving character of the law than just the use and justification of

[62] ibid 28.

coercion.[63] Sometimes abiding by the law is a way to express our commitment to a community, or a sense of gratitude or respect, and so on. There are, to use Joseph Raz's term, 'expressive reasons' to abide by the law.[64] Nonetheless, many of my arguments are framed in sufficiently diplomatic terms so that they can be acceptable from different philosophical perspectives. If I may offer a piece of advice for reading this book, it would be to keep in mind that there are those two possible readings. As long as the reader accepts the richness of resources we as agents have for practical deliberation, there will be enough to deliver the claims of the book, at least in the spirit of the first reading, which means that this book will be of use even for those that are not convinced by the more specific picture of practical reasoning I provide.

III. The Map of the Argument

In this final section of the chapter, I will present a rough sketch of the whole book. This section by no means covers all the topics of the upcoming chapters, but is useful, I think, to provide a bird's-eye view. First, let us recall the two central claims made in this chapter: that agents have dispositions, motivations, values, and the like that are central to practical deliberation; and that law characteristically demands respect from its subjects. Those two central claims will permeate the whole text, giving it unity.

I will present my revised version of reasons internalism, *open-minded reasons internalism*, in the second chapter.[65] According to Williams, reasons for action must be capable of explaining individual action. To do so, they must be somehow connected to the motivations and dispositions that people have through a sound deliberative route. This account is contrasted with reasons externalism, the view according to which there can be reasons for action that are independent of any 'subjective motivational sets' that individuals might have.[66] Roger Teichmann, however, has recently argued that Williams has an ambiguous view on the role of desires in practical reasoning and that this in turn makes his account a poor explanation of the phenomenology of practical reasoning.[67] I will defend Williamsian internalism against this criticism, but in doing so I will also borrow a page or two from Harry Frankfurt's discussion of care and from Joseph Raz's

[63] A point that will be discussed in further detail in my detailed analysis of Dworkin in the fifth chapter.

[64] Raz, 'Respect for Law' 255. We will come to the idea of expressive reasons later in this book.

[65] Among the main texts discussed: B Williams, 'Internal and External Reasons' in B Williams, *Moral Luck* (Cambridge, Cambridge University Press, 1981); B Williams, 'Internal Reasons and the Obscurity of Blame' in B Williams, *Making Sense of Humanity* (Cambridge, Cambridge University Press, 1995).

[66] The expression appears in Williams, 'Internal and External Reasons'. It is used in all of his discussions on the matter.

[67] R Teichmann, 'How Should one Live? Williams on Practical Deliberation and Reasons for Acting' in SG Chappell and MV Ackeren (eds), *Ethics Beyond the Limits* (London, Routledge, 2018).

views on what it means to be an agent.[68] The general claim will be in favour of a more nuanced view on the role of desires in practical deliberation that will dissolve Teichmann's criticism.

In the internalist model, we have a reason for action if this reason can be connected to a person's subjective motivational set via a sound deliberative route. After defusing Teichmann's criticism, I will analyse in more detail the idea of a deliberative route in practical reasoning. One of the appeals of a Williamsian approach is the flexibility it has in explaining what can count as a procedure of reasoning. As I understand it, a sound deliberative route for Williams is any kind of narrative that can make sense of an action of an agent for herself and for third parties that share enough of her form of life. After presenting the idea of sound deliberative routes, I will defuse criticisms regarding it. There are four kinds of criticism: that the Williamsian model is arbitrary because it narrows down the kinds of reasoning without presenting an argument for that, that the model is arbitrary because it does not consider the case of the Aristotelian *phronimos*, that there are societal or institutional reasons that are external to the agents, and that our practices of blame demand external reasons.[69]

Once we are done with those four criticisms, I will address a more general concern in the next section of the chapter. It is usually believed that a view such as Williams' deprives ethics or morality of their critical bite. Ethics or morality, one could say, are supposed to have ultimate importance, but this does not seem to be the case in an internalist model. There are two versions of this claim. The first one, illustrated by Christine Korsgaard and Catherine Wilson, is a helpful criticism of sorts. They argue that there is more space for ethical or moral considerations in internalism than the model suggests. The second version of the claim is in the sense that the internalist model has a wrong view about what it is to have a reason, and Ronald Dworkin figures as a good example of someone endorsing this claim.[70] I will argue that Korsgaard's and Wilson's concerns can be easily taken

[68] H Frankfurt, *The Reasons of Love* (Princeton, Princeton University Press, 2004); H Frankfurt, *The Importance of what we care about* (Cambridge, Cambridge University Press, 1988); H Frankfurt, *Necessity, Volition, and Love* (Cambridge, Cambridge University Press, 1999); J Raz, *Engaging Reason* (Oxford, Oxford University Press, 1999).

[69] Among the texts analysed in this bit are J McDowell, 'Might there be external reasons?' in JEJ Altham and R Harrison (eds), *World, Mind, and Ethics: Essays on the Ethical Philosophy of Bernard Williams* (Cambridge, Cambridge University Press, 1995); B Hooker, 'Williams' Argument against External Reasons' in E Millgram (ed), *Varieties of Practical Reasoning* (Cambridge, MIT Press, 2001).

[70] C Korsgaard, 'Skepticism about Practical Reason' in C Korsgaard, *Creating the Kingdom of Ends* (Cambridge, Cambridge University Press, 1996); C Wilson, 'Moral Authority and the Limits of Philosophy' in SG Chappell and MV Ackeren (eds), *Ethics Beyond the Limits* (London, Routledge, 2018); R Dworkin, *Justice for Hedgehogs* (Cambridge, Harvard University Press, 2011). There are replies by Williams to some of those arguments in: B Williams, 'Postscript: Some Further Notes on Internal and External Reasons' in E Millgram (ed), *Varieties of practical reasoning* (Cambridge, MIT Press, 2001); B Williams, 'Values, Reasons, and the Theory of Persuasion' in B Williams, *Philosophy as a Humanistic Discipline* (AW Moore ed, Princeton, Princeton University Press, 2006); B Williams, 'Replies' in JEJ Altham and R Harrison (eds), *World, Mind, and Ethics: Essays on the Ethical Philosophy of Bernard Williams* (Cambridge, Cambridge University Press, 1995) 187–91.

onboard, and that Dworkin's method confuses what is at stake in the discussion. Underlying their concerns, however, is an assumption about ethics' supreme value in deliberation, and I will have something to say about this as well.

The corollary of the second chapter is that practical reasoning is a complex and often obscure process. If a reason is to be a reason for action, then it will necessarily have the right kind of relation to the person's subjective motivational set. In my favourite parlance, we can only explain individual action through an intelligible narrative that connects reasons for action to the things that this agent cares about. Important consequences follow from this regarding the reason-giving character of the law.

The third chapter is, in a sense, an exercise of landscape cleaning, as it is all about understanding what legal positivists have said and about what they haven't said. Its focus is on the way some positivists explain (or, to be more accurate, could have explained) the reason-giving character of the law. I will argue that legal positivism – or, to be more precise, the positivism inspired by HLA Hart – presents a story about the law that is, in terms of what Williams calls a 'fictional genealogy'. This means that legal positivism presents us with a schematic narrative that explains how something (the law) could have emerged from very basic human needs.[71] The problems for positivists emerge on two fronts.[72] On the one hand, they might even be right about their fictional genealogies, but because they do not move beyond them, their theories cannot explain how law affects the practical reasoning of concrete agents. This is so because the picture of the agent presupposed by positivism is, to use Williams' term, 'characterless', that is, it is an agent that has none of the contents that make up for real agents. On the other hand, the accounts of legal normativity we can extract from positivism fail to capture

[71] The main reference in this will be B Williams, *Truth and Truthfulness* (Princeton, Princeton University Press, 2002). It should be said from the outset that I am not the first to use Williams' genealogy to understand legal normativity. Sylvie Delacroix has made extensive use of Williams' genealogical method in her work, and as far as I know, she pioneered the use of Williams in jurisprudence. See S Delacroix, *Legal Norms and Normativity – An Essay in Genealogy* (Oxford, Hart Publishing, 2006). I will say a bit more on her take on genealogy and normativity later in the book, especially in the third chapter, but I believe that it is worth pointing out some of our differences here. Firstly, we diverge about Hart's engagement with genealogy, since I believe that there is indeed a genealogical account in *The Concept of Law*, and Delacroix holds the opposite view. Secondly, Delacroix's own take on legal normativity stresses the contribution of civic engagement with the law and draws heavily from Christine Korsgaard's constructivism. My own take is more strictly Williamsian and more sceptical about the relevance of morality to our understanding of normativity.

[72] In this chapter, I will analyse not only Hart, but also other positivists such as Jules Coleman, Scott Shapiro and Joseph Raz. Hart, *The Concept of Law* (1994); Coleman, *The Practice of Principle – In Defence of a Pragmatist Approach to Legal Theory* (2001) and SJ Shapiro, *Legality* (Cambridge, Harvard University Press, 2011). My arguments regarding those authors draw from Shapiro, 'What Is the Internal Point of View'; Kaplan, 'Attitude and the Normativity of Law' (2017); Deigh, 'Emotion and the Authority of Law'; Rodriguez-Blanco, *Law and Authority under the Guise of the Good* (2014); V Rodriguez-Blanco, 'The Moral Puzzle of Legitimate Authority' in S Bertea and G Pavlakos (eds), *New Essays on the Normativity of Law* (Oxford, Hart Publishing, 2011); M Bratman, 'Reflections on Law, Normativity and Plans' in S Bertea and G Pavlakos (eds), *New Essays on the Normativity of Law* (Oxford, Hart Publishing, 2011).

the characteristic aspect of law's demand for respect. Positivism explains nicely what it means for a practice to be rule-guided, but legal normativity involves more than that.[73] At the end of this chapter, what I hope to have made intelligible is the claim that legal positivism either does not present an account of legal normativity, or if it is taken as presenting such an account, then it is an insufficient one. That being said, Hart's internal point of view is a valuable tool, one that I will develop in different directions in the fourth chapter.

The fourth chapter is the core of the book and presents my account of the reason-giving character of the law. I will begin the chapter with a discussion of Williams' book on political philosophy, *In the Beginning was the Deed*.[74] This discussion will provide us with a better understanding of what it means to say that the law is part of a story or narrative of political rule. Once that is understood, I will recast Hart's original argument of the internal point of view in terms of the more concrete attitude of respect for the law. I will, in the sequence, present working definitions of the ideas of respect, character and identity. Roughly speaking, we have a more specific sense of respect that entails at least reasons for action to not act against a given value, institution, or practice; and a sense of identity or character that entails that the agent sees some value, institution, or practice as impinging on her sense of self.

The combination of all those ideas will allow me to present my account of the reason-giving character of the law. There is, firstly, a thick case in which the agent identifies herself with the law in the sense of seeing law as part of her character. For this agent, to break the law is 'unthinkable' because she fully identifies herself with the political community and with its law. In the thick case, there is mutual support between the possible senses of identification an agent might have. We can 'peel' this thick case, so we can have cases in which the agent respects the law and the community or identifies herself with the community and only respects the law, and many other combinations. The picture I am proposing admits of many degrees, given the number of items it has: the idea of respect for law will be present as long as the agent recognises some sort of good or value in the law and that this provides her with at least a reason to not act against the law. We can finally peel it down to only notions of prudential reasons and of what Williams has called 'loss of power', that is, a perception of being diminished in relation to others,[75] and to prudential reasons.

In a sense, what I intend to do in the fourth chapter is to bring together different insights by Williams, Raz, and Deigh in order to present a more realistic view of the reason-giving character of the law. Raz's discussion of respect for law,[76]

[73] To make this point, I will rely heavily on Deigh, 'Emotion and the Authority of Law'.

[74] B Williams, *In the Beginning was the Deed* (G. Hawthorn ed, Princeton, Princeton University Press, 2005). Other essays that will be important are in Williams, *Philosophy as a Humanistic Discipline* (2006) and in B Williams, *Essays and Reviews 1959-2002* (Princeton, Princeton University Press, 2014).

[75] Williams, *Shame and Necessity* (1993) 219–23.

[76] Raz, 'Respect for Law'; J Raz, 'The Obligation to Obey: Revision and Tradition' in J Raz, *Ethics in the Public Domain: Essays in the Morality of Law and Politics* (Oxford, Clarendon Press, 1995).

I contend, is a nice starting point for our understanding of how agents engage practically with the law, but it is an insufficient account. Deigh is helpful in pointing out that the law has a distinctively political function and that individuals often have 'emotional bonds' with it, but he never develops what can be the contents of those bonds.[77] Their insights are combined with the political narrative Williams tells in *In the Beginning was the Deed* in a way that provides content to the second of the central claims made in this chapter and that will be underlying the whole book. The first claim, as already pointed out, is developed in further detail in the second chapter, about reasons internalism, but will receive its more concrete content in the discussion of what it means to respect something and of what it means to identify oneself with something in the fourth chapter. When we put all those pieces together, we get a view on the reason-giving character of the law that is fit for the kind of beings that we are.

The fifth chapter is offered in the spirit of a supplement to the analyses of the limits of morality in practical deliberation in the second chapter and of the objections against my account discussed in the fourth chapter. It also concludes our inquiry. Many authors have argued that if there is anything to legal normativity, this must be moral normativity. The chapter starts with an analysis of Ronald Dworkin's view that legal obligations are, at the end of the day, moral obligations. I will start by presenting Dworkin's theory, and then I will expose it to criticism. Dworkin's view, in a nutshell, is that the law is an interpretive concept, and that the best interpretation of the law presents it as a moral phenomenon capable of providing moral reasons for action.[78] The main problem in Dworkin's view is that it overestimates the role and power of moral considerations, and this causes his account to ignore the possibility of nonmoral obligations. As I will try to show, people sometimes feel that they have genuine obligations that cannot be traced back to morality. If there are nonmoral obligations, then there is also the possibility for legal normativity to be at least partly based on those nonmoral considerations.[79]

The chapter then continues with an analysis of John Finnis' Natural Law account. According to Finnis, the reason-giving character of the law can be traced back to basic goods through the requirements of practical reasonableness.[80] How this can be so is a quite complex matter, so I will spend some time in the chapter attempting to reconstruct Finnis' argument. My criticism of it will be threefold. We have, firstly, radical indeterminacy when it comes to the basic goods and their content. Secondly, Finnis fails to make a convincing case for his requirements of practical reasonableness. Thirdly, Finnis' theory is committed to an ideal of

[77] Deigh, 'Emotion and the Authority of Law'.

[78] The main texts analysed in my discussion of Dworkin are R Dworkin, *Law's Empire* (Cambridge, Harvard University Press, 1986) and Dworkin, *Justice for Hedgehogs* (2011).

[79] My criticism of Dworkin relies heavily on Williams' claims in B Williams, 'Persons, Character and Morality' in B Williams, *Moral Luck* (Cambridge, Cambridge University Press, 1981).

[80] My discussion on Finnis takes as its focus J Finnis, *Natural Law and Natural Rights*, 2nd edn (Oxford, Oxford University Press, 2011) and J Finnis, 'Law and What I Truly Should Decide' (2003) 48 *The American Journal of Jurisprudence* 107.

transparency in practical reasoning (in the sense that law's function must be accessible to agents through reasoning) that is implausible.[81] By the end of the fifth chapter, I hope to have highlighted how Dworkin and Finnis commit the same mistake, although in different ways. Both authors believe that the reason-giving character of the law can be grounded in morality, morality here understood as reasons that are either external or supremely important or properly rational to the concrete agents. This presupposition induces the authors to lose sight of the full story of the reason-giving character of the law. Real-life agents are messier and more imperfect than much moral philosophy presupposes. We do legal philosophy a favour if we remember how obscure we are, even to ourselves.

[81] Central to my criticisms of Finnis are Williams, *Ethics and the Limits of Philosophy* (2011) and B Williams, *Morality – An Introduction to Ethics* (Cambridge, Cambridge University Press, 1993).

2

Open-Minded Reasons Internalism

I. Introduction

A main claim in this book is that individuals have dispositions, motivations, projects, and so on, and that those elements must figure in an account of the reason-giving character of the law. In this chapter I will develop this claim through an account of practical reason that is a version of reasons internalism, which I will label *open-minded reasons internalism*.

In general, reasons internalism is contrasted to reasons externalism, but this does not seem to me very enlightening once we understand what it means for a reason to be a reason *for action*. A part of my argument will be to say that at the end of the day, when it comes to reasons *for action*, we are all at least partly internalists. Be it as it may, there is no need for a reader to reject all views on practical reason but internalism for her to accept much of what I am going to say later in the book. Still, if what I am saying in this part of the book turns out to be true, not only will my account of the reason-giving character of the law become more plausible, but all other accounts will become a variation of what I have to say.

What does it mean to say that we engage in practical reason? R Jay Wallace defines practical reason as 'the general human capacity for resolving, through reflection, the question of what one is to do';[1] and Harry Frankfurt defines it as 'any of the several varieties of deliberation in which people endeavor to decide what to do, or in which they undertake to evaluate what has been done'.[2] Bernard Williams, in turn, has famously claimed that the only possible reasons for action are of an internal kind.[3] 'Internal reasons', as he calls them, are reasons that are somehow connected to the 'subjective motivational sets' of individuals, subjective motivational sets here understood as comprising not only desires that an individual might have, but other items as well, such as 'dispositions of evaluation, patterns of emotional reaction, personal loyalties, and various projects, as they may be

[1] RJ Wallace, 'Practical Reason' in N Zalta (ed), *The Stanford Encyclopedia of Philosophy* (Spring 2018 Edition), available at plato.stanford.edu/archives/spr2018/entries/practical-reason/, accessed 03 December 2019.

[2] H Frankfurt, *The Reasons of Love* (Princeton, Princeton University Press, 2004) 5–6.

[3] B Williams, 'Internal and External Reasons' in B Williams, *Moral Luck* (Cambridge, Cambridge University Press, 1981) 111. See also B Williams, 'Internal Reasons and the Obscurity of Blame' in B Williams, *Making Sense of Humanity* (Cambridge, Cambridge University Press, 1995) 35.

abstractly called, embodying commitments of the agent'.[4] So, says Williams, in order for a given reason to be a reason for action for a given agent, it must be grounded on her subjective motivational set.[5] Williams's more mature and favoured statement of his *reasons internalism* is the following one: 'A has a reason to φ only if he could reach the conclusion to φ by a sound deliberative route from the motivations he already has.'[6]

I will develop this statement and propose some amends to it. In the next section, I will explain in greater detail what a subjective motivational set is. As we will see, there is some obscurity in Williams' original formulation, and this makes him liable to the kind of criticism elaborated by Roger Teichmann, namely, that desires play an ambiguous role in the Williamsian model. As a way of amending the model, I will suggest that we understand Williams' subjective motivational sets through Harry Frankfurt's structure of care. After doing that, I will focus on the second item in Williams' account, the idea of a 'sound deliberative route'. One of the appeals of a Williamsian approach is the flexibility it has in explaining what can count as a procedure of reasoning. In my discussion of sound deliberative routes, I will engage with different forms of possible criticism, the most notable of them being John McDowell's. With the two elements of a Williamsian account of practical reasoning clear in mind, I will discuss the role and limits of ethical considerations in practical reasoning. A common worry regarding models like the one I am going to defend is that they do not give enough power to ethical and moral considerations. I will argue that this is not really the case. The model gives ethical and moral considerations as much power as they actually have, and this is not the same thing as having as much power as we would want them to have.

The picture of practical reasoning that will emerge from this chapter, open-minded reasons internalism, can thus be summarised: it is a kind of Williamsian reasons internalism, with the important addendum that I am recasting the subjective motivational sets of individuals as the things agents care about, in Frankfurtian terms. This means, roughly, that someone has a reason for action if and only if this reason is somehow connected to the things that the agent cares about. This connection is provided by what Williams calls a sound deliberative route. As I interpret this term, it refers to intelligible narratives that present that reason for action as the conclusion of the deliberative process for that agent. Among the things that someone might have reason to do are moral or ethical requirements, but this will only be the case if the agent cares about ethics or morality in the first place. According to the view that I will defend, there can be no reasons *for action* that are free-floating from the agent.

As I have mentioned, there is no need for the reader to follow me all the way with reasons internalism. There are two reasons for this. Firstly, the main claims that

[4] Williams, 'Internal and External Reasons' 105.
[5] ibid 102.
[6] Williams, 'Internal Reasons and the Obscurity of Blame' 35.

I will develop later in this book demand only that the reader accept the importance of internal reasons and how they function in our lives. Even if there are external reasons, those will not render my account of the reason-giving character of the law a false one. Secondly, as I will explain in further detail later, there is a *sense* in which we can talk about reasons for action that are external to agents, but that is not the sense I am interested in, as reasons for action in that other sense play no role in the explanation of action.[7]

II. Individuals, Desires, and Care

A. Williams' Original Claim

Reasons internalism is more complex than the basic Humean argument that if I have a desire, then I have a reason to act on that desire, if by desire we mean a passion or want.[8] The subjective motivational set of an individual contains – as we have just seen in the quote in the Introduction – much more than just desires, and even though it is possible to say that the Williamsian picture is a more sophisticated descendant of Hume's, this in my view only confuses things. To begin with, there is an important normative element involved here.[9] There is room in internalism for corrections of fact and of reasoning regarding the sound deliberative route.[10] This can be seen in Williams' classical case of the glass containing gin or petrol. Let's say I am thirsty and want to drink gin and tonic, and to my surprise there is a glass of a transparent liquid on the table, a liquid that resembles gin and tonic. Unknown to me, however, is the fact that the glass actually contains petrol.[11] The question that emerges is this: do I have a reason to drink from the glass?

The answer is no, because *what I actually want* is gin and tonic, and not petrol. A sound deliberative route connects my motivational set to action, and there is no sound deliberative route from wanting gin and tonic to drinking petrol. If a deliberation is to be sound, then it must have elbow room for this kind of correction pertaining to facts or reasoning (I will discuss the idea of a sound deliberative

[7] Since I think that the version of reasons internalism I defend is correct, unless otherwise specified, I will write the next chapters of the book presupposing the relevant sense of reasons for action and the truth of my account.

[8] In 'Internal and External Reasons', Williams builds his interpretation using the 'sub-Humean' model as its starting point. He then adds many provisos and details to this more primitive model. See Williams, 'Internal and External Reasons' 101–104.

[9] Williams, 'Internal and External Reasons' 101–102; Williams, 'Internal Reasons and the Obscurity of Blame' 36. Indeed, it could be asked if Hume's own view was as crude as some of his commentators believe.

[10] Williams, 'Internal Reasons and the Obscurity of Blame' 36.

[11] The example appears in Williams, 'Internal and External Reasons' 102–103. He also repeats it in other texts.

route in more detail later).[12] In this, we can say that there is a sense of normativity in practical reasoning, a sense in which corrections are possible because individuals in general want to achieve their goals, fulfil their desires and projects, and so on, and they can only do that if they possess the pertinent correct beliefs. For instance, I can only achieve my goal of drinking gin and tonic if I know that the glass on the table contains gin and tonic. It is fair to say that I have an interest or disposition in acquiring correct beliefs regarding the interests and goals I might have, and this, says Williams, is a quite general interest or disposition shared by every rational agent.[13]

B. Teichmann's Criticism: The Ambiguity of Desire

Roger Teichmann in 'How should one live? Williams on practical deliberation and reasons for acting'[14] takes issue with the prominent role Williams attributes to desires in practical reasoning. Teichmann's main complaint against Williams's account is that desires play an ambiguous role in it. Williams, he says, endorses the view that someone can present a desire she has as a reason for action.[15] Now, according to Teichmann, 'The problem is that in deliberating whether to φ, I am *ipso facto* deliberating whether to want to φ; my already wanting to φ had better not be taken as a given.'[16] The ambiguity is that in a Williamsian account desires apparently figure as reasons *and* as facts in the deliberation, depending on my *identification* (that's Teichmann's use of the term) with them. If I do not identify myself with a desire and want to get rid of it, then I will treat the desire as one more element in my practical reasoning, in the same way I treat things like the weather or the violence in the neighbourhood. This is easily illustrated with the case of someone that has nasty desires and repudiates them. This person might say things like 'this is not who I am' or 'those desires are not part of my self'. If someone asks John's wife why he is going to therapy, she can simply say 'Oh, he wants to quit smoking', and the person will immediately grasp the meaning of John's actions.

On the other hand, when the agent identifies herself with a desire, the role of the desire in her practical deliberation is that of the conclusion or the reason that emerges at the end of deliberation. According to Teichmann, and in this he is echoing GEM Anscombe, we can still press the question 'why?' regarding this

[12] Williams, 'Internal Reasons and the Obscurity of Blame' 36.

[13] B Williams, 'Postscript: Some Further Notes on Internal and External Reasons' in E Millgram (ed), *Varieties of practical reasoning* (Cambridge, MIT Press, 2001) 91–92; Williams, 'Internal Reasons and the Obscurity of Blame' 37.

[14] R Teichmann, 'How Should one Live? Williams on Practical Deliberation and Reasons for Acting' in SG Chappell and MV Ackeren (eds), *Ethics Beyond the Limits* (London, Routledge, 2018).

[15] ibid 211. Quoting B Williams, *Ethics and the Limits of Philosophy* (London, Routledge, 2011).

[16] Teichmann, 'How Should one Live? Williams on Practical Deliberation and Reasons for Acting' 211.

agent in this case.[17] Teichmann has the following example to explain his point. Think about the case of a daughter that identifies herself with the desire to murder her parents and proceeds in doing so. She is liable to the question 'why?'. If she replies that she wanted to do that, that she so desired, this is not enough for us to understand her action. According to Teichmann, the question 'why?' here actually means 'Why did you want to kill your parents?'.[18] This means that a desire is not enough as a conclusion of a practical deliberation. Teichmann's conclusion is that 'Williams is surely wrong to say that one's desire to do something is a reason for doing it'.[19] Evidence in favour of Teichmann's reading of Williams is presumably taken from *Ethics and the Limits of Philosophy*. In that book, Williams claims (and Teichmann quotes) the following: 'Desiring to do something is of course a reason for doing it.'[20]

Teichmann's complaint – that Williams has an ambiguous view on the role of desires – is in part motivated by Williams' lack of clarity regarding what the 'subjective motivational sets' of agents are. Teichmann's objection has important implications for our understanding of practical reasoning. Desires are first-personal, and we usually think of them as something an agent has. We do say things like 'I have this desire.' When we are talking about reasons, however, it seems that this way of talking is off. If I understand Teichmann correctly, he is claiming that there is more to the phenomenology of reasons than what Williams accounts for. Reasons seem to be good or bad independently from people's motivational sets. They have an *external aspect*[21] that cannot be cashed in in terms of desires one person happens to have.[22] Reasons for action appear to agents as things that were already there, independently of their motivational sets or desires.

C. Internalism and What We Care About

Williams' original claim was that the subjective motivational sets of agents can contain desires, dispositions, projects and values. I believe that we can refine the model in a way that addresses Teichmann's criticism if we borrow a page or two from Harry Frankfurt's discussion about what it means for an agent to care about something.[23] How can the structure of care help us in the understanding of

[17] ibid 212.
[18] ibid.
[19] ibid 213.
[20] Williams, *Ethics and the Limits of Philosophy* (2011) 21.
[21] It is important to not confuse the *external looks* that a reason might have for the agent that has the reason for action with a different thing, namely, that there are *external reasons* for action. I will come back to external reasons later in this chapter.
[22] Teichmann, 'How Should one Live? Williams on Practical Deliberation and Reasons for Acting' 215–17.
[23] His lectures collected in H Frankfurt, *The Reasons of Love* (Princeton, Princeton University Press, 2004) are going to be the most important source on this for my purposes. Besides those, the essays collected in H Frankfurt, *The Importance of What we Care About* (Cambridge, Cambridge University

practical reason? To answer this question, we must first understand what it is to care about something and how it relates to other evaluative categories we use in our daily lives.

We evaluate things in different ways, and not all of those are the same thing as caring about something. Here is a first way: sometimes we recognise that a given object has intrinsic value, that it is good in itself, without this meaning that we care about it. For instance, I can recognise the value of opera, believe that it is a good thing for opera to exist, but not care myself about it. We recognise value in this mode quite frequently; we can see that a collection has value for a collector, and yet not be moved to think that it is *important to us*.[24] Merely recognising the importance of something lacks a conative component that somehow connects me to that thing in question.

To care about something is more than to simply desire something as well, even though it is in a sense a desire. To merely desire something is to want it.[25] This accounts for the conative component I just mentioned, but to desire something is not the only element in our engagement with practical reason (part of Teichmann's objection was based on this point). We can have desires and act on them because they are strong enough to motivate us, but we can also have desires and not act on them, and this is so for at least three different reasons. Firstly, the desire might be too weak, so it has no power to move us out of our way in order to pursue it. Secondly, it can be weaker when compared to other desires that we have and that are incompatible with the fulfilment of the first desire, so we pursue what we desire more. Thirdly, we can reject, or even despise, the desire we have, independently of its intensity, and decide to not act on it, and even attempt to free ourselves of the desire.[26] Let me give quick examples of those situations. The first case is quite common. I desire to have a sip of coffee before class, but because I can't be bothered to walk to the coffee shop, I just skip it altogether. It is, I believe, a variant of the second case. The second case is nicely illustrated by the scenario in which I want to lose weight and to eat a cheeseburger. Because the first desire is stronger, I do not fulfil my second desire. The third case is this. Imagine a religious person that has sexual desire towards someone she is not supposed to desire. She can desire the other person in a quite intense way, but because she despises that desire, she does not act on it. On the contrary, she will try to get rid of the desire through penitence, prayer and so on.

So, what does it mean to care about something? According to Frankfurt, to care about something involves not merely a desire, but also a kind of reflexivity towards

Press, 1988) and H Frankfurt, *Necessity, Volition, and Love* (Cambridge, Cambridge University Press, 1999) are also relevant. Sophie-Grace Chappell and Nicholas Smyth used the expression 'to care about' to explain Williams' view, but not in the Frankfurtian terms I am proposing here. See SG Chappell and N Smyth, 'Bernard Williams' in N Zalta (ed), *The Stanford Encyclopedia of Philosophy* (Fall 2018 Edition) section 5, available at plato.stanford.edu/archives/fall2018/entries/williams-bernard/, accessed 03 December 2019.

[24] Frankfurt, *The Reasons of Love* (2004) 12–14.

[25] ibid 10.

[26] ibid 11–12.

this desire. When an agent cares about something, says Frankfurt, 'he is willingly committed to his desire. The desire does not move him either against his will or without his endorsement. He is not its victim; nor is he passively indifferent to it. On the contrary, he himself desires that it move him.'[27] This means that to care is to have an attitude of wilful endorsement of the desire. In the Frankfurtian view, the agent that cares about something desires this something, but in addition to that, she also wants to sustain and foster this desire for this something. In caring about something, we commit ourselves to this or that desire or object of want.[28]

The attitude of wilful endorsement I have mentioned comes in the shape of what Frankfurt has called 'higher-order desires'. In a sense, they consist in a desiring whose objects are other desires. They correspond to the stand we take towards our first-order desires, and in this they are, for Frankfurt, an important hallmark of agency. Differently from animals and toddlers, fully developed agents can evaluate their own desires and endorse them.[29] Think about Frankfurt's case of the smoker, and to keep the name from my previous example, let us call him John: he has two desires, one to stop smoking and another one to keep smoking. He can evaluate and take a stand about his desires; he can identify himself with the desire to stop smoking and work to make that desire a reality.[30] This attitude of wilful endorsement, it is important to notice, is not necessarily the same thing as a choice between two or more possible courses of action. Some very important cases present themselves as practical necessities for the agent, cases in which he feels constrained, in which he feels that there is only one way to go, but he still identifies himself with that way and makes it *his* way. Later I will develop this point further.[31]

It is this kind of reflexivity that, according to Frankfurt. is not available for toddlers or animals. They have desires and can act on them (and even refrain from acting on them), but they cannot identify themselves with this or that desire. Of course, the fact that John identifies himself with the desire to stop smoking and says to himself that this is what he really wants does not mean that he will not end up having a cigar after all. John can fail to restrain himself and fall into temptation. Note that John is not lying; he really wants to stop smoking and believes that to be his will, but the intensity or power of a desire has no necessary relation to our identification with it. Someone can try to resist some desire that she does not believe

[27] ibid 16.

[28] ibid 16. See also H Frankfurt, 'On Caring' in H Frankfurt, *Necessity, Volition, and Love* (Cambridge, Cambridge University Press, 1999) 155–62; H Frankfurt, 'On the Necessity of Ideals' in H Frankfurt, *Necessity, Volition, and Love* (Cambridge, Cambridge University Press, 1999) 110–11; H Frankfurt, 'The Importance of What we Care About' in H Frankfurt, *The Importance of What we Care About* (Cambridge, Cambridge University Press, 1988).

[29] Frankfurt, *The Reasons of Love* (2004) 18–19. See also H Frankfurt, 'Freedom of the Will and the Concept of a Person' in Frankfurt, *The Importance of What we Care About* (1988) 16–19; H Frankfurt, 'Identification and Wholeheartedness' in Frankfurt, *The Importance of What we Care About* (1988) 164–67.

[30] Frankfurt discusses this example in Frankfurt, 'Identification and Wholeheartedness' 164–67.

[31] This is an important point for both Williams and Frankfurt.

worthy but fail in this. This is why Frankfurt says that if someone does her best to not act on a given desire but ends up acting on it nonetheless, then this person acted against her will.[32]

The things I care about, says Frankfurt, are those regarding which I have this sort of higher-order desire. I take a stand about my desires and endorse some of them as really mine, and in doing so I find out what I care about.[33] This gives us, I think, a neat explanation of what Williams calls the subjective motivational sets of individuals, albeit one that gets some distance from his original formulation. This case is strengthened because of situations like the following one, raised by Frankfurt himself. There are things that can have intrinsic value, but intrinsic value is not enough to make things important *to a specific agent*. Now, Frankfurt adds the following complication: sometimes, things can be important to an agent without her knowing that. Here is Frankfurt's example: if an agent lives close to radiation – let's say that there was a leak of radioactive material near her house in the past – the fact that this radiation damages her health is important to her even if she is not aware of it, but this is so *only if* the agent cares about her health or something like that. The sense of importance of things for us depends on what we care about. If an agent cares about her health, the levels of radiation near her house are important to her even if she is not aware of them.[34] Conversely, if the agent does not care at all about her health, the radiation will not be important to her. To someone insisting that she ought to move to a better place due to the radiation, she could reply: 'So what?'. This is another way to bring home the point made by Williams, that people might have reasons to do or to not do things that are not obvious to them because they are in error of fact or deliberation.[35]

I believe we can recast what Williams calls a subjective motivational set as the things that we care about in Frankfurtian terms. There are some advantages in doing so. Firstly, Williams' original argument seems to me correct, but by saying that elements in the agents' subjective motivational sets are the things we care about, we can explain how we move from having a plethora of dispositions, values, projects and so on to action; that is, Frankfurtian resources can explain how having those motivations can ensue action. The idea of care (and of second-order desires more generally) helps us to understand how agents navigate their subjective motivational sets. Agents do not merely react to their desires; they take

[32] Frankfurt, *The Reasons of Love* (2004) 18–20. See also H Frankfurt, 'Autonomy, Necessity, and Love' in H Frankfurt, *Necessity, Volition, and Love* (Cambridge, Cambridge University Press, 1999) 136–37.

[33] Frankfurt, *The Reasons of Love* (2004) 20–21.

[34] ibid 21–22. See also H Frankfurt, 'On the Usefulness of Final Ends' in H Frankfurt, *Necessity, Volition, and Love* (Cambridge, Cambridge University Press, 1999) 87–88.

[35] For a view on the vicinity of Frankfurt's, notwithstanding important differences, see G Watson, 'Free Agency' in G Watson, *Agency and Answerability – Selected Essays* (Oxford, Oxford University Press, 2004). Whereas Frankfurt introduces a distinction between different orders of desire, Watson introduces a distinction between what he calls the 'valuational' and 'motivational' systems of the agent.

a stand regarding them, and in doing so, they differ from wantons. Secondly, it adds simplicity without compromising plurality. One of Williams' insights was that we can be motivated by many things – desires, values, projects and so on – but by focusing on the structures of care, we can cash out all those things in terms of desires and higher-order desires. Take values and projects. Something is a value or a project for *us* only if we care about it. Unless I am somehow committed to that value or project, this value or project will not present itself as a source of potential reasons for action for me.

How can this discussion about the structure of care help us regarding Teichmann's criticism? Recall that his complaint was that desires were functioning as both reasons and facts in the model. The distinction between basic desires and higher-order desires can explain away the ambiguity identified by Teichmann. Basic desires, like John's desire to smoke or the daughter's desire to kill her parents, function as *facts* in someone's deliberation. John, for instance, can stop and 'see' that he wants to smoke. On the other hand, when someone identifies herself with a desire and acts on it, that is, when someone cares about it, then this desire functions as a *reason* or a conclusion to a practical deliberation. When this is the case, the agent takes a stand regarding her desire; she commits herself to the sustenance of that 'configuration of the will', to use Frankfurt's term. To quote Williams somewhat out of the original context, 'in this sort of case, what I think I have most reason to do, taking all things together, is the thing I very much desire to do, and if I *should* is taken to refer to what I have most reason to do, this is what I should do'.[36]

III. Further Developments: Necessity, Goodness, and Reasons-Responsiveness

A. Satisfaction and Necessity

More must be said. If I care about something and this motivates me to act in a given way, I am still liable to the 'why' question of Teichmann and Anscombe. The ambiguous role of desire has been clarified, but there is also need for an argument that can give an intelligible reply to the 'why' question. The problem can be stated like this: Frankfurt has introduced higher-order desires that explain what it means to care about something, but why shouldn't those desires also be exposed to the 'why' question? Those are, after all, desires that a person has. The fact that I care about something, it seems, is not enough to provide us with a reason for action. Think about the murderous daughter. She can answer the first question, 'why', by saying 'Because I wanted to kill them'. We can ask her

[36] Williams, *Ethics and the Limits of Philosophy* (2011) 21.

again, 'why', and this second time she would reply 'Because I wanted to have that desire.' One can ask now why she wanted to have this higher-order desire, and this can go on creating desires of higher orders indefinitely.[37] We have, it seems, a problem of infinite regress.

Frankfurt's first solution to this sort of problem was to say that at some point of the deliberation we make a decision that 'resounds' across the will, putting an end to our engagement in the deliberative process.[38] As he recognises later, this answer is at best incomplete, because there is a need for an answer to the question of *when* a decision that resounds across the will can be made (that is, there must be more to this decision than merely an *ex nihilo* choice, for how could this choice resound by itself?). This point makes him add that an agent can make such a decision when she manages to overcome doubt, that is, when the agent concludes that this or that higher-order desires are the ones that she ought to commit herself to. This does not mean that the person does not feel the sting of her other desires anymore, merely that she has confidence in the course of action that she adopted as her own. That is why a sense of conflict might remain. The person feels the temptation of doing things differently, but in her mind, there is no doubt anymore.[39] In later writing, Frankfurt explains this same point by talking about a sense of satisfaction. Satisfaction, he says, 'is a state of the entire psychic system – a state constituted just by the absence of any tendency or inclination to alter its condition'.[40]

When a person achieves this state of satisfaction, she not only identifies herself with some of her desires but also sees no reason to keep deliberating about what she cares about or about what she ought to do.[41] This, as Frankfurt points out, is not the same thing as believing that her state and her situation in the world are the best possible ones. It merely means that the agent is confident that the decision she is taking is supported by the best available reasons given her circumstances. This is the terrain of confidence: the agent sincerely believes that she has done enough in terms of reasoning.

For many cases, that will be more than enough as an explanation. But for others, one can insist on keeping the inquiry going, wondering why the person has found herself satisfied or confident about her desires, and if that is enough to warrant an answer to the 'why' question. As I have anticipated, I think that one of the key aspects of Teichmann's criticism is that when an agent provides us with a reason for doing whatever she is doing, this might not take the form 'I have this desire and I will do so-and-so'.[42] There is an aspect in which the reason seems to

[37] For Frankfurt's presentation of this problem (one he tries to address), see Frankfurt, 'Freedom of the Will and the Concept of a Person' 21–22; Frankfurt, 'Identification and Wholeheartedness' 166–67.

[38] Frankfurt, 'Freedom of the Will and the Concept of a Person' 21–22.

[39] Frankfurt, 'Identification and Wholeheartedness' 166–69.

[40] H Frankfurt, 'The Faintest Passion' in H Frankfurt, *Necessity, Volition, and Love* (Cambridge, Cambridge University Press, 1999) 104.

[41] ibid 102–06.

[42] Teichmann, 'How Should one Live? Williams on Practical Deliberation and Reasons for Acting' 215–17.

come first; that is, when an agent makes a statement about a reason, this statement 'has explanatory priority over the one about his acceptance of the reason, either in its first-person or its third-person form'.[43]

When faced with the 'why' question, the agent presents *the reason* as an answer, not *her acceptance* of the reason. This is an aspect of the phenomenology of practical reasoning that apparently a Williamsian model cannot account for. Some reasons for action might look like external requirements to the agent that entertains them in the sense that they do not appear to the agent as dependent on her. There are three things I would like to say about this further step in the dialectic. The first point has to do with practical necessity. The second point is about the phenomenology or perception of the good. The third and final point concerns reasons-responsivity. In demanding that a reasons-internalist account say something about those points, Teichmann's criticism is, I think, very successful. In answering to those demands, my Williamsian account will narrow the gap between what is usually understood as internalism and externalism, hence the monicker *open-minded internalism*.

Let us begin with practical necessity, and to do so let us take a look at an example from Williams' *Shame and Necessity*, the case of Aeschylus' *Agamemnon*. The play opens up with the retelling of the dilemma faced by the Greek commander at Aulis: Agamemnon must either give up the war on Troy or sacrifice his own daughter so that the goddess Artemis will allow the Greek armies to travel to Troy. After painful deliberation, the Greek leader decides to sacrifice Iphigeneia, his daughter. Agamemnon 'put[s] on the harness of necessity', in Williams' translation of the line.[44] Williams calls our attention to the fact that the wording in the original lines of Aeschylus uses an active vocabulary. Agamemnon is not described as passive towards the dilemma; he engages in it. This example is interesting because, in a sense, there were two possible courses of action. This is how a third party looking at it would see it. However, through Agamemnon's eyes, once he had made his decision, there was only one possible path. The path that he must follow appears to him as an external requirement in the sense that he does not see it as a mere whim of his, but *as a necessity*.[45] Now, it is important to notice that a different person facing the same dilemma would not necessarily see the same necessity as Agamemnon. Another king could 'put on the harness of necessity' of fleeing in order to save his daughter, and he would also express himself in the language of necessity and of the 'I *must* …'. How are we to explain this?

The idea of necessity is an important one here, and it deserves careful unpacking. There are some 'incapacities of character' that – according to Williams – set up the boundaries of what we can seriously consider as a course of action for us. Some courses of action are, in a sense, 'unthinkable', not in the sense that we

[43] ibid 215.
[44] B Williams, *Shame and Necessity* (Los Angeles, University of California Press, 1993) 132–35.
[45] See, for instance, Frankfurt, *The Reasons of Love* (2004) 64–67.

cannot imagine them, but in the sense that we could not follow them or consider them as alternatives for *us*. The positive counterpart of an incapacity of character, we may say, is a *necessity of character*. Such a necessity presents us with a demand that we cannot do anything but endorse. This is so because the demand made by a necessity of character is an expression of the persons we are. As Williams puts this, it is a necessity that not only shapes our character but also provides part of its content.[46] Since they are connected to our character, those necessities are not the kind of thing we can actively try to get rid of. When we get to a situation in which we can actively try to get rid of a necessity, then it is not a necessity *of character* anymore. As Williams says, it can be a 'psychological' necessity, like a compulsion, but in that it will lack the identificatory element that ties it with character and with our will.[47] Because of their constitutive role in who we are, those necessities present themselves to us as if they were external to us, but they actually come from within ourselves.[48]

A comparison with the Frankfurtian treatment of love might help here. According to Frankfurt, to love someone or something is a particular kind of care, one that is a deeply personal matter. No one supposes that a given instance of love can be universalised in the way we universalise matters of logic. Yet, from the point of view of the lover, her love towards the beloved is not seen as a choice of hers. It would not be love if she could opt out of it at any time and without any effort. Her love is, in a sense, pressed upon her, but it is also deeply personal, and because it is a kind of care, when we love something, we have an attitude of wilful endorsement towards it.[49] There is a further complication, however, because the idea of loving someone or something and at the same time not wanting to love this someone or something makes sense, but I will not develop this point here, since what interests me is the parallel between love and necessity.

Just like with love, when we identify ourselves with a given desire or course of action in the sense of necessity, this will appear to us as something that was *already there* independently of my will and that we also *voluntarily embrace*.[50] This is, possibly, the reason why Aeschylus' language regarding Agamemnon is in terms of his *activity*; he is voluntarily embracing his path (the only one available to him), in the same way as someone puts on armour, as Williams remarks. In a discussion somewhat connected to this, Williams makes the following point:

> Ever since the Enlightenment a recurrent aspiration of distinctively modern politics has been for a life that is indeed individual, particular, mine, within the reach of my will, yet

[46] B Williams, 'Practical Necessity' in B Williams, *Moral Luck* (Cambridge, Cambridge University Press, 1981) 129–31.

[47] B Williams, 'Moral Incapacity' in B Williams, *Making Sense of Humanity* (Cambridge, Cambridge University Press, 1995) 54.

[48] See, for a similar point in a slightly different context, Williams, *Ethics and the Limits of Philosophy* (2011) 57–58.

[49] See Frankfurt, *The Reasons of Love* (2004) ch 2.

[50] B Williams, 'Identity and Identities' in B Williams, *Philosophy as a Humanistic Discipline* (AW Moore ed, Princeton, Princeton University Press, 2006) 63–64.

> at the same time expresses more than me, and shapes my life in terms that mean something because they lie beyond the will and are concretely given to me. It is the politics, if you like, of self-realization. That term contains in itself obvious difficulties: it is even grammatically ambiguous between activity and passivity, and illuminatingly so.[51]

For Williams, some desires are part of the *ethos* of the agent. They are part of who she is, yet at the same time they present themselves as necessities for that agent.[52] This accounts *for part* of the phenomenology of practical reasoning that Teichmann was alluding to, the external aspect of some reasons for action (this is only a partial answer because necessities of this kind are not all that there is to practical reason). To step outside those necessities would be the same thing as stepping outside of who one is, and this is not feasible when it comes to action. I can, of course, entertain how it would be for me to belong to a certain religion and what would be a necessity for someone that sincerely professed that faith, but given that this is not about my religion, this kind of reasoning will not bear on my action. When we get to the necessities that an agent has, on the other hand, they circumscribe the limits of what she sees as possible action.[53]

B. The Perception of the Good

The second point is related to an important phenomenological aspect about the role of the good in practical deliberation. Think about the following conversation. John and Mary are discussing what John ought to do. At a certain point, Mary says something like this: 'Well, if you care about X, then you ought to do Y.' This sort of argument is neatly captured by the internalist model. The problem is that in many cases the exchange between the agents involves pointing out *the good or value* of a given course of action. Mary might say something like 'you ought to Y because that's the right thing to do' or 'you ought to Y because that's good', and so on. Conversely, John could argue either by pointing out the good of another course of action or by calling into question the goodness of Y. Agents argue as if they perceived the good in a given course of action. This is an important aspect of our practices of reasoning, one that seems off the hook of the account developed so far.[54]

How can my account explain this? Think for a moment: what does it mean for something to be seen as good by a given agent? Why does this given agent see this thing as good? The good cannot be something free-floating from the agent;

[51] ibid 64. See also Williams, 'Practical Necessity' 130–31.

[52] See, for instance, Williams, *Shame and Necessity* (1993) 103.

[53] See, in general, Williams, 'Practical Necessity'.

[54] I am perfectly content with Raz's definition of reasons for action as 'facts in virtue of which those actions are good in some respect and to some degree'. J Raz, 'Agency, Reason, and the Good' in *Engaging Reason* (Oxford, Oxford University Press, 1999) 22–23. The point I will emphasise in this section (and, as far as I know, a point that is compatible with Raz's general views on practical reason) is that what counts as 'good in some respect and to some degree' depends on the subjectivity of the agent.

otherwise, it would not be a good from her perspective. The question that emerges is this: how can something be judged good by an agent from her perspective? The answer must be from her motivations, dispositions, and values, that is, from her subjective motivational set. For an agent to have any view on something, she must have enough in her to go around the world.[55] Unless there is enough in us to enable us to judge and evaluate, the idea of the good is out of our grasp. There seems to be a paradox looming in the background: the things we deem good appear as good to us independently of who we are, but the reason we can judge them good is that we have enough in us to make those judgements, judgements that are informed by our subjectivity.

Here is no more than a suggestion of a solution for the paradox. We have already analysed the idea of practical necessity, the idea that there are some demands that present to us as necessary because they are connected to whom we fundamentally are. Those demands are dependent on who we are, on our motivational sets, but they are in a sense external in that they do not present themselves to us as free choices. This was neatly captured by Harry Frankfurt's treatment of love: we do not choose what we love; love presents itself to us as a necessity. However, we at the same time recognise that love is deeply personal, that it cannot be universalisable.[56] The good, on the other hand, looks pretty much universalisable. How so? Here is the suggestion. Just like love or necessity, the idea of the good is an important feature of our shared forms of life. It is part of who we are, not in the sense that we are committed to the same content of the good, but that we have widespread agreement about what it means for something to be good. That is, whatever the content is taken as the good, we take the good to have this and that feature in our engagement with it (eg, we take it to be universalisable etc). I believe this to be a possible application of Wittgenstein's cryptic remark in paragraph 241 of *The Philosophical Investigations*:

> 241. 'So you are saying that human agreement decides what is true and what is false?' – What is true or false is what human beings say; and it is in their *language* that human beings agree. This is agreement not in opinions, but rather in form of life.[57]

It is part of the beings we are, part of our forms of life, that the good – if it is to be good – must be something more than just the judgement from my own subjective motivational set. At the same time, we can only perceive the good as a judgement made from the standpoint of the things we care about. This judgement, however, receives a different status through our shared forms of life. When we recognise something as good, we perceive its goodness as something external to us, but this is enmeshed in our own judgement transfigured by our internalised practices

[55] See H Frankfurt, 'Rationality and the Unthinkable' in Frankfurt, *The Importance of What we Care About* (1988).

[56] See Frankfurt, *Reasons of Love* (2004) ch 2. See too Frankfurt, 'Autonomy, Necessity, and Love'.

[57] L Wittgenstein, *Philosophical Investigations*, 4th edn (PMS Hacker and J Schulte eds, London, Willey-Blackwell, 2009) para 241, but see also para 242.

of evaluation. Just like love or necessity makes something internal into something external, the evaluation or judgement of something as good claims for itself an aspect of externality, of 'being there' independently of our judgement. Once we realise that our judgements about the good are inescapably dependent on whom we are, important questions emerge regarding relativism and the confidence we are entitled to have in our evaluations, but this is not the place for developments on this point.[58]

One very brief remark seems in place, however. My argument about the role of the good in practical deliberation could be running together two kinds of issues. The first one is reasons internalism (the main topic of this chapter), but the second one is internalism about the good (ie, subjectivism). How so? One could insist that the good exists objectively in a manner that is independent from our internal reasons and subjective motivational sets. Nothing that I have said denies this possibility. Let us assume that the good exists in such a manner. This objective good, then, would be unable to provide reasons for action for us because we could not see it as the good. The sketchy internalist account of the good I offered avoids this, as it allows the good to provide reasons for action at the cost of giving up a strong (or even Platonic) sense of objectivity. It does not, in any case, provide an argument against the existence of good beyond us, but it is mysterious how such good could manifest itself in the world.[59]

C. Reasons-Responsiveness and the Semblance of Rationality

A third and final argument I would like to discuss regarding Teichmann's challenge concerns reasons-responsiveness and the Frankfurtian idea of satisfaction. This is also connected to Teichmann's insight that we usually see ourselves as beings that act in the world because of the reasons we believe that we have; that is, we do not see ourselves as acting merely because we accept such reasons. Earlier in this chapter I discussed Frankfurt's idea of being satisfied. The idea was that satisfaction is a 'condition in which we willingly accept and endorse our own volitional identity'.[60] There is more that must be said, I think, about how we can get ourselves into the state of satisfaction and how we can maintain it.[61]

[58] See, for instance, Williams, *Ethics and the Limits of Philosophy* (2011) ch 9.

[59] I am in debt to Steve Bero for pointing this out to me.

[60] Frankfurt, *The Reasons of Love* (2004) 97.

[61] I discuss this point in DP Murata, 'What Does it Take to be Oneself?' [2024] *Res Publica* (DOI: 10.1007/s11158-024-09700-z). Here, I am drawing from that article and expanding a bit on its ideas. In the article, I argue that Raz' seminal paper 'When We are Ourselves' is a plausible starting point for our views on action and activity when supplemented with some ideas from Bernard Williams and David Velleman. The route I try in the article is different from the one I am deploying here, but the conclusions are essentially the same.

Frankfurt himself was eager to highlight that satisfaction is not the same thing as complacency, but how can we maintain the distinction?

The key is our own practical engagement. I can only get to a state in which I am satisfied after an exercise in practical deliberation. I need to be able to see that there are some forms of good or value in the actions I decide to take (as seen in the previous section). We can only get to the state of satisfaction if I manage to recognise goodness or value in how my volitional identity is shaped. Equally, I can only maintain such a state if I keep recognising such goodness or value. Also, as already discussed, what can be recognised as good or valuable depends fundamentally on our subjective motivational sets. At this point, I would like to add an important idea suggested by Joseph Raz, that of a 'semblance of rationality':

> [W]e are ourselves so long as, as we see it, we are responsive to reason. We may be irrational in thinking that we are responsive to reason. What counts, however, is not the justification or rationality of our view, but the view itself: We are ourselves and we lead our own life so long as we see ourselves as rational agents, so long as we conduct our life under the semblance of rationality.[62]

Raz' point is that *we see ourselves as agents* in the world when we understand that *our actions have been done under what we take to be reasons*. This is what he means by living under the semblance of rationality, and this is, I think, a necessary condition for our state of satisfaction. Think about it: in general, you would not be satisfied with yourself and your actions unless you were able to present reasons for being in such a state, and the presentation of such reasons involves pointing out their good or value. Now, as already discussed, we can only recognise goods and values through reasoning that starts from our own subjective motivational sets. Frankfurt wanted to distinguish his picture of satisfaction from mere complacency,[63] however satisfaction indeed becomes complacency when we fail to present reasons that justify (at least to ourselves) our state. My point is that we have the resources to present those reasons, and they start from our own selves. This is not to say that we cannot be mistaken: we can incur deliberative error (wishful thinking and delusional states, for instance), or we can be misinformed regarding facts, and so on. I will discuss this in further detail in this same chapter.

We now have all the pieces that enable a more sophisticated version of reasons internalism to account for the important phenomenological aspect highlighted by Teichmann. Reasons indeed appears to come first, and, indeed, our 'acceptance' of them appear to be of secondary importance. However, considerations appear as reasons for action to us only because of their connection to our subjective

[62] J Raz, 'When We are Ourselves' in J Raz, *Engaging Reason* (Oxford, Oxford University Press, 1999) 19. This quotation is the focus of my article 'What Does it Take to be Oneself?'.

[63] Frankfurt, *The Reasons of Love* (2004) 94. For Frankfurt's analysis of Raz, see H Frankfurt, 'Disengaging Reason' in RJ Wallace, P Pettit, S Scheffler and M Smith (eds), *Reason and Value – Themes from the Moral Philosophy of Joseph Raz* (Oxford, Oxford University Press, 2006).

motivational sets. Sometimes those reasons can even take the shape of practical necessities, but in general, they will be tracking what we take to be good or valuable, and what we take to be good or valuable is independent of whatever external goodness or value there might be out there (and there might be good out there).

IV. Teichmann's Challenge Answered

We covered much ground in our path to answer Teichmann's challenge. The ambiguity of desires in a Williamsian model was put to rest through the use of Frankfurt's structure of care and the distinction between desires and higher-order desires. The way that Frankfurt himself framed the argument, however, was in need of supplement, notably regarding the 'external' aspect of the practice of giving reasons. So, I have tried to supplement the account with three further claims. Firstly, there was a claim made in terms of the inner necessities that an agent has, and of how those necessities appear to her. Secondly, a claim in terms of an explanation of the good as dependent on our shared forms of life. Thirdly, a claim about how we understand ourselves as being responsive to reasons.

There are some things I want to say before moving to the next point, the idea of practical deliberation itself. Firstly, the emerging picture moves quite a bit from Williams' original account but manages to keep its advantages. It is independent of any belief in the existence of external reasons but at the same time, it accounts for the complexity of our practical engagements (I will have a lot more to say about external reasons in what follows). Secondly, although I have explained the external aspect of reasons according to my internalist model, I have said nothing in the sense that there can be no external reasons. Rather, one of my objectives was to show that we are all at least partly internalists. Thirdly, it is a bit ironic that in the end the internalist model is still pretty much under Aristotle's influence. We have discussed at length what it means for some action to be perceived as good or valuable by concrete agents, and in this score, we built some distance between the internalist model and Aristotle. However, we are still committed to the idea that every action is done under some semblance of the good. Just as we are all at least partly internalists, it seems to me that we are all at least partly Aristotelians.

V. The Workings of the Sound Deliberative Route

We must now analyse the idea of a sound deliberative route. This was the second important item in Williams' original account of reasons internalism, and as one might expect, Williams does not provide a clear definition of what he understands by it. There are good reasons for this lack of clear boundaries. People might deliberate in many different ways without any of those ways being necessarily unsound. They can resort to reflection, in the sense of diving inward and thinking hard about what one wants to do. But they can also resort to persuasion of either themselves or others, and this (as we will see shortly) usually takes the form of 'If I were you …' propositions. Significantly for Williams, people can be imaginative in their deliberations; that is, the person can imagine paths that were not presented to her at all, and those might bear on deliberation. A use of imagination in deliberation, says Williams, is the situation in which a person finds out a third possibility that avoids a dilemma presented to her.[64]

A sound deliberative route, therefore, is not something that can be defined a priori because its soundness will depend on what can make sense as an intelligible route between what we care about and the reason for action. Indeed, there are two traits of a deliberative route that deserve mention here.

Firstly, Williams invites some confusion by his use of the term 'deliberation'. It comprises more than what is usually understood by the term. As I understand it, *a sound deliberative route is any kind of narrative that can make sense of an action of an agent for herself and for third parties that share enough of her form of life.* An agent does not necessarily stop and 'deliberate', putting cards on the table and then deciding what she ought to do. Sometimes the sound deliberative route can be more visceral. The agent merely sees what must be done, and if someone were to demand an explanation of her (or if she were to think about it later), this could be given in terms of a narrative that makes sense, taking into account her motivational set. This relates to what I have said in the first chapter. For Williams, to make sense of things 'involves relating them intelligibly to human motivations, and to the ways in which situations appear to agents'.[65] Another way to put this point is this: just because the agent didn't stop to deliberate, it does not mean that there is no sound deliberative route that makes sense of her action in terms of reasons for action.

Secondly, sound deliberation should not be taken as a one-way track as well. Deliberation is capable not only of getting to reasons from the motivational sets, but also of changing the motivational sets themselves.[66] Think about the following scenarios. An agent wants to pursue a career as a judge because this was her father's dream for her, but once she deliberates about that, facts such as her father's recent death and her distaste for bureaucracy strike her as severely weakening that desire she had in her motivational set; she might even conclude that she does not desire that anymore. Sometimes, it is through the exercise of deliberation that we find out what we really want. An agent is being helped by an advisor to figure out what she ought to do. This advisor is well-intended and is trying his best to not manipulate the agent. In their engagement, the agent discovers that she fell in love with the advisor, and this changes her motivations.

[64] Williams, 'Internal and External Reasons' 104–105; Williams, 'Internal Reasons and the Obscurity of Blame' 38.

[65] Williams, *Shame and Necessity* (1993) 161.

[66] Williams, 'Internal and External Reasons' 104105; Williams, 'Internal Reasons and the Obscurity of Blame' 38.

There are now reasons for action tracked in her new motivations that were not there when she started.[67]

Someone might complain that the model is obscure because it does not provide us with a strict protocol of practical reasoning that would enable us to know for sure what we have reason to do. For Williams, however, the model is useful *because* it is indeterminate in this sense.[68] To know what one has reason to do is not like the application of formulas. Sometimes we will have a clear picture of our reasons; on other occasions, this is not the case, and we feel like we are in the dark about what to do, and our way out of darkness might deploy all of the resources I've mentioned earlier.[69] As Williams says, 'Practical reasoning is a heuristic process, and an imaginative one, and there are no fixed boundaries on the continuum from rational thought to inspiration and conversion.'[70]

Significantly, reasons internalism allows us to *explain individual action* in a convincing way. In this resides what I take to be the greatest appeal of the Williamsian account. This point can be seen through the case of Henry James' Owen Wingrave, a favourite of Williams. Owen's family is proud of their military tradition. Every man of the Wingraves went to the army, and now the family is pressing Owen to follow this path as well. The problem is that Owen has absolutely no interest in joining the army; all of his family's rhetoric about honour and service sounds like noise to him. He has no reason to join the army, because nothing in his motivations inclines him towards that action,[71] or in the Frankfurtian terms that I have suggested, he does not care at all about it. What would be necessary for Owen to be convinced that he has reason to join the army?

It would take, I think, a persuasive uncle to articulate materials in Owen's own motivational set, someone insightful enough to present a sound deliberative route from the things that Owen cares about to a reason to join the army. For instance, if Owen cares about the respect he has in the family, this is the kind of element in his set that can be mobilised in the deliberation. This would take something like the form: 'Well, if you care about this, then you should ….' In the case that Owen decides to join the army, we can say that he did that because of the reason he found himself to have. This is an internal reason that can be tracked to things he cares about. When someone asks us why Owen joined the army, we can offer the reason. Sometimes, the back-and-forth between Owen and his uncle will be more indirect, in the sense that their exchange will unfold in terms of pointing out the rightness or goodness of this or that course of action. Regarding such attempts at persuasion,

[67] This second example is used by Williams in a slightly different context in B Williams, 'Values, Reasons, and the Theory of Persuasion' in B Williams, *Philosophy as a Humanistic Discipline* (AW Moore ed, Princeton, Princeton University Press, 2006) 116.

[68] Williams, 'Internal and External Reasons' 110; Williams, 'Values, Reasons, and the Theory of Persuasion' 110.

[69] B Williams, 'Postscript: Some Further Notes on Internal and External Reasons' in E Millgram (ed), *Varieties of Practical Reasoning* (Cambridge, MIT Press, 2001) 92.

[70] Williams, 'Internal and External Reasons' 110.

[71] ibid 106–107.

success hangs on the possibility of a given side getting a route from their desired action to the subjective motivational audience of their addressee, of getting the other to see things as they see.

The lessons from the preceding remarks can be encapsulated in what I will call the requirement of explanation: 'If something can be a reason for action, *then it could be someone's reason for acting on a particular occasion, and it would then figure in the explanation of that action.*'[72] This is the point that means trouble for the opponents of internalism. Williams calls them externalists, and in their view there can be reasons for action for a given agent that are not connected to their motivational sets in any way.[73] The trouble is this: if this reason has no connection to the concerns of the agent through some deliberative route, how can this reason be a reason for action *for* this given agent? The reason would be something free-floating, apart from the agent, and would not help to explain why he did whatever he did.[74] Reasons externalism cannot account for the *requirement of explanation* (I have already presented a version of this same claim earlier in this chapter, in our discussion about the good). Williams is not saying that there are no external reasons, merely that they do not play a role in the explanation of the actions of agents, and therefore they cannot be reasons *for action.*[75]

It is not clear who would count as an externalist in Williams' view. His first paper on the matter, 'Internal and External Reasons', has no clear foe, and the only one mentioned in his more mature paper, 'Internal Reasons and the Obscurity of Blame', is John McDowell, who can be reinterpreted without much violence to his ideas as an internalist, as I will try to show in a moment. Also, in this later paper, Williams says that he has no real disagreement with Christine Korsgaard's argument about practical reason, an argument of Kantian flavour to which I shall also return later. Sophie-Grace Chappell and Nicholas Smyth argue, to my mind correctly, that all that Williams is claiming is that if we are to understand something as a reason for action for someone, then this something necessarily has a connection with the things that have some kind of importance to the agent. 'If this thesis is true', say Chappell and Smyth, 'then perhaps we should not expect to find any definite examples of clear-headed external reasons theorists'.[76]

[72] ibid 106, my emphases.

[73] ibid 101–102.

[74] ibid 107. In this same page, Williams presents this point in the following, useful terms: 'The whole point of external reason statements is that they can be true independently of the agent's motivations. But nothing can explain an agent's (intentional) actions except something that motivates him so to act.'

[75] By the end of *Truth and Truthfulness*, Williams claims that 'A lot of very interesting history is itself the history of reasons for action, of considerations that at a given time or place could count for or against doing various things.' See B Williams, *Truth and Truthfulness* (Princeton, Princeton University Press, 2002) 248.

[76] SG Chappell and N Smyth, 'Bernard Williams' in N Zalta (ed), *The Stanford Encyclopedia of Philosophy* (Fall 2018 Edition) section 5, available at plato.stanford.edu/archives/fall2018/entries/williams-bernard/, accessed 03 December 2019. A point also noted by Stephen Finlay and Mark Schroeder. See S Finlay and M Schroeder, 'Reasons for Action: Internal vs. External' in N Zalta (ed), *The Stanford Encyclopedia of Philosophy* (Fall 2017 Edition) section 2.1.2, available at plato.stanford.edu/archives/fall2017/entries/reasons-internal-external/, accessed 03 December 2019. It seems to me

In what follows, I will develop the idea of a sound deliberative route through the analysis of a series of general objections to internalism. The criticisms come in four kinds: that the Williamsian model is arbitrary because it narrows down the kinds of reasoning without presenting an argument for that, that the model is arbitrary because it does not consider the case of the Aristotelian *phronimos*, that there are societal or institutional reasons that are external to the agents, and that our practices of blame demand external reasons.[77] After presenting and discussing the objections, I will take some time to focus on the relationship between reasons internalism and moral or ethical considerations.

VI. Four General Objections against Internalism

A. Is the Model too Narrow?

Let us begin with the first kind of criticism, about arbitrariness. Two different versions of it have been advanced. The first one is by Brad Hooker, who argues that Williams' account is too arbitrary in two different ways. Firstly, according to him, Williams fails to explain why there is no way for practical reason to start from a point external to the motivational set or cares of the agent. Secondly, he claims that Williams fails to account for other modes of deliberation that go beyond his model, and if Williams opens up to those other modes, then he has no reason to exclude external reasons from practical reasoning, since those other modes of deliberation might have a role for them.[78]

Hooker's criticism does not do justice to Williams' argument, and to show why this is so, I will take the reverse order and start with his second point. Recall that the notion of a sound deliberative route is, for Williams, quite permissive. The only constraints in practical reasoning are those covered by the corrections of fact and reasoning, and that the reasoning must be intelligible for individuals in the sense that it explains for them what they did. I have explained Williams' view by saying

that the only theories that could be coherently externalist are those of Socratic/Platonic colours and, as pointed out by Chappell and Smyth, some kinds of utilitarianism. At least on some interpretations of Socrates and Plato, to know the good means the same thing as to be good. When the agent knows the good, the good impresses on him and therefore he has reason to act according to it. According to those interpretations, the good is something independent of the idiosyncrasies of the agents, it bears no relation to the kind of person an agent concretely is. The Socratic/Platonic argument is an intelligible form of externalism, but its metaphysical assumptions are too strong for it to be plausible for us. It would need Plato's argument of the forms, for instance. I have benefitted from discussion with Veronica Rodriguez-Blanco and Kenneth Ehrenberg on this point.

[77] Regarding those criticisms, Williams has said things about all of them and in the following I will explain what he said. In some cases, however, I will also draw from other sources. For instance, even though Williams has written replies to John McDowell, my answer to McDowell will draw from Chappell and Smyth as well.

[78] B Hooker, 'Williams' Argument against External Reasons' in E Millgram (ed), *Varieties of practical reasoning* (Cambridge, MIT Press, 2001) 100–101.

that a sound deliberative route is merely an intelligible narrative that connects actions to reasons. More importantly, any account of practical reasoning must tackle the *requirement of explanation*. Reasoning that starts from '(…) from some objective ('external') values or requirements, fixed independently of the agent's present motivations',[79] to quote Hooker himself, cannot connect reasons to motivations, and therefore to actions. This means that this form of reasoning cannot be *practical* reasoning, unless those values or requirements are already things that the agent cares about (or things that, through a sound deliberative route, this agent could come to care about),[80] but if this is the case, then we are talking about internal reasons for action in the relevant sense again.

Regarding the first point, even if objective or external values exist, and even if we can talk and reason about these values, they will not figure in explanations we provide for actions undertaken by agents, unless they are related in the requisite way to what agents care about. If that is not the case, then reasoning about such values will be like the kind of reasoning an insightful anthropologist engages in (again, I am not arguing that objective or external values do not exist). The anthropologist can grasp the values of alien cultures and reason with them, but they will not motivate her to act in any way. She can, for instance, reason with a thick concept like 'chastity', but this concept will not be reason-giving for her unless she somehow endorses the concerns of chastity.

It is at this stage that it makes sense, I think, to talk about a sense of reasons for action that is appropriately external. The ways in which we use the language of reasons are not uniform, and this can be the cause of much confusion. The sense of reasons for action in which I am interested is the one related to the explanation of action. This was captured by the requirement of explanation. A given consideration can be a reason for action if and only if it can figure in an explanation of why a concrete agent engages (or could have engaged) in a certain action. We can, for purposes of clarity, refer to those reasons as *proper* reasons for action. We do use the language of reasons in another sense, however. Sometimes we use the language of reasons to refer to considerations that could be invoked in favour of or against certain actions, but those considerations have no connection to the subjective motivational sets of agents. Having no connection to subjective motivational sets, those reasons cannot bear on the action of agents, so they cannot be *proper* reasons for action. When dealing with this kind of reasons, we can reason with 'values or requirements, fixed independently of the agent's present motivations', to bring Hooker's phrase once more, but they will fail to meet the requirement of explanation. Now, being considerations in favour of or against a certain action, they *can* be called reasons for action, but they are not the kinds of reasons I am interested in, as they do not have the right fit; that is, they will play no role in the explanation of action. Later in this chapter I will say a bit more about those reasons, and about

[79] ibid 100.
[80] I thank Steve Bero for pressing me on this point in order to make it clearer.

how many authors, in talking about them, have managed to change the subject of practical reason.

B. McDowell and the Argument from the *Phronimos*

The second version of the criticism of arbitrariness is John McDowell's.[81] For McDowell, there is an important difference between getting to reasons by deliberation – the thing that, according to him, Williams is talking about – and the discussion about the *correct way to deliberate*. McDowell presents the idea of 'proper upbringing' in this connection.[82] For him, someone that has been properly educated – the Aristotelian *phronimos*[83] – deliberates correctly in the same way someone who has mastered some skill can execute it without further thinking. For the *phronimos*, correct deliberation just happens to be the way she thinks; it is a combination of 'a way of seeing things and of a collection of motivational directions or practical concerns, focused and activated in particular cases by exercises of the way of seeing things'.[84] Now, and this is the important point, for McDowell this process of upbringing is not in itself a deliberative procedure, because it demands things like emotional education and inculcation of patterns of thought.[85]

As pointed out by Chappell and Smyth, McDowell's argument is not a criticism of reasons internalism. Indeed, the argument might even demand it. To see this, think about what it means for an agent to receive an ideal education. The upbringing of this agent does not provide her with external reasons for action; much to the contrary, by educating an agent, we provide her with materials for her subjective motivational set: we teach her how to evaluate things in the 'right' way, how to have the 'right' dispositions, and so on. The *phronimos* is not someone that acts based on external reasons, but a person that received an education that allows her to have the 'right' internal reasons.[86] The content of those 'right' internal reasons is not what interests us here, but the fact that those reasons are only reasons *for action* because this particular agent happens to care about the materials they are connected to and that this agent only cares about those things because she was taught to do so.

What happens when an agent is not the *phronimos*? According to Williams, unless the agent is deluded, she will have some understanding of her limitations

[81] J McDowell, 'Might There be External Reasons?' in JEJ Altham and R Harrison (eds), *World, Mind, and Ethics: Essays on the Ethical Philosophy of Bernard Williams* (Cambridge, Cambridge University Press, 1995).

[82] ibid 73–77.

[83] The term *phronimos* is used by Williams in his discussion of McDowell. McDowell himself does not use the term in this specific paper. See Williams, 'Postscript: Some Further Notes on Internal and External Reasons'; B Williams, 'Replies' in Altham and Harrison (eds), *World, Mind, and Ethics: Essays on the Ethical Philosophy of Bernard Williams* (1995).

[84] McDowell, 'Might There be External Reasons?' 73, footnote omitted.

[85] ibid 78.

[86] Chappell and Smyth, 'Bernard Williams' section 5.

and vices and will take those things into account in her deliberation. For instance, if an agent is married and intends to be loyal to her partner, and she knows that she has a weak spot for pretty people, this might give her reason to avoid going to a wild party at the weekend. Presumably, the *phronimos* has no weak spot whatsoever, and could go to the party (assuming she has reason to do so) without being worried about being unfaithful. This, however, is not the case with the person in the example.[87] She might say something like this: 'I wish I were that kind of person! Alas, I am not, so I better stay at home.'[88] It might be useful to present Williams' own words on this matter: 'Just because I am, and can know myself to be, an imperfect agent, it may be that I have reason not to try things which a better agent would indeed have reason to do.'[89]

C. Are Institutional or Societal Reasons External?

What about the third form of criticism? A plausible candidate for an external reason is the idea of an institutional or societal reason. The argument would be something like this: society in general or more concrete institutions can provide reasons for action, and those reasons are supposed to be reasons for action that are not dependent on whatever is in the motivational set of individuals. Arguably some legal philosophers think that the law can provide us with reasons for action that are independent from our motivational sets. You have legal rights and duties, they might say, from the 'legal point of view'.[90] This line of thought seems compelling but will not be enough to vindicate external reasons in the relevant sense as well. This is so because either the legal (or any other institutional) point of view has already been accepted by the agent, and thus reasons from this point of view will be internal, or the legal point of view is not accepted by the agent, and thus its reasons will lack any force for her. To present this in slightly different terms: from the fact that institutions claim that we have reason to do or not to do something, we cannot derive that we actually have such reason.[91]

In 'Formal and Substantial Individualism' Williams claims that 'deliberative or practical questions are radically first-personal (…) and, to the extent that his or her action [the agent's] is intentional, it can be explained in terms of a deliberation that the individual could have conducted'.[92] This means that institutions will only have a claim on us if this is somehow connected to what we care about through a deliberative route. In real life this is often the case, of course, and we often

[87] See Williams, 'Postscript: Some Further Notes on Internal and External Reasons' 94; Williams, 'Replies' 187–91.

[88] See also Finlay and Schroeder, 'Reasons for Action: Internal vs. External' section 2.4.

[89] Williams, 'Postscript: Some Further Notes on Internal and External Reasons' 94.

[90] This is, of course, a simplification. For a discussion on the legal point of view, see the next chapter.

[91] Williams, 'Postscript: Some Further Notes on Internal and External Reasons' 94–95.

[92] B Williams, 'Formal and Substantial Individualism' in B Williams, *Making Sense of Humanity* (Cambridge, Cambridge University Press, 1995) 125.

come to think that some institutions have a claim on us thanks to education and internalisation of values and beliefs. In many cases, however, as Critical Theorists correctly remind us, our motivations are the result of complex social phenomena of which we are unaware, but this does not mean that Williams is wrong. If we want to explain why the proletarian acts in a way according to bourgeois ideology, we need to look at how the proletarian deliberates.[93] Because the proletarian has been educated within the confines of bourgeois values, those are the values that she cares about. The proletarian does not care about revolution or anything like that, but cares about being able to buy a new car by the end of the year. We make sense of her actions in a way that not only is compatible with reasons internalism but rather presupposes it.[94]

D. The Practices of Blame and Reasons Internalism

The fourth form of criticism that I will analyse in this section comes from our practices of blame, and this criticism demands more attention than the others. Reasons internalism sounds exasperating when we confront what Williams calls 'hard cases', like this one: a brutal, inconsiderate husband that does not care at all about his wife and mistreats her horribly. This husband has no item in his motivational set that would provide him with an internal reason for action to be a better person, so he has no reason for that.[95] At this point, someone could complain that this cannot be right. Indeed, the situation is not right. There are many ways in which we can criticise the husband, and of course, we can act. For one thing, we can throw him in jail. What we cannot do, according to internalism, is to claim that the husband *had a reason* to behave otherwise.

This scenario raises a powerful suspicion about reasons internalism. We do say things like 'The husband has reason to be better!' If such statements are not taken to mean what they mean at face value, how are we to interpret them?[96] According to Williams, as 'optimistic internal reason statements': 'I suspect what are *taken for* external reason statements are often, in fact, optimistic internal

[93] In general, see Williams, 'Formal and Substantial Individualism' 127–31. There is a very interesting discussion about what Williams calls the 'Critical Theory Test' and how it can displace some beliefs in *Truth and Truthfulness*. The Critical Theory Test also appears in Williams' more positive takes on political philosophy. See B Williams, 'Realism and Moralism in Political Theory' in B Williams, *In the Beginning was the Deed* (G Hawthorn ed, Princeton, Princeton University Press, 2005) 6; see also B Williams, 'From Freedom to Liberty: The Construction of a Political Value' in Williams, *In the Beginning was the Deed* (2005) 88–89.

[94] A useful discussion of Williams's individualism and its place in his philosophy is Lorenzo Greco's. See L Greco, 'Reflection and the Individual in Williams' Humanistic Philosophy' in A Perry and C Herrera (eds), *The Moral Philosophy of Bernard Williams* (Cambridge, Cambridge Scholars Publishing, 2003). Greco argues, to my mind correctly, that reflexivity and 'formal individualism' are both parts of a 'positive philosophical program' in Williams.

[95] Williams, 'Internal Reasons and the Obscurity of Blame' 39–40.

[96] This paragraph is indebted to M Jenkins, *Bernard Williams* (Chesham, Acumen Press, 2006) ch 5.

reason statements: we launch them and hope that somewhere in the agent is some motivation that by some deliberative route might issue in the action we seek.'[97] They are like a lottery of sorts: we make our best guesses about the numbers in the box, hoping to be right.

It is at this point that an externalist might try to press a dilemma against the internal reasons account: if we believe that blame is the attitude we should have towards the abusive husband, then we should allow for external reasons; on the other hand, if we stick with internalism, then we should give up blame. This dilemma arises because we see blame as a justified attitude against the abusive husband, but at the same time, if blame is to be a justified reaction, then it must be towards acts or omissions the agent had reason to do or not do. It would make no sense, or so the objection goes, to blame someone for doing something that she had no other option but to do. Now, if internalism is true, there is no sound deliberative route from the abusive husband's motivational set to a reason to be better with his wife; he simply does not care about her. It seems, therefore, that reasons internalism would have the unsavoury conclusion that blame directed towards this husband is unjustified.[98]

According to Williams, the case of the abusive husband is an irredeemable one. There is nothing that we can say *to* him; we cannot reason *with* him. But this is not the general case. In general, it is not correct to assume that either people's reasons are straightforwardly evident to them, related in a clear and unambiguous way with what they care about, or that people have no reasons at all. Practical reasoning, as we have seen earlier, has room for much indeterminacy, and we should be open to the many cases in which people realise that they have reason to do or not to do something when such reason was not evident at the beginning of the deliberative process. According to Williams, *proleptic mechanisms* play an important role here: they try to articulate the materials in the motivational sets in order to provide reasons indirectly, so to say.[99] Regarding blame, this is how this works:

> People (…) have a general desire to be ethically well related to people they respect, and the expression of blame serves to indicate the fact that in virtue of this, they have a reason to avoid these things they did not have enough reason to avoid up to now. In these circumstances, blame consists of, as it were, a proleptic invocation of a reason to do or not do a certain thing, which applies in virtue of a disposition to have the respect of other people. To blame someone in this way is, roughly, to tell him he had a reason to act otherwise, and in a direct sense this may not have been true. Yet in a way it has now become true, in virtue of his having a disposition to do things that people he respects expect of him, and in virtue of the recognition, which it is hoped that the blame will bring to him, of what those people expect.[100]

[97] Williams, 'Internal Reasons and the Obscurity of Blame' 40. Also quoted by Jenkins, *Bernard Williams* (2006) 103.

[98] Williams, 'Internal Reasons and the Obscurity of Blame' 40–41.

[99] ibid 41–43. Jenkins discusses the proleptic mechanisms in Jenkins, *Bernard Williams* (2006) 103–05.

[100] Williams, 'Internal Reasons and the Obscurity of Blame' 41–42.

I believe that it is fair to say that proleptic mechanisms work as indirect, sound, deliberative routes. They go beyond the obvious in order to make a case for a certain reason for action. This adds many shades between the two extremes of the dichotomy pressed by the externalist. An abusive husband might not care at all about his wife, but he might care about other things, like the impact of his behaviour on their children, and at the very minimal level, he might care about being respected by people he cares about. Those materials, according to Williams, are a point of entry for ethical considerations, and they explain how we can get a reason for action that will stick to the abusive husband.[101] Of course, this picture of proleptic mechanisms is far from the situation we would want as the ideal. We would like this husband to become a better person because of considerations about his wife, not because of his longing for respect, but real agents are far below our wishes.

Another way to understand Williams' views is through Kate Manne's depiction of the process of giving reasons to someone as a kind of idealised conversation. According to her view, 'the process of reasoning with someone will be depicted as constrained by those motivations which the agent herself would have if the process of reasoning with her were to be perfected and completed. We are idealizing not the agent, but the relevant interpersonal process.'[102] The kind of idealisation Manne has in mind neatly accounts for the normative aspect of reasons internalism we saw earlier in this chapter. It enables us to provide important information regarding which the agent was unaware and to fix bits of her reasoning that are deficient.[103] Idealised conversations can bring about the reasons that the agent actually has and that are not, empirically speaking, obvious to her.[104]

There is an important consequence of this: an agent might have an internal reason for action even if she is unaware of it, granted that this reason bears a connection to the subjective motivational set of the agent through a sound deliberative route. The agent could have realised she had this reason had she been properly informed and reasoned correctly.[105] This is quite congenial to

[101] Miranda Fricker usefully refers to the desire for respect mentioned by Williams as a 'baseline disposition'. According to her, this is a 'baseline' because it enables further work to be done by deliberation, it can ground more complex motivations on the basic material of the agent's longing for respect. Absent this baseline, there is no starting point for the deliberation, and this agent will be, presumably, outside the reach of ethical considerations of any kind. As she puts in her keynote speech 'Postscript: On Having a Reason' in the Conference *Agency, Fate and Luck – Themes from Bernard Williams*, at Lund University (Sweden), June 2019, available at www.youtube.com/watch?v=kQgh6fjFADw, accessed 25 January 2025.

[102] K Manne, 'Internalism About Reasons: Sad but True?' (2014) 167 *Philosophical Studies* 89, 105.

[103] ibid 104–105.

[104] This is how she summarises the argument: 'a reason for an agent A to φ can hold only if A would become (somewhat) motivated to φ, following an idealized process of being reasoned with in this way'. Manne, 'Internalism About Reasons: Sad but True?' 112.

[105] This, too, is something that has been suggested earlier as well. To see this, recall our discussion of Frankfurt's example of the person living in a radioactive place and the reasons she had to move.

Williams's own later arguments on this matter. Williams at times speaks of a 'sympathetic adviser' or a 'deliberative assistant' that could help the agent to navigate its own world of reasons,[106] and he also explains that 'The stance towards the agent that is implied by the internalist account can be usefully compared to that of an imaginative and informed advisor, who takes seriously the formula "If I were you …".'[107]

What about an agent that is immune even to such proleptic mechanisms? She really is a 'hard case', an impossible one, even. We might want to blame this agent as well, but then the question is: what is the point of blame in such a case? She will not recognise it, be moved by it, feel remorse, or anything like that. Our blaming will simply not stick to her. Williams says that in cases like this, we simply stop blaming. In a way, we stop caring: we see this agent as someone that is not fit for our social practices and relationships.[108] Towards those agents, we adopt something like PF Strawson's objective stance: agents that are totally out of reach for our practice of giving reasons are the ones we manage, avoid, protect or isolate; but they are not the ones we actually engage *with*.[109] This is the reason why sometimes it makes no sense to blame psychopaths. They do not care at all about anything, and blame is meaningless to them.

It is important to keep in mind, however, that blame plays other roles besides this one in our practices of giving reasons. It can also be an expressive practice. In this mode, blame is less about the blamed person, and more about our expression of anger, resentment and emotions of this sort. This is illustrated by cases in which we put our fingers in the chest of the one we want to blame and exclaim: 'This is your fault!', and then simply walk away from the person. This expressive role is not necessarily connected to recognition by the blamed party. Someone might tell us: 'She does not care'. To this, we might also reply: 'I know, but I wanted to throw it at her face nonetheless.' In such an expressive role, blame is not connected to the reasons an agent might have and can be present in both usual cases and Williams' 'hard cases'. It seems to me that to believe that blame has just one function is an unwarranted restriction. Our practices of blame can be more complex than that; they can serve a multitude of purposes, and their 'obscurity', to use Williams' word, might very well be constitutive of them. We wouldn't be the kind of beings we are without some practice of blame, even though we are not really sure about what blame does for us. Be it as it may, we do not need to give up our practices of blame just because internalism is true.

[106] Williams, 'Values, Reasons, and the Theory of Persuasion' 115, 117.

[107] Williams, 'Postscript: Some Further Notes on Internal and External Reasons' 94. Also quoted in a footnote in Manne, 'Internalism about Reasons: Sad but True?' (2014) 99.

[108] Williams, 'Internal Reasons and the Obscurity of Blame' 43.

[109] PF Strawson, *Freedom and Resentment and Other Essays* (London, Routledge, 2008). For a text connecting reasons internalism with Strawsonian arguments, see Manne, 'Internalism about Reasons: Sad but True?'.

VII. Internalism and Ethical Considerations

A. Korsgaard and Wilson on the Role of Ethical Considerations

The most appealing objection to an internalist model of practical reasoning is that it leaves too limited a space for ethical and moral considerations. Because of its relevance, this objection deserves a section of its own. There are at least two versions of it. In a first version, internalism – as presented until now – does not pay enough attention to the role of ethical considerations and ought to make amends for that. In a second version, the internalist view is misguided in its own structure, because its account of what it is to have a reason is misguided. The first kind of criticism is about the content of internalism, and it is more of a helpful criticism; the second one is about the structure or form of internalism, and it challenges the presuppositions of the model. This sub-section will discuss the first criticism, and the following one will discuss the second criticism. A further sub-section will approach the issues raised in a different manner, highlighting a hidden premise in the criticisms discussed in this and in the next sub-section.

A good example of this first kind of criticism is given by Christine Korsgaard. In her view, there is nothing in Williamsian internalism that makes it incompatible with Kantian pure practical reason.[110] This claim, surprising at first sight, is actually very reasonable and made up of three steps. Firstly, and in agreement with Williams, she endorses what she names the 'internalism requirement', according to which 'Practical-reason claims, if they are really to present us with reasons for action, must be capable of motivating rational persons.'[111] This is roughly equivalent to what I have called the requirement of explanation. Secondly, and still in agreement with Williams, Korsgaard adds that since people can care about more things than just egoistic desires and means-end reasoning, people can also care about ethical values.

It is at the third step that there is room for disagreement with Williams. Once we have admitted that people might care about ethics, she says that there is no reason for us to 'close off without argument the possibility that reason could yield conclusions that every rational being must acknowledge and be capable of being motivated by'.[112] To put it in other words, from the fact that people care about many different things, there is no reason for us to derive the conclusion that people cannot share – in virtue of human rationality – a concern with the ethical. As I interpret her claim, Korsgaard means that there might be a deliberative route

[110] C Korsgaard, 'Skepticism About Practical Reason' in C Korsgaard, *Creating the Kingdom of Ends* (Cambridge, Cambridge University Press, 1996).
[111] ibid 317.
[112] ibid 328.

available to every agent that will show her that she cares about the ethical. Reason in itself would commit us to the ethical.[113]

Korsgaard's argument provides us with a way into the ethical that would be open to anyone due to reason. However, as Williams remarks, this argument must be made, and it is a very hard one to spell out. It must be shown that ethical concerns can be grounded through a sound deliberative route to the subjective motivational sets of *any* rational being.[114] This is, indeed, the project of ethical constitutivism: the project of showing that in virtue of our own agency we would necessarily be committed to some form of ethical content. In its shape, this project is similar to the one Williams himself deploys to explain why there is a general interest in the acquirement of correct beliefs and in corrections of reasoning. The important thing to notice, however, is that if the project of ethical constitutivism succeeds, it will ground internal reasons, as its ethical content is entirely derived from the subjective motivational sets of agents.[115]

A similar story unfolds for Aristotelian arguments. In rough terms, for Aristotelian views, there is the idea of well-being or *eudaimonia*, and this idea provides us with a measure for the good life. This can be interpreted in more than one way. In the more conventional reading of Aristotle, the content of *eudaimonia* was defined in part through a *telos*, or purpose, that was dependent on Aristotelian metaphysics. Under this reading, the idea of *eudaimonia* would provide external reasons for action since the *telos* is independent of particularities of individuals. There is a right way to live that is given by facts of nature. Even this reading can be recast in internalist terms, however. If an Aristotelian committed to this view manages to provide us with an argument that shows why what every agent *actually* wants is to live according to a given understanding of *eudaimonia*, then this Aristotelian would have succeeded in showing an internalist route to *eudaimonia*.[116] It is worth mentioning, however, that this same Aristotelian could reject the requirement of explanation. She could say that she is concerned with an account of reasons that is not about the explanation of action. As we have seen in our discussion of Hooker's criticism of Williams, this is in principle a possibility. The resulting account, however, would not be about reasons for action in the sense I am exploring in this chapter. This is why earlier I said that this move would amount to a change of subject.

[113] For further analyses of Korsgaard's constitutivism, as well as JD Velleman's, see P Katsafanas, *Agency and the Foundations of Ethics* (Oxford, Oxford University Press, 2013) 68–108.

[114] John Deigh believes that there is no need for Williams to concede even this. See J Deigh, 'Williams on Practical Reason' in J Deigh, *From Psychology to Morality: Essays in Ethical Naturalism* (Oxford, Oxford University Press, 2018).

[115] Williams, 'Postscript: Some Further Notes on Internal and External Reasons' 94; Williams, 'Internal Reasons and the Obscurity of Blame' footnote 3; Williams, 'Values, Reasons, and the Theory of Persuasion' 111. See also the discussion in Jenkins, *Bernard Williams* (2006) 105–109.

[116] For Williams' discussion of *eudaimonia*, see B Williams, *Ethics and the Limits of Philosophy* (London, Routledge, 2011) ch 3. My argument in this paragraph is based on Williams' general discussion in that chapter.

On other (and, to my mind, subtler) readings of Aristotle, what counts as *eudaimonia* is heavily influenced by the particularities of agents. As Teichmann observes, a more sophisticated, richer understanding of *eudaimonia* is available for an Aristotelian. This richer view treats it not as a one-dimensional kind of development, but as a kind of 'human flourishing' that might involve things like arts, creativity, spontaneity, and more. Through human flourishing, says Teichmann, there can be pluralism regarding *eudaimonia*. This means that the Aristotelian is not necessarily stuck with the idea that there can be only one proper conception of a good life.[117] The content of *eudaimonia* can be different for different people. Now, and here is the important point for my purposes, if that were to be the case, then we would be within the confines of internalism from the start. *Eudaimonia* would be equivalent to what a particular agent really wants, after considerate deliberation.[118] Different people would flourish in different ways, and they find out how they do that through their first-personal practical deliberation.

Another argument in the vicinity of Korsgaard's is Catherine Wilson's in her recent and interesting paper 'Moral Authority and the Limits of Philosophy'. Like Korsgaard, she believes that Williams is essentially right, but that there is more room for moral criticism than he originally thought. Wilson's argument takes as its starting point the fact that moral theorists, Kant and Bentham are her examples, are in a position quite similar to Owen Wingrave's relatives. Both Kant and Bentham have moral advice for people, but if people fail to care about moral or ethical considerations, their advice will not connect to them, and they will pay them no attention. To bring her point home, Wilson recalls Williams' Gauguin. The painter was deliberating if he should abandon his family and move to Tahiti in order to pursue his passion as an artist. If a moral theorist were to advise Gauguin against his departure, she would need to somehow tap on things that Gauguin cares about; otherwise she would sound just like Owen's parents.[119] Gauguin works as a focal point for Wilson's main worry, which she calls the 'exceptionalist threat': 'Because I am so clever, attractive, appetitive, visionary, and charismatic, or possessed of such an extraordinary mission (…) conventional morality does not apply to me.'[120]

Since morality or ethics is supposed, according to Wilson, to 'protect the weak from the strong',[121] how can it tackle the 'exceptionalist threat'? Wilson's proposal is a distinction between two kinds of narratives, 'condemnatory' and 'vindicative'. People's actions, says Wilson, are explained by means of different narratives that mobilise concepts that make sense for us, notably thick concepts

[117] Teichmann, 'How Should one Live? Williams on Practical Deliberation and Reasons for Acting' 219–20.

[118] Later in the book I will discuss John Finnis' views. The remarks made here anticipate some of the troubles we will identify in Finnis' theory.

[119] C Wilson, 'Moral Authority and the Limits of Philosophy' in SG Chappell and MV Ackeren (eds), *Ethics Beyond the Limits* (London, Routledge, 2018) 240–42.

[120] ibid 244.

[121] ibid 243.

that are part of a given form of life. We can say of Gauguin that he is acting like a 'selfish bastard', for instance, or that the brutish husband is nasty, disgusting and so on.[122] Because most people 'have been inculcated into a framework that makes use of condemnatory and exculpatory narratives',[123] those narratives will have the necessary authority over them. I think that Wilson frames the matter in an illuminating manner, but her solution does not advance when compared to Williams' original claims.

There is some obscurity caused by the indeterminacy regarding *the audience* of the narratives. If the narrative is directed towards the agent (eg, Gauguin), to the extent that those narratives depend on what the agent concretely cares about, I fail to see how they differ from Williams' original argument of sound deliberative routes. Let's say I present to Gauguin the 'condemnatory narrative' according to which abandoning his family will make him a 'selfish bastard'. If he hears my narrative and ends up agreeing with it, he might also end up giving up his plans to leave. This, however, is not different from Williams' original claim: if I can present a sound deliberative route from what Gauguin cares about to the reasons against his departure, then I have a chance of dissuading him. To go beyond Williams' original claim, Wilson needs to provide an argument that explains *why* an agent that is not persuaded by the condemnatory narrative *should* change his mind. Absent this argument, it is open to Gauguin to tell her the same thing he tells his other critics: 'I see your reasons, I just happen to not care about them.' It is true that Wilson appeals to thick concepts by claiming that they are part of the narratives, but thick concepts only have authority over those that already accept them. There is a story involving Oscar Wilde that Williams once quoted that nicely illustrates this. When enquired by those that reprimanded his work if he thought it to be obscene, Wilde replied: 'obscenity is not a word of mine'.[124]

The more interesting alternative sees the audience of the narratives as third parties observing the situation.[125] After listening to the condemnatory narrative, people will either distance themselves or punish the agent. In this scenario, the narratives people tell about the agent might have influence over the way the agent acts. Someone might say this to Gauguin: 'If people find out that you abandoned your family in a state of misery to create your art, no one will see any value in your paintings, nor will you be recognised as the genius that you are.' Now, if Gauguin finds himself moved by this argument, we should note that its authority over him is not necessarily ethical or moral. It can be instrumental.[126] The only thing that the argument *necessarily* shows is that people can have

[122] ibid 245.
[123] ibid 245.
[124] B Williams, 'Truth in Ethics' (1995) 8(3) *Ratio* 227, 237.
[125] We can say that the narratives fuel their reactions to the agent in a way similar to PF Strawson's 'vicarious attitudes'. See PF Strawson, *Freedom and Resentment and Other Essays* (London, Routledge, 2008).
[126] Wilson herself recognises the importance of these kinds of arguments but fails to connect them with her own solution. See Wilson, 'Moral Authority and the Limits of Philosophy' 244.

non-ethical reasons to act according to the demands of ethics. The effects of narratives whose audience are third parties on the agents *might* develop into an ethical form, however.[127] If such 'condemnatory narratives' succeed in connecting a certain action to the things that the agent cares about, they might become ethical *if* among those things that the agent cares about we have ethical considerations. If this is what Wilson had in mind, she is probably right, but then her account fails to add more leverage to moral criticism than what was originally available in Williams' original account.

B. Categorical Reasons and Interpretive Reasoning

What about the second form of the criticism adumbrated at the beginning of the previous sub-section, about the structure of internalism? Ronald Dworkin figures as a good example of this.[128] In *Justice for Hedgehogs*, Dworkin engages explicitly with Williams's internalism, contrasting it with his own view, that someone has a reason to do something 'if (but only if) doing that would be *good* for him'.[129] Dworkin's view favours the existence of 'categorical reasons', that is, reasons for action that exist for the individual and that are independent from what he cares about.[130] This is so because what is *good* for the agent does not necessarily coincide with anything that can be drawn from the agent's motivational set. What is *good*, says Dworkin, is defined by our best understanding of our ethical considerations, which, in turn, depends on constructive interpretation. I will come back to this idea in a moment. It is fair to say that a categorical reason in Dworkin's terms is an external reason in Williams'.

Dworkin's argument in favour of external reasons and of his model proceeds in the following way. Firstly, he claims that 'The concept of having a reason is an interpretive concept.'[131] A Dworkinian interpretive concept is a concept subject to what he calls constructive interpretation. Constructive interpretation 'is a matter of imposing purpose on an object or practice in order to make of it the best possible example of the form or genre to which it is taken to belong';[132] and an interpretation is correct or true for Dworkin when it can 'form a large interconnected and interdependent system of principles and ideas'.[133] This is a kind of coherence theory: an interpretation is better than another when it is more coherent, and its many parts support each other. Secondly, equipped with

[127] See, for instance, Williams' discussion about in Williams, *Truth and Truthfulness* (2002) 120.
[128] Dworkin will be discussed in much more detail later in the fifth chapter.
[129] R Dworkin, *Justice for Hedgehogs* (Cambridge, MA, Harvard University Press, 2011) 50, my emphasis.
[130] ibid 49.
[131] ibid 51.
[132] R Dworkin, *Law's Empire* (Cambridge, MA, Harvard University Press, 1986) 52. Dworkin's parlance seems to treat 'rationality' and 'practical reasoning' as the same thing.
[133] Dworkin, *Justice for Hedgehogs* (2011) 117.

this method, Dworkin proceeds by saying that his account – which has space for external reasons – is preferable to Williams' because it 'ties rationality to ethics',[134] it makes practical reason and ethics mutually supportive, and it brings together the explanation of practical reason with its justification:

> A conception of rationality would be a poor one – it could serve no *justifying purpose* – if it declared that someone has a reason to get what he wants even if getting it would be bad for him. So an ethical theory – a theory about what is good or bad for people – must be part of a successful theory of reasons and rationality.[135]

Dworkin's argument against Williams appeals to his theory of interpretation to say that our very notion of practical reason is constructively interpretative; this is why it challenges the very structure of internalism. The problem is that Dworkin's attempt to bring together explanation and ethical justification is unwarranted. Dworkin rightly points out that our use of the terminology of reasons is not univocal. We came across this idea earlier: during my discussion of Hooker's criticism of Williams, I have mentioned different senses of the term reasons for action. We do say that 'Stalin had no reason to kill his subjects' and that the 'brutish husband had no reason to mistreat his wife'. In such contexts, we usually mean with those propositions that there are no 'external' or 'objective' considerations in favour of those actions (killing the subjects, mistreating the wife). However, in other contexts we also formulate propositions that mean that those agents, Stalin and the brutish husband, had no reasons to act differently from what they did, that is, that they had no *proper* reasons for action to act in a different way. 'Reason' can be used in many ways.

From this correct claim, Dworkin moves to the unwarranted conclusion that, since we disagree about what it means to say that someone has a reason, we should look for the all-things-considered best interpretation; but the idea that 'The concept of having a reason is an interpretive concept'[136] cannot be taken for granted. Because the best interpretation for Dworkin is the one that reveals a given phenomenon in its best moral light, he ends up conflating the criteria for success at the *justification* of something and the criteria for success at the *explanation* of something, but this is not something that can be assumed without further argument.

Dworkin's argument has an important gap. From the fact that we are in the dark about what it means to have a reason, he infers that to have a reason must be an ethical matter. This would be true if the way to go in deciding about what it means to have a reason were the same way to go in moral disagreements, but there is no evidence of that. In moral disagreement, says Dworkin, we try to present the most coherent interpretation of our moral values that shows how they support each other. Now, even if this were true in ethics, this is not what the

[134] ibid 51.
[135] ibid 51, my emphasis.
[136] ibid 51.

philosophical discussion about reasons for action is about, or to be more precise, this does not exhaust the discussion. The category of having a reason involves not only normative considerations broadly conceived (in the sense that there can be corrections of fact and reasoning) but also phenomenological aspects in the sense that the category is concerned with an accurate description of our experience from our point of view as agents. This is what I have tried to capture with the requirement of explanation. There is no reason to prefer an account of practical reason simply because this account best justifies, morally speaking, the exercise of practical reason.

Dworkin might reply by saying that he is concerned with normative reasons and not with motivational reasons. This is something that is made clear in the following excerpt:

> If I am right, then someone who lives as Stalin did has a bad life: his life is bad for him *even if he does not recognize that it is*. Williams had a different ethical theory. He thought that what is good or bad for people depends only on what they genuinely want. He was skeptical about any more objective ethical or moral truth, and he therefore denied the possibility of categorical reasons.[137]

This is a good time to consider the distinction that is often presented between normative and motivational reasons. Practical reasoning has a normative component since it allows for corrections of beliefs and of deficits in reasoning. However, when someone says that practical reasoning is about normative reasons, this person might mean something more. She might mean that there are reasons that can be justified independently of the contingent motivations of the agents. The claim is that there are reasons for action for the agent that do not motivate him to act. The discussion some paragraphs ago of the examples of the husband and of Stalin seemed to be capturing this. There seems to be that additional sense of reasons for action that is not accurately described by the model I've been defending.

Williams insisted, to my mind correctly, that '[i]t must be a mistake simply to separate explanatory and normative reasons'.[138] As I have tried to argue previously in this chapter, reasons that are independent from the motivations of the agents cannot be proper reasons *for action*, and an account of those reasons cannot be an account of *practical* reasoning. This is so because they fail to account for the requirement of explanation. For a reason to be normative (or external) in Dworkin's sense, this must be a reason for action that would be there for the agent, even if this reason is never recognised or acted upon (because it bears no connection to the subjective motivational set). To say that this reason is a reason for action in the sense that this reason plays a role in that agent's deliberation about what she ought to do would be incorrect. Note that I am not claiming that a reason not recognised by an agent does not exist, nor that we cannot call it a reason

[137] ibid 51, my emphasis.
[138] Williams, 'Internal Reasons and the Obscurity of Blame' 38–39.

for action in a certain sense. I am claiming that it cannot exist as a *proper reason for action for that specific agent* because it cannot explain her action, either actual or potential (it is worth remembering that there can be internal reasons about which the agent is unaware). Proper reasons for action must be based on what an agent cares about and they must be acceptable to her through a sound deliberative route.[139]

Now, there is no logical impediment in the case a Dworkinian decides to bite the bullet and give up the requirement of explanation from the start. Her claim that there are reasons for action that are not connected to what people care about, however, would be about something else entirely, not about proper reasons for action, that is, the kinds of reasons that can bear on what an agent does (or could do). Like one of the hypothetical Aristotelians I have introduced earlier, the Dworkinian would have changed the subject, and her argument would be about something that my argument (and Williams') is not.

C. Practical Reasoning and the Supreme Value of Ethical Considerations

There is a shared premise in Korsgaard, Wilson and Dworkin that will reward further commentary. The authors share a concern that Williamsian internalism is ill-equipped to criticise behaviour (and at least in one case, Dworkin's, the rationality and the morality of the behaviour were tied together, so to criticise behaviour as immoral would be tantamount to criticising it as being irrational). The underlying premise is that moral or ethical considerations have supreme value, that if they are present and that this can be shown to agents, then agents will have overriding reasons to do what ethics or morality commands.[140] This premise is important because without it moral or ethical considerations are not as powerful as moralists would like them to be. In turn, this would mean that even if moral or ethical considerations could be present for every agent, this fact in itself would not be enough to warrant the importance of ethics or morality for the agents. Here is the problem with it: real agents care about other things besides ethics or morality.[141] They care about personal projects, goals, relationships, and so on. It is far from clear why we should accept the supremacy of ethics or morality if the only

[139] Veronica Rodriguez-Blanco also sees this distinction between normative and motivational reasons as a problem. For her, this distinction obscures the explanation of practical reasoning. V Rodriguez-Blanco, *Law and Authority under the Guise of the Good* (Oxford, Hart Publishing, 2014) 2.

[140] Another way to make the same point is to claim that the premise is misguided insofar as it treats moral or ethical reasons as what Williams has called a 'moral obligation', a consideration to do or not to do something that is overridingly important. See Williams, *Ethics and the Limits of Philosophy* (2011) 7, 194–201.

[141] See, for instance, S Wolf, 'Moral Saints' (1982) 79(8) 8 *Journal of Philosophy* 419.

reason for doing so is that ethics or morality themselves tell us to do that.[142] This is how Williams puts this point:

> For impartial morality, if the conflict really does arise, must be required to win; and that cannot necessarily be a reasonable demand on the agent. There can come a point at which it is quite unreasonable for a man to give up, in the name of the impartial good ordering of the world of moral agents, something which is a condition of his having any interest in being around that world at all.[143]

An example might be useful here. At the Prologue of Euripides' *Hippolytus*, the goddess Aphrodite presents her case. She was gravely offended by Hippolytus, the illegitimate son of Theseus. Because of that, she made Theseus' wife, Phaedra, fall madly in love with Hippolytus, thus triggering the events that would cause Phaedra's own death and that of Hippolytus. This is what Aphrodite says:

> Renowned shall Phaedra be in her death, but none the less die she must.
> Her suffering does not weigh in the scale so much
> that I should let my enemies go untouched
> escaping payment of that retribution
> that honor demands that I have.[144]

A contemporary reader might find Aphrodite's lack of concern for Phaedra shocking, but given what she cares about, the honours that she understands are due to her thanks to her godly nature, could she have wanted something different? Aphrodite cares about her honour; her honour was violated, so she takes this as a reason to punish the offender. As a piece of practical reasoning, Aphrodite's deliberation is irreproachable. It seems off the mark to insist that Aphrodite should have acted according to moral or ethical considerations, especially if by this we mean *our* moral or ethical considerations. They would be free-floating entities that cannot connect themselves with what she cares about; they would be like the radiation in Frankfurt's example: if someone does not care at all about their health, the radiation is simply not important to them. Aphrodite recognises that Phaedra will die, but that this is not as important as the restitution of her honour. In other words, the goddess cares more about her status than about Phaedra's life. Ethical considerations do not have the force that sometimes moral theorists claim them to have. Aphrodite's 'too bad' style of answer is unnerving, but it is certainly rational and an example of agency.

Cases like Aphrodite's might make us want to believe that ethics or morality enjoy some sort of authority in practical reason, but there is no way to ground this belief. Indeed, even if there are external reasons, they would not suffice to ground that authority, as those external (moral) reasons would still

[142] See also H Frankfurt, *The Reasons of Love* (Princeton, Princeton University Press, 2004) 6–8.
[143] B Williams, 'Persons, Character and Morality' in B Williams, *Moral Luck* (Cambridge, Cambridge University Press, 1981) 14.
[144] Euripides, *Hippolytus*, trans D Greene (Chicago, The University of Chicago Press, 1942) lines 46–50.

need to compete with all other reasons an agent might have. As remarked by Susan Wolf,[145] the belief in the supremacy of morality or ethics flies in the face of how we actually reason. We should notice that much of the richness of our lives comes from things that we care about that are not related to ethics or morality: aesthetical appreciation, gastronomic experiences, beauty both physical and intellectual – all those things are not required by ethics or morality.[146] If moral or ethical considerations were supreme, the agent would be rationally demanded to do whatever it takes and to sacrifice anything so that he could follow the reasons of ethics or morality. This demand, obviously enough, is not reasonable. As Williams says:

> Life has to have substance if anything is to have sense, including adherence to the impartial system; but if it has substance, then it cannot grant supreme importance for the impartial system, and that system's hold on it will be, at the limit, insecure.[147]

VIII. Open-Minded Internalism: A Summary

In a very compelling essay, David Velleman describes himself as a 'fainthearted externalist'.[148] Velleman's claim is made in the context of his argument that the dichotomy between reasons internalism and reasons externalism is false.[149] According to him, all (full-blooded) actions share a basic aim, that of autonomy, understood here as 'being in control of one's behavior'.[150] Velleman's point, as I understand it, is that this basic aim (in other writings he speaks of a 'drive')[151] is behind the motivational powers of whatever reasons we come to have. Velleman sees no reason why such a basic aim (that every agent has due to their very status as an agent) could not motivate one to act 'on considerations that aren't based on desires at all',[152] hence his suspicions about the dichotomy. He might have a point. We might even wonder if Velleman's basic aim is not, at the end of the day, a very general desire or disposition we all share, in the same sense we all have a general desire to acquire correct beliefs regarding our more specific interests or goals (remember our discussion of Williams' example of the glass containing petrol/gin and tonic).

[145] Wolf, 'Moral Saints'.
[146] Unless, of course, we extend those categories in a way that would make them very different from what moral theorists have in mind. If this turns out to be a plausible option, then I would have no quarrel at all.
[147] Williams, 'Persons, Character and Morality' 18.
[148] JD Velleman, 'The Possibility of Practical Reason' (1996) 106(4) *Ethics* 694, 704.
[149] ibid 695–96.
[150] ibid 719.
[151] See, in general, JD Velleman, *The Possibility of Practical Reason*, 2nd edn (Michigan, Michigan Publishing, 2014).
[152] Velleman, 'The Possibility of Practical Reason' 726.

I am myself more inclined to a different label, that of an *open-minded internalist*. The reasoning behind this label is that we can get ourselves to new reasons for action (or to abandon some reasons for action we originally had) through the exercise of practical reason. Our desires, projects and the like are not set in stone: we deliberate in order to achieve those things, but deliberation also affects the reasons we have to achieve those things. Furthermore, deliberation is not a game in which every move is valid. There is space for corrections regarding facts (as in the case of the glass containing petrol) but also regarding reasoning (as in cases of wishful thinking and self-deception). All of this means that, as agents, we can deliberate well or badly, and that we can change who we are when we deliberate about what we will do.

There is a silver lining to the somewhat depressing discussion of this chapter. Given the openness of practical deliberation, people can change for the better. Not always, of course, but in many cases that is a real possibility. The realisation that practical reasoning is open-ended and that we can shape ourselves through its exercise also opens new and exciting questions for both moral and political philosophy.[153] Crucially, we need to think hard about the kinds of persons we want to be and that we want other members of our community to be. We also need to think about what we find justifiable in terms of education. Still, for reasons well discussed in political philosophy – from alienation to the conditions of Modernity, to pluralism and stability to resentment – we should be careful in our aspirations to change ourselves and others.[154]

It is a good idea at this stage to summarise the view on practical reason I've been developing in this chapter, the so-called *open-minded reasons internalism*:

1. Williams' original statement is the following: '*A has a reason to φ only if he could reach the conclusion to φ by a sound deliberative route from the motivations he already has*'.[155]
2. There are two elements in this original formulation: 'sound deliberative routes' and the 'subjective motivational set'.
3. Against Teichmann's worry that Williams' argument was ambiguous regarding desire, I proposed that we treat the subjective motivational set as the things that an agent cares about (following Frankfurt).
4. To this picture, I added considerations about practical necessity, about the perception we have of the good, and about reasons-responsiveness. Together, those considerations addressed the phenomenological blind spots of the Williamsian account.

[153] Veronica Rodriguez-Blanco made much effort to convince me of this. I am thankful for all our conversations about this topic.

[154] See, in general, B Williams, *In the Beginning was the Deed* (G Hawthorn ed, Princeton, Princeton University Press, 2005). See too DP Murata, 'Justification, Coercion and Political Responsibility: Remarks on Ethical Environmentalism' (2025) 16(2) *Jurisprudence* 352.

[155] Williams, 'Internal Reasons and the Obscurity of Blame' 35.

5. I also claimed that all plausible candidates for external reasons, such as institutional reasons and moral reasons, could be either described as internal reasons, or that they were not proper reasons for action due to the *requirement of explanation*.
6. The idea of a 'sound deliberative route' was explained as any kind of narrative that can make sense of an action of an agent for herself and for third parties that share enough of her form of life.
7. Deliberation admits of corrections of both facts and reasoning. Not everything goes, since one can deliberate badly (ie, wishful thinking) or have misguided information (ie, the gin and tonic case).
8. The upshot is that an agent might have an internal reason for action even when she is unaware of its existence.
9. Our subjective motivational sets are not fixed. They can change with our engagement in practical reason (ie, we can abandon some projects and values, start to endorse some new goal, etc). In this sense, practical reason moves in two ways.

Given all of the above, we might wonder if at the end of the day Velleman is right by claiming that the dichotomy between internalism and externalism is false. It might very well be. Labels aside, the position I have been developing under the name of 'open-minded reasons internalism' sounds plausible enough to orient our enquiries going forward.

IX. Preliminary Remarks about the Reason-Giving Character of the Law

This chapter provided us with a picture of how the agent deliberates. She starts from her subjective motivational set and moves to reasons for action through a sound deliberative route. When it comes to the reason-giving character of the law, this means that for law to provide reasons for action to a given agent, there must be some connection between the law and the subjective motivational set of this agent; that is, there must be something in the agent that can ground law's normativity. To the extent that there are general or shared elements that belong to the motivational sets of different individuals, those shared elements can be connected to their reasons via a sound deliberative route in such a way that they will play a part in their answers to practical questions. This means an explanation of the reason-giving character of the law will have its generality proportional to the generality of the items on which it is based. The more widely spread the item, the more general the answer.

The question that arises is this: given the account of practical reasoning defended here, what kinds of items can account for the reason-giving character of the law? Those are considerations that move from the agent towards the law; they are related to what it means for an agent to respect the law. They belong to the issues that I will explore in the fourth chapter of this book. Before advancing my positive account, however, I want to turn my attention to an influential account of the reason-giving character of the law, the one offered by legal positivism, or, to be more accurate, the account that *could* be provided by it.

3

Practical Reason, Political Rule, and the Limits of Legal Positivism

I. Introduction

There are two broad claims underpinning this book. Firstly, there is a claim about the agent that engages in practical reason. Agents have projects, values, dispositions, and motivations that are, in a sense, subjective, and those play a central role in the explanation of reasoning and action. I've developed this claim in the previous chapter; through the view I have called open-minded reasons internalism.

Secondly, there is a more jurisprudential claim. The law as we know it is part of a broader story or narrative of political rule.[1] To rule over others is more than just being able to control them, it also involves the idea that there is a demand for *respect*[2] from its subjects. Putting the two claims together, if we want to understand the relationship between law and reason and action, we need to understand how law can demand respect from its concrete subjects, subjects that have projects, values, dispositions and so on. As just mentioned, the first claim was discussed in the previous chapter. In this chapter, I will start the discussion of the second claim in connection with the limitations of legal positivism, although a more comprehensive analysis of it will have to wait until the next chapter.

There are two things I want to do in this chapter. Firstly, I will lay down Hart's basic insight about the internal point of view since this idea will be helpful to frame our inquiry. Secondly, I will argue that legal positivists following Hart's lead presented insightful functional[3] accounts of the law, but that because legal positivism was committed to what Williams has called a 'fictional genealogy', it ended up being a theory ill-equipped to explain the reason-giving character of the law. This is so due to two reasons related to the claims just stated. Firstly,

[1] See J Deigh, 'Emotion and the Authority of Law' in J Deigh, *Emotions, Values and the Law* (New York, Oxford University Press, 2008). I take my overall project to be in tandem with Deigh's article.

[2] I am using the term 'respect' in a quite broad sense here. Later I will add much more detail to this. Deigh speaks of something similar to this very broad notion of respect when he talks about 'allegiance' to the law. As far as I know, the most important discussion of respect for the law is that of Joseph Raz. I will analyse it in detail in the next chapter.

[3] I will develop in greater detail what Williams meant by the idea of a function a few paragraphs below.

legal positivism pays little attention to the more concrete, contingent aspects of ourselves. When we attempt to get an explanation of how law affects our practical reasoning from positivism, we are fated to get explanations that are at best incomplete; that is, positivists are not in the business of providing an account of the first, agential, claim above. Secondly, the narratives that the positivists present of law's origin do not pay enough attention to law's dimension as 'a political institution', to use John Deigh's wording.[4] This means that accounts of the reason-giving character of law extracted from positivist philosophers tend to ignore the second claim made above and, in effect, a central aspect of law as it appears to us.

Three preliminary remarks are needed. Firstly, as many authors have already pointed out,[5] legal positivism today is somewhat of a misnomer. The school has authors as diverse as HLA Hart, Joseph Raz, Jules Coleman, Andrei Marmor and Scott Shapiro in their ranks, and there is also the contentious case of normative or ethical positivism, with Jeremy Waldron and Liam Murphy being two of its defendants.[6] Williams was fond of quoting a remark by his former teacher, Gilbert Ryle, that he (Ryle) was 'Not interested in isms: we can talk about some things positivists say.'[7] This sounds like the right approach. In this chapter, I will analyse what some positivists said, notably Hart, Jules Coleman, Scott Shapiro and Joseph Raz (although it should be mentioned from the outset that I will discuss Raz in further detail in the next chapter as well), and after that, I will make more general claims based on the common traits detected in those authors.[8]

Secondly, it is sometimes claimed that legal positivism is not concerned with legal normativity or practical questions at all. If this were really the case, then my effort in this chapter would be misguided from the start. The claim is a half-truth for the reasons already mentioned. It is true that legal positivists do not attempt to directly answer how law can be reason-giving. Still, as I will try to show, they fail to describe an aspect that is *characteristic* of law, its part in a narrative of political rule; and more generally, underlying positivism there is an overly thin view of the agent that fails to explain how the law can be reason-giving. Stated at this abstract

[4] Deigh, 'Emotion and the Authority of Law' 145.

[5] See, for instance, D Dyzenhaus, 'The Genealogy of Legal Positivism' (2004) 24(1) *Oxford Journal of Legal Studies* 39.

[6] HLA Hart, *The Concept of Law*, 2nd edn (Oxford, Oxford University Press, 1994); J Raz, *The Authority of Law* (Oxford, Oxford University Press, 2009); J Coleman, *The Practice of Principle* (Oxford, Oxford University Press, 2001); A Marmor, *Philosophy of Law* (Princeton, Princeton University Press, 2010); SJ Shapiro, *Legality* (Cambridge, MA, Harvard University Press, 2011); J Waldron, 'Normative (or Ethical) Positivism' in J Coleman (ed), *Hart's Postscript: Essays on the Postscript to 'The Concept of Law'* (Oxford, Oxford University Press, 2001); L Murphy, 'The Political Question of the Concept of Law' in Coleman (ed), *Hart's Postscript: Essays on the Postscript to 'The Concept of Law'* (2001).

[7] B Williams, 'Replies' in JEJ Altham and R Harrison (eds), *World, Mind, and Ethics: Essays on the Ethical Philosophy of Bernard Williams* (Cambridge, Cambridge University Press, 1995) 186.

[8] When I use the word 'positivism', therefore, I am mostly referring to the authors that wrote under Hart's influence. This use does not cover all of the 'positivisms' in jurisprudence.

level, those claims do not amount to much, but I intend to make them sounder as we look at what positivists have said. At any case, my intent in this chapter is not a criticism of positivism per se, but an analysis of the limitations that would plague an account of the reason-giving character of the law that does not account for the two central claims presented. I believe that it is fair to say that I am deploying the resources of positivism to see if they can help us with the issue of the reason-giving character of the law. It would be a misguided verdict to say that they themselves have tried and failed to tackle that issue.

Thirdly, I am not the first to rely on Bernard Williams' genealogical method as a way to engage with the problem of legal normativity. Sylvie Delacroix, in the preface of *Legal Norms and Normativity*, claims that 'If anything distinguishes this book, it is the attempt to import into the theory of legal normativity a method which Williams has brilliantly developed in relation to the concept of truthfulness. (…) The narrative of this book seeks to explain how law, as a normative phenomenon, comes about. Likewise, it relies on what Williams calls a 'genealogy''.[9] As it will become clearer at a later moment, I am using Williamsian genealogy in a different way from Delacroix's. Most importantly for this chapter, we seem to disagree on whether Hart was committed or not with a genealogical approach (roughly, I think that he is; she thinks otherwise).[10] Before the conclusion of this chapter I will comment on Delacroix's ingenious use of Williams' genealogy and on her views about legal normativity.

I will begin this chapter by briefly presenting the genealogical method as it was developed by Williams. Equipped with the genealogical method, I will be able to present what I take to be a Hartian genealogy of the law and the idea of the internal point of view. Drawing from Jeffrey Kaplan and Scott Shapiro, I will claim that Hart was correct in saying that the internal point of view is an attitude adopted by the agents that helps to explain the rule-guided nature of the law, but I will add that this argument, by itself, is not an account of the reason-giving character of the law. To know *that* the law is reason-giving is one thing; to know *how* it is reason-giving is another. The remaining sections of the chapter have two purposes. Firstly, they will analyse attempts to 'remedy' Hart's original account, attempts made by Jules Coleman, Shapiro, and Joseph Raz. Secondly, the later bits of the chapter and its conclusion will recast the piecemeal discussion of the previous sections in a more general argument.

Before moving to the explanation of the genealogical method, I take another remark to be important. Once I've heard a legal theory professor say that regrettably jurisprudence sometimes sounds like the *Highlander* movie, in which a recurrent motto is the claim that 'there can be only one'. By that he meant that it is a common attitude in jurisprudence to present one's theory as if the theory were the only

[9] S Delacroix, *Legal Norms and Normativity – An Essay in Genealogy* (Oxford, Hart Publishing, 2006) xvi.

[10] In a later footnote I will discuss this again.

correct one.[11] I think his remark was onto something true, and one thing that I would like to avoid is to be misinterpreted as saying that the whole of Hart's or Shapiro's or Coleman's accounts is mistaken. What I am claiming is much more circumscribed. *I am claiming, firstly, that an overly abstract view of the practical agent cannot help us in understanding the reason-giving character of the law, and secondly, that there is a characteristic aspect of law as a political institution – its demand for respect – that is downplayed by legal positivism.* I have nothing to say here about the debate between exclusivist and inclusivist positivists, or about the role of moral considerations in the definition of our concept of law, for instance. Indeed, nothing that I will say is necessarily at odds with the main tenets of positivism. Some might even say that the upshot of this chapter can be seen as a defence of sorts for positivism, in the sense that we cannot demand from it an explanation that it didn't set up for itself to provide.

II. Genealogy and the Hartian Internal Point of View

A. The Genealogical Method

In the Introduction I have claimed that legal positivism is, in general, committed to a fictional genealogy of the law that enabled them to present insightful functional accounts of the law. What are we supposed to understand by that claim? In *Truth and Truthfulness*,[12] Williams explains what a genealogy is: it is 'a narrative that tries to explain a cultural phenomenon by describing a way in which it came about, or could have come about, or might be imagined to have come about'.[13] This definition actually contains two different kinds of genealogy. When a narrative explains how something came to be, we can have a 'real genealogy', a piece of real, contingent, history. On the other hand, when a narrative tells us how something could have appeared, we have a 'fictional genealogy'. This prompts the question: why would someone be interested in this kind of fiction? This is Williams' answer: a fictional genealogy 'helps to explain a concept or value or institution by showing ways in which it could have come about in a simplified environment containing certain kinds of human interests or capacities, which, relative to the story, are taken as given'.[14] In a fictional genealogy, we tell a story about how something – let's say X – could appear, taking into account the needs we take for granted that

[11] If I am not mistaken, the professor was Noel Struchiner, from the Pontifical Catholic University of Rio de Janeiro.

[12] B Williams, *Truth and Truthfulness* (Princeton, Princeton University Press, 2002). For a good review of the book, see T Nagel, 'Williams: The Value of Truth' in T Nagel, *Secular Philosophy and the Religious Temperament* (Oxford, Oxford University Press, 2010).

[13] Williams, *Truth and Truthfulness* (2002) 20.

[14] ibid 21.

the agents have. This X that appears somehow attends to those human needs. This is where *function* enters.[15]

We can say that a fictional genealogy is a narrative that presents how X could have appeared, taking into account its function in relation to human interests or capacities. This story will have some characteristics. Firstly, this narrative does not presuppose that the agents involved acted in a purposive or intentional way in creating this X that has a function for them. If that were the case, they would already have a concept or idea about X, and this would make the account redundant: it would presuppose the existence of the very thing it is trying to explain how it came to exist. Secondly, this genealogy usually has the shape of an explanation of an achievement. People that now have X can see their current situation as an improvement when compared to when they did not have X; that is, they can in principle see that X has some function for them considering their needs.[16]

Now we get to the important twist: a fictional genealogy is not enough to explain the value that something has for us *at the present moment*. We are not the agents depicted in the fictional genealogy. We can see an illustration of this point through Williams' own use of fictional genealogies to understand the virtues of truth. Williams tells us about the function of the virtues of truth through the narrative of a 'State of Nature'. This State of Nature is a stylised primitive society, characterised by its simplicity and lack of written language.[17] In such a primitive society, the virtues of truth are important for the survival of the group: they need to gather and transfer truthful information.[18] However, the functional value of the virtues of truth in that society might not be the same value that they have for us in our lives. If we want to explain this part of the value of the virtues of truth, we need to engage with their 'real history'.[19] What we need, from this point onwards, is a supplement of 'real genealogy'; the real, contingent narrative of those virtues.[20]

To summarise, in the case of the virtues of truth, Williams starts from the State of Nature, that is, a fictional and schematic scenario in which the origins of a given phenomenon can be explained through basic human needs.[21] In this scenario, those virtues fill a function in enabling the survival and flourishing of the group. In the State of Nature, the question asked is 'why do we have the virtues of truth?'; and to this, the answer is 'we have them because they enable us

[15] ibid 31–32.
[16] ibid 33–34. To be accurate, Williams presents three characteristics, but this makes no difference for my explanation.
[17] ibid 41.
[18] ibid 41–44.
[19] ibid 60.
[20] ibid 39.
[21] ibid 21. In another place, Williams usefully defines the State of Nature as 'a stripped-down and explicitly fictional account of an elementary society'. B Williams, 'Why Philosophy needs History' in B Williams, *Essays and Reviews 1959-2002* (Princeton, Princeton University Press, 2014) 408.

to both rely on the information we receive from others and to share the information we have'. The functional account, however, is in the best case incomplete. In the case of the virtues of truth, Williams highlights that they are not valuable *only* because they are useful for other purposes.[22] People value them also for intrinsic reasons; they recognise that those virtues have value in themselves. To explain why this is so, we need other resources. We need to grasp the kind of motivations and dispositions that individuals have, and in order to understand those, we need to look at contingent elements such as cultural developments.[23] Without appeal to such materials, we are destined to have an incomplete (or even distorted) understanding of what we are trying to explain. This is what Williams says about this:

> If you stop at the schematic picture, you may be left with the idea that truthfulness is a merely functional quality, and then be puzzled by the fact that it manifestly is not. Perhaps you will move to the general idea that it is a functional quality that needs to be understood as not merely functional. Philosophy without history will not get you much further than that (…).[24]

Bringing the point back to jurisprudence, I will argue that underlying Hartian positivism there is a fictional genealogy that explains the functional value of the law. Other authors such as Coleman and Shapiro seem to endorse – either explicitly or implicitly – Hart's general narrative. I will then argue that this kind of account is insufficient to explain the reason-giving character of the law. Positivist authors advance stories that resemble Williams' State of Nature and in doing so neatly account for the function of the law. They lack, however, a realistic understanding of who the agent deliberating is, and from which materials she deliberates. Those elements bring much contingency into jurisprudence, since they are dependent on the kinds of beings we are and on how we were, to a significant extent, shaped by our cultural landscape. As a result, the kinds of accounts of the reason-giving character of law we can get from the resources developed by the positivist are incomplete.

B. Positivism and Genealogy

It is time to present the Hartian fictional genealogy.[25] I think we should begin in the same way as Hart, with his criticism of John Austin's command theory. Austin famously defined the law as commands enacted by a sovereign. The key ideas

[22] Williams, *Truth and Truthfulness* (2002) 60.

[23] Williams, 'Why Philosophy needs History' 408.

[24] ibid 408.

[25] Any commentary on Hart faces a challenge from the start, namely, that there is so much written about him and so many different interpretations of his claims that it is no exaggeration to claim that every legal theorist has her 'personal Hart'. This is a point made by Dworkin about John Rawls in R Dworkin, *Justice in Robes* (Cambridge, MA, Harvard University Press, 2006) 261.

here are 'command' and 'sovereign': a command is an 'order backed by threats',[26] whereas a sovereign is someone (or some group) that is habitually obeyed and that does not obey anyone else in turn.[27] Hart's criticism of Austin is devastating because it starts from everyday facts about the law as we know it and shows how the Austinian model fails to explain them. Here is a first fact pointed out by Hart: after a long and successful reign, King Rex I dies, and his son, Rex II, takes the crown. This fact presses an explanatory challenge against the Austinian model, because Rex II is not habitually obeyed; he is not sovereign in the sense that his father was. Of course, as soon as he sits on the throne, his commands become law, independently of a former habit of obedience of citizens towards him. How can we explain this?[28] A second fact is this: in our lives, we make contracts, marry and divorce, open businesses and so on. The idea of a command seems accurate as a description of law when the paradigm is criminal law, but we use legal tools for many other things. Legal directives that tell us how to make a binding contract are better described not as commands, but as mechanisms that award us power to make contracts. To present them as commands backed by sanctions is artificial at best.[29]

Hart argues that the troubles in the Austinian picture have a common origin. Austin lacks an account of what *legal rules* are. To understand Hart's point, we must unpack the notion of a legal rule. It is in the development of this idea that I believe we can see his use of fictional genealogy. Let us follow Hart's strategy, beginning with the basic notion of a *habit*, and from it, we will move to the notion of a *social rule* and finally to *legal rules*. For Hart, a habit is merely a repeated pattern of behaviour that can be either individual or social. We can say that Immanuel has the habit of going for daily walks, or that the British have the habit of drinking tea in the afternoon. In the unlikely situation in which Immanuel does not go for a walk or that a British person skips tea, people might wonder why this happened. There is some expectation that has been frustrated. The non-conformity to a mere habit, however, does not ground any sort of serious criticism; at most, people might say things like, 'that's not usual of him!'[30]

This is different in the case of a social rule. According to Hart, a social rule is a pattern of behaviour that is accepted by people as a criterion for evaluation and criticism of conduct. This is Hart's own parlance:

> [I]f a social rule is to exist some at least must look upon the behaviour in question as a general standard to be followed by the group as a whole. A social rule has an 'internal' aspect, in addition to the external aspect which it shares with a social habit and which consists in the regular uniform behaviour which an observer could record.[31]

[26] Hart, *The Concept of Law* (1994) 20.
[27] This is discussed mostly in the second chapter of Hart, *The Concept of Law* (1994).
[28] Hart, *The Concept of Law* (1994) 51–55.
[29] ibid 32–42.
[30] ibid 55.
[31] ibid 56.

This excerpt adds three important ideas. The first one is the 'external aspect' that is shared by both social rules and habits; this is the pattern of behaviour that can be noted by an observer. The second idea is the 'internal aspect' that sets social rules apart from habits. This aspect means that those that accept the rule use it as a reason[32] in the assessment of the conduct of themselves and others. The 'internal aspect' corresponds to an acceptance of the pattern from an 'internal point of view', and imports what Hart calls a 'reflective critical attitude'.[33] The third and often overlooked idea in the excerpt is that a pattern is a social rule if and only if enough people take it to be applicable to the whole community. Some pattern is not a social rule if it is accepted by individuals as a criterion for their own conduct but is not used as a criterion for others. As I have said before, the internal point of view is one of Hart's key insights, and I will come back to it many times throughout the book. For now, we can stick to this quite underdeveloped take on it.

The idea of a social rule adds the needed complexity to explain the kingly succession mentioned before. We can say that there is a social rule accepted by enough subjects saying that the eldest son of the former king is to inherit the crown. Social rules can, therefore, account for the problem of the continuity of a legal system. It is evident, however, that what we understand as law is not comprised of social rules alone. There are many legal rules that are not accepted in a way that makes them *social*. How can we explain those? It is at this point that Hart introduces what I take to be his fictional genealogy and his functional account of the law.[34]

Here is the fictional genealogy.[35] Hart invites us to think about a primitive society that has a group of social rules for guidance. Social rules alone can successfully guide the conduct of individuals in this society as long as the society maintains strong levels of homogeneity. When this primitive society starts to get more complex, let's say their numbers are now too big for everyone to know everyone, or that they received immigrants from other communities, or developed more sophisticated economical practices; social rules alone will not suffice.[36]

[32] ibid 89–90.

[33] ibid 57.

[34] Jules Coleman and Scott Shapiro also argue that Hart has a functional account of law in the fifth chapter of *The Concept of Law*. My understanding of what amounts to a functional account is slightly different from theirs, but I believe that on this I am roughly on the same page as them, regarding Hart's exegesis. My own presentation on the following paragraphs is quite influenced by Coleman's. See Coleman, *The Practice of Principle* (2001) 206–207.

[35] In this point, there is an important disagreement between my understanding of Hart and its relationship with genealogy, and Delacroix's. Differently from me, she claims that Hart was not committed to any kind of genealogy whatsoever. After rightly pointing out that Hart was not a moral realist (much to the contrary, he was deeply suspicious of moral realism), she adds that 'One may thus be tempted to think that nothing stood in the way of his developing some kind of genealogical story, had he been interested. The fact is, though, he wasn't interested. (…) The specificity of Hart's project, his endeavour to analyse the meaning of a normative statement such as 'it is the law that', simply did not require him to look into the various social practices contributing to bringing law into existence.' Delacroix, *Legal Norms and Normativity – An Essay in Genealogy* (2006) 124–125, see also 113–114. In what follows up, I will argue precisely that Hart indeed had a fictional genealogy to tell.

[36] Hart, *The Concept of Law* (1994) 91–92.

Hart points out three problems that emerge in this scenario. Firstly, a more complex society will have difficulties identifying which patterns of behaviour are actual social rules. That's the problem of 'uncertainty', and it creates the need for some 'pedigree test', to use Ronald Dworkin's expression.[37] Secondly, this more complex society will develop itself in ways that make their current social rules obsolete. Their rules belong to a former epoch, and their application to the new context is bound to be disastrous, so there is need for some remedy to the problem of 'the static character of rules'. Thirdly, there is the problem of 'inefficiency'. There can be disagreements about the violation of rules, since one party can claim that the rule was violated, and the other defend herself, claiming that this was not the case. If rules are to be efficient, they demand some sort of mechanism to guarantee their application.[38]

According to Hart, the problems presented are corrected by the introduction of different kinds of secondary rules that he defines as rules that 'specify the ways in which the primary rules may be conclusively ascertained, introduced, eliminated, varied, and the fact of their violation conclusively determined'.[39] Secondary rules are, in a sense, rules that tell us what to do with other rules and how to identify them. It is the introduction of those rules that, for Hart, separates what he calls a pre-legal situation (our primitive society example) from a legal situation. For Hart, the 'union of primary and secondary rules' is 'the heart of a legal system'.[40] There are three kinds of secondary rules: (1) 'rules of change' that address the difficulty in changing, amending and creating rules; (2) 'rules of adjudication' that establish procedures for the application and enforcement of rules; and (3) 'rules of recognition' that establish the ways in which we identify which rules count as part of the legal system.[41]

In introducing the secondary rules of recognition, change and adjudication, Hart presupposes that those rules – combined with the primary ones – have a function for us; that's *why* we need them. Having only primary rules plagues us with the problems he detected. Now, those problems are problems *because* rules are supposed to do something for us; that is, they have a function. He makes this function explicit in the text, as we can see in the following quotation:

> *The principal functions of the law as a means of social control* are not to be seen in private litigation or prosecutions, which represent vital but still ancillary provisions for the failures of the system. *It is to be seen in the diverse ways in which the law is used to control, to guide, and to plan life out of court.*[42]

[37] R Dworkin, *Taking Rights Seriously* (Cambridge, MA, Harvard University Press, 1977).
[38] Hart, *The Concept of Law* (1994) 92–94.
[39] ibid 94.
[40] ibid 98.
[41] ibid 94–98.
[42] ibid 40, my emphasis. I became aware of this paragraph thanks to Veronica Rodriguez-Blanco's use of it in her discussion of Hart's internal point of view. See V Rodriguez-Blanco, *Law and Authority under the Guise of the Good* (Oxford, Hart Publishing, 2014) 78.

Hart's argument, rephrased, would look like this: 'the law – made by the union of primary and secondary rules – has a function of social control or guidance, as it is explained in the fictional genealogy of the emergence of secondary rules'.[43] This reading is strengthened by what Hart says just before introducing the problems he identifies in the pre-legal context:

> More important for our present purpose is the following consideration. It is plain that only a small community closely knit by ties of kinship, common sentiment, and belief, and placed in a stable environment, *could live successfully* by such a regime of unofficial rules. *In any other conditions such a simple form of social control must prove defective and will require supplementation in different ways.*[44]

In the same section from the quotation above, Hart also repeats his view of groupings of rules as 'means of social control',[45] and in his discussion about the 'minimum content of natural law',[46] he says that he is concerned with 'social arrangements for continued existence'.[47] This, I believe, is enough to make the case for understanding Hart as presenting the functional/fictional account Williams talked about.[48]

Someone could put the following point against Hart: he has introduced the idea of secondary rules to account for the problems of uncertainty, lack of dynamism and inefficiency; however, this is not enough. If those rules are not accepted by the community, they will not be able to perform their function; and the problem with the simpler picture in which we only have primary rules is that acceptance is a messy business in a more complex community. Insofar as the secondary rules depend on acceptance, Hart's solution is question-begging. If Hart stopped his account at this point, the objection would be true, but he has more to say, especially about the rule of recognition.

The rule of recognition stands apart from other rules due to a number of characteristics. Firstly, the rule of recognition is responsible for the identity of a legal system. It is this rule that establishes the *criteria of validity*, that is, the criteria that makes something into law. To use Hart's example, the rule of recognition is law in the same sense that the standard metre in Paris is a metre. That's why he calls the rule of recognition the 'ultimate' criteria of validity.[49] The idea of validity introduces the needed tool to tackle the objection of the previous paragraph. Something is valid, and therefore is law, if and only if it attends to the criteria established by the rule of recognition. This means that we can have legal rules that

[43] Stephen Perry and Jeremy Waldron claim something analogous to this in S Perry, 'Hart's Methodological Positivism' in Coleman (ed), *Hart's Postscript: Essays on the Postscript to 'The Concept of Law'* (2001); Waldron, 'Normative (or Ethical) Positivism'.
[44] Hart, *The Concept of Law* (1994) 92, my emphasis.
[45] ibid 92.
[46] ibid 192–200.
[47] ibid 192.
[48] For a discussion on the meaning of 'social control', see Delacroix, *Legal Norms and Normativity – An Essay in Genealogy* (2006) 140–143.
[49] Hart, *The Concept of Law* (1994) 107–10.

are not necessarily accepted by people through the internal point of view, but that are law nonetheless because they are valid. Traffic laws can figure as an example of this. Even when most people disregard them, they are still valid as laws because of their connection to the rule of recognition of that legal system.

Secondly, the rule of recognition *is* a social rule; it is not a rule that received its validity from another source (for there is no other source). This means that the rule of recognition *must* be accepted through the internal point of view. This, however, should not be confused with acceptance by the populace at large. For a rule of recognition to exist, it suffices that the relevant officers accept it, and that the populace at large obey what such officers say.[50] This is how Hart presents it: 'The assertion that a legal system exists is therefore a Janus-faced statement looking both towards *obedience by ordinary citizens* and to the *acceptance by officials* of secondary rules as critical common standards of official behaviour.'[51]

We can now grasp the complete account. Hart presents us with a narrative that explains why we moved from the pre-legal scenario to the legal one, and in so doing he attributes a function (social control or guidance) to the law. For the law to discharge this function, it suffices that the relevant officers accept its rule of recognition, and that people by and large obey what the officers tell them. This is how Hart explains the foundations of a legal system and how we got legal rules that are not dependent on acceptance. Both Jules Coleman and Scott Shapiro endorse something akin to Hart's account. For instance, Coleman says that 'the basic idea is that law's capacity to guide conduct effectively is part of the explanation of its existence and persistence, as well as of the shape law takes in its mature forms'.[52] Shapiro says something similar when he claims that 'Legal institutions are supposed to enable communities to overcome the complexity, contentiousness, and arbitrariness of communal life by resolving those social problems that cannot be solved, or solved as well, by nonlegal means alone.'[53] The three authors seem to endorse the claim that the law has a function of social ordering or organisation that enables people to pursue their goals and that this can be seen in a fictional genealogy that shows how law can fulfil its function.

An account of the reason-giving character of the law that draws on the Hartian functional argument would say that the law is reason-giving for agents *because* the law plays an important function of social control. This is a straightforward functional answer that can be derived from the fictional genealogy of the law. Now, it might be true that the law has this function, but this function by itself does not tell us how and why the law affects the practical reasoning of an agent. Consider for a moment what this answer would mean. You ask me: 'why

[50] ibid 114–117. See also G Postema, *A Treatise of Legal Philosophy and General Jurisprudence*, Vol 11 (Dordrecht, Springer, 2011) 311.
[51] Hart, *The Concept of Law* (1994) 117, my emphasis.
[52] Coleman, *The Practice of Principle* (2001) 206.
[53] Shapiro, *Legality* (2011) 171.

do you abide by the law?'. I reply, 'I abide by the law because it is a form of social control'. Your reaction probably will be another question: 'that's true, but why do you care about that?'.[54] This second question demands an answer that is not given by the mere fact that the law plays a function of social control. As Hart himself points out, social control is not in itself a good thing because it can be used for oppression.[55] There are many things that one can say as an answer to this second round of questions, but those go beyond the functional account presented by Hart. I can say that 'I care about the social control because it enables me, in my legal system, to achieve my goals'[56] or that 'I care about it because its regulations are fair.' Those tentative answers have more concrete content than the functional account, for they demand that we know something about a concrete legal system and something about ourselves.[57]

Equally important, there is the second claim made at the beginning of this chapter: it is a characteristic feature of the law that it demands respect from its subjects, and this is somehow obscured in the answers an agent could give that we have been discussing in the last couple of paragraphs. Arguably, there is more to law's claim than just being that of a party in a transaction. Those remarks take us back to Williams' point about the limits of functional accounts: if all we have is the functional argument, then we are bound to be puzzled by the fact that our answers to practical questions (eg, an explanation of legal reason-giving) appeal to elements that are extraneous to it.

To recall something I have said earlier, what is at stake here is not if the functional account is strictly speaking correct or not, but if it can explain relevant aspects of the reason-giving character of the law. The claim is that there is need for something else. Indeed, as Scott Shapiro and Jeffrey Kaplan have convincingly argued[58] – and I will develop this in the next sub-section – Hart was not in the business of presenting a theory of legal normativity as this term is understood now, as law's power to provide someone with justifying reasons to obey the law. Nonetheless, his arguments lay the frame for an inquiry into legal normativity. This is done through what I take it to be Hart's greatest insight, his idea of the internal point of view.[59]

[54] My strategy here roughly follows Veronica Rodriguez-Blanco's argument. See Rodriguez-Blanco, *Law and Authority under the Guise of the Good* (2014) 75–100.

[55] Hart, *The Concept of Law* (1994) 202. This is also emphasised by Coleman and Shapiro. See Coleman, *The Practice of Principle* (2001) 207.

[56] Something like this will be part of Shapiro's argument below.

[57] Much of Delacroix's case against Hart draws on a similar point. For her, 'While any society will have to rely, as a prerequisite, on a structure allowing the peaceful coexistence of divergent interests, the agenda calling for the emergence of a legal order may include further moral ambitions which do not easily fit under the banner of 'social control'.' Delacroix, *Legal Norms and Normativity – An Essay in Genealogy* (2006) 142.

[58] J Kaplan, 'Attitude and the Normativity of Law' (2017) 36 *Law and Philosophy* 469; SJ Shapiro, 'What Is the Internal Point of View' (2006) 75 *Fordham Law Review* 1157.

[59] See, eg, Shapiro, 'What Is the Internal Point of View' for a similar claim.

C. Hart's Insight: The Internal Point of View and its Importance

What Hart actually meant by an 'internal aspect' of rules is far from uncontentious. I think that there are at least two different understandings of Hart's text, and attention to those will reward us. We have, first, what we might call a *minimalist interpretation* of the internal point of view. According to this view, which has Scott Shapiro and Jeffrey Kaplan as its exponents, Hart never sought to explain what we usually refer to as legal normativity in the jurisprudential debate nowadays, but merely to explain how law is a rule-guided practice, and how this can be better accounted for through the internal point of view.

This is how Shapiro defines the internal point of view: 'the internal point of view is the *practical attitude of rule acceptance* – it does not imply that people who accept the rules accept their moral legitimacy, only that they are disposed to guide and evaluate conduct in accordance with the rules'.[60] This view is also shared by Kaplan, who in turn says that 'To take the internal point of view toward a rule is to take that rule as a source of reasons (or as itself a reason) for or against the behavior governed by the rule'.[61] According to this interpretation, the internal point of view is an 'attitude'[62] or 'disposition'[63] to evaluate, criticise or justify conduct by reference to a given pattern of behaviour.

Kaplan argues that it is because of this attitude that a given 'pattern of behaviour' becomes a rule.[64] He and Shapiro treat the internal point of view as a way of granting 'intelligibility' to legal practices.[65] The point is that when agents engage with the law, the ways in which they act and think about it presuppose something like the internal point of view, that is, an attitude of endorsement of the rules of the law as reasons for evaluation and criticism of conduct. We can say that the minimalist interpretation is an attempt to *make sense* of legal practices. We need something like the internal point of view if we want to explain how the law is understood by agents.

The minimalist interpretation stands contrasted with Gerald Postema's view, which I will call the *expressivist interpretation*.[66] In this view, Hart's account is incomplete in the sense that his argument about social acceptance is not enough

[60] Shapiro, 'What Is the Internal Point of View' 1157. My emphasis.

[61] Kaplan, 'Attitude and the Normativity of Law' 476.

[62] Both Shapiro and Kaplan refer to the internal point of view as an attitude.

[63] Shapiro indicates textual evidence for Hart's use of this term regarding the internal point of view. See Shapiro, 'What Is the Internal Point of View' 1163.

[64] Kaplan, 'Attitude and the Normativity of Law' 473. See also Shapiro, 'What Is the Internal Point of View' 1164–65. This is also defended by Jules Coleman. See Coleman, *The Practice of Principle* (2021) 81–82.

[65] Shapiro, 'What Is the Internal Point of View' 1165–67.

[66] The term 'expressivist' is used here because Postema claims that Hart is committed to a kind of expressivism, as I will explain below. This is not to be confused with the standard use of the term in ethics.

to actually ground reasons for action. In order for us to get to Postema's view, let us take a look at the following excerpt by Hart, in which he presents his view on the acceptance of the legal system:

> Not only may vast numbers be coerced by laws which they do not regard as morally binding, but it is not even true that those who do accept the system voluntarily, must conceive of themselves as morally bound to do so, though the system will be most stable when they do so. In fact, their allegiance to the system may be based on many different considerations: calculations of long-term interest; disinterested interest in others; an unreflecting inherited or traditional attitude; or the mere wish to do as others do.[67]

As the excerpt makes clear, in the Hartian picture there is no need for moral or ethical considerations when it comes to the acceptance of something through the internal point of view. This, combined with the Janus-faced structure of the law, creates problems for Hart, or so Postema argues.[68] In the Hartian account, those subject to the law are under no necessity to accept the legal rules from the internal point of view. People under the law can be 'deplorably sheeplike'[69] and be totally alienated from the law. For law to discharge its function of social control, it suffices that legal officers accept it from the internal point of view for whatever reasons they might have. Once the officers accept the law from the internal point of view, they proceed to apply it over the subjects, independently of the subjects' views on the matter. It is perfectly possible and consistent with Hart's argument that the subjects will then be merely coerced by the law. They do not see themselves bound by the law, except maybe in the minimal prudential sense ('if I want to avoid punishment, I ought to obey the law').

Legal officers claim that subjects are under legal obligations, but the subjects do not recognise them; they see themselves as coerced or even fail to have a picture of themselves in this scenario (alienation or indifference are also possible here). To the claim 'you have a legal obligation to perform x', this subject might reply 'why should I care about this?' If the answer given to this is 'because otherwise I will punish you', then the classical Hartian distinction between 'having an obligation' and 'being obliged' is lost, at least regarding those subject to the law. A kind of gap opens since legal officials argue that subjects have obligations that the subjects themselves do not accept from an internal point of view. The upshot of this, according to Postema, is that Hart fails to explain how the law can provide reasons for action for its subjects.

Postema explains this point nicely when he claims that Hart is committed to what he calls 'expressivism' regarding the reason-giving character of the law. Expressivism claims that 'Social rules are *normative for* those who accept them, but they are not normative *because* (for the reason that) they accept them. Hart's

[67] Hart, *The Concept of Law* (1994) 203.

[68] G Postema, 'Norms, Reasons, and Law' (1998) 51(1) *Current Legal Problems* 149. Much of my discussion in this part draws from Postema's paper.

[69] Hart, *The Concept of Law* (1994) 117.

theory of social normativity rests essentially on an expressivist, non-cognitivist metaethics.'[70] We can rephrase the problem in the following way: from the fact that legal officials accept the law and enforce it against the subjects, it does not follow that the law is reason-giving for the subjects. The expressivist interpretation of Hart argues, in a nutshell, that Hart's account of the reason-giving character of the law faces a problem trying to move from non-moral acceptance of the law by officials to the reason-giving character of the law for everyone else. Postema's demand, in a sense, can be read as a consequence of what I take to be his view about normativity, that the only 'real' normativity is moral in character. In the ethical or moral debates, the recognition of moral reasons by individuals plays a key role. For instance, we can wonder if someone can be blamed for violating a moral principle that she does not recognise. Discussions about the fairness or the point of blame depend on how we understand the scope of moral reasons. Postema ingeniously brings this point to the law.[71]

I think that Postema's argument is *too strong*. To see this, let us take a look at what Kaplan says about rule-guided practices like the law and etiquette. The existence of those practices, he says, depends on their acceptance by the relevant groups. For a practice of etiquette to exist, the relevant group should accept their norms as reason-giving for them. There is, however, a catch. For this to be the case, there is no need for acceptance from *everyone* across the board. When one individual does not accept a given rule, this does not mean that she is out of the scope of the rule and of criticism targeted at her based on that rule.[72]

A common case illustrates this. It is usual in Latin American countries to greet people of the opposite sex with a kiss on the cheek, but this is not the case in Asian countries like Japan. If a Latin man greets a woman with a kiss on the cheek without warning in Japan, he will be considered rude – and some might even mistake that for harassment. Japanese etiquette rules establish that the appropriate greeting of strangers is through bowing. The clueless foreigner violated this rule, and he obviously did not accept it from the internal point of view. The minimalist interpretation is capable of making perfect sense of this situation: etiquette is normative in the sense of being rule-guided. Those that accept the social rule of etiquette were able to use it intelligibly; that is, they criticised the foreigner's conduct, taking the etiquette rule as a reason. This is how they perceive what happened, and also how we third parties would describe the situation.

It seems to me that the expressivist interpretation is trying to get more from Hart than what he intended to offer (a point connected to my remarks at the

[70] Postema, 'Norms, Reasons, and Law' 158.

[71] For a view that is similar to Postema's, see S Perry, 'Hart on Social Rules and the Foundations of Law: Liberating the Internal Point of View' (2006) 75 *Fordham Law Review* 1171, 1173–74. Among Perry's many claims in his piece is that 'Legal normativity is moral normativity, and the law's claim to authority is a moral claim'. For a discussion of Perry's views in contrast to Shapiro's, see B Zipursky, 'Legal Obligations and the Internal Aspect of Rules' (2006) 75 *Fordham Law Review* 1229, 1234–37.

[72] Kaplan, 'Attitude and the Normativity of Law' 486.

beginning of this chapter, that maybe positivists were not talking about legal normativity at all). As the etiquette example above shows, there are good reasons to suppose that Hart's internal point of view is meant to capture only what it means for a behaviour to be rule-guided.[73] It is more charitable to Hart to agree with Kaplan and Shapiro and say that the original Hartian argument was merely about the intelligibility of law as a rule-guided practice. This is how, following Kaplan, we could formulate this point: the internal point of view is the acceptance of patterns of behaviour as reasons. This is not the same thing as the endorsement of reasons that could potentially justify the application of the rule to others.[74] Still, an account of the intelligibility of a practice as rule-guided does not amount to an account of its reason-giving character, and therefore Hart's account is incomplete if it is taken as an instance of the latter.

Knowing *that* law provides reasons for action is not enough as an explanation of *how* it does that. At this point, we only know about law what we know about etiquette or games, yet, as John Deigh rightly points out, there is more to legal normativity than that. Differently from those other practices, law purports to provide reasons for action that apply to all that are subject to it. Additionally, the reasons for action provided by it must be more than the mere threat of force; otherwise the distinctive aspect of having an obligation (in contrast with being obliged) will be lost, as Postema emphasised. This is why Deigh says that the law has authority in a sense that is distinct from the sense in which we can meaningfully speak about the authority of the rules of chess.[75]

The issue seems to be that Hart's explanation of the origin of a legal system in a rule of recognition obscures a characteristic aspect of law, namely, its role in a narrative of political rule. Differently from etiquette or games, law's reasons for action are supposedly of a more important kind; they purport to claim the subject's allegiance (to use Deigh's term) or respect (to use my preferred term).[76] I will say more on the role of law in a narrative of political rule in the next chapter, but for now, the important point is that the account of the reason-giving character of the law we can get from Hartian resources is not an account of its characteristic aspects; it does not do much in terms of illuminating the differences between law and other rule-guided practices, and as a result of that, there is an aspect of law that is unaccounted for. Now, if we want to understand what is missing, we need to understand *how* the law relates to the exercise of practical reason on the part of the concrete agents that are subject to it. It is at this point that the two claims made in the first paragraph of this chapter come together: law is part of a broader story of political rule; to rule over others entails the capacity

[73] ibid 475–80.

[74] ibid 476.

[75] Deigh, 'Emotion and the Authority of Law' 144–47. It is worth mentioning that Deigh himself frames the issue in terms of a discussion about law's authority, but this has no effect on the argument here.

[76] ibid 144–47.

to demand their respect; and therefore, if we want to explain what is characteristic of law's normativity, we need to account for the psychological makeups of the concrete agents subject to it.[77]

Delacroix captures those concerns neatly when she claims that Hart's 'focus is on the surface phenomena flowing from the fact that law is normative, not on what it takes for law to be normative in the first place'.[78] Veronica Rodriguez-Blanco stresses a similar point when she claims that the rule-guided nature of the law (the 'thing' we can call law's 'social normativity') is only part of a broader story, and it will misguide us if 'it is presented as a *comprehensive* explanation of the normativity of law'.[79] We must investigate this broader story if we want to find a more compelling explanation of the reason-giving character of the law.[80]

This concludes the initial discussion of Hart's account of the internal point of view and its limits, which I take to be the most important sub-section in this chapter. For the next section, I will engage with some philosophical tools that were developed by other positivists that could be used to remedy Hart's original account in the sense of providing a more substantial view on the reason-giving character of the law. The general issue will be that those tools, notwithstanding their refinement, fail to account for the reason-giving character of the law because they merely move the limitations we originally identified in Hart to a later stage of the argument.

III. Attempts to Remedy Hart

A. Shared Cooperative Activities and the Practical Difference Thesis

One way of interpreting Jules Coleman's aim in *The Practice of Principle* is to see him as providing remedies that allow Hart's positivism to explain what he takes to be the peculiar normativity of the rule of recognition.[81] The first remedy, the argument that the law is a shared cooperative activity, can be understood once we see how Coleman frames some of Hart's limitations. There are two things that Coleman finds troublesome in Hart's original account. Firstly, he points out that

[77] As I have said before, I believe that Deigh's project and mine are congenial.

[78] S Delacroix, 'Tracing a Genealogy of Legal Normativity: Responsibility, Authorship and Contingency' in S Bertea and G Pavlakos (eds), *New Essays on the Normativity of Law* (Oxford, Hart Publishing, 2011) 314.

[79] Rodriguez-Blanco, *Law and Authority under the Guise of the Good* (2014) 77.

[80] In this sense, even though my analysis of Hart is quite different from Delacroix', the conclusions are congenial. See Delacroix, *Legal Norms and Normativity – An Essay in Genealogy* (2006) 68–69, 89–91, 142.

[81] For a concise and somewhat critical summary of Coleman's views regarding legal normativity, see M Giudice, *The Normativity of Law* (Cambridge, Cambridge University Press, 2024) 37–41.

rules that exist because of the internal point of view are in principle capable of being extinguished by the individual if she ceases to endorse the rule. If my acceptance through the internal point of view ceases, that pattern of behaviour ceases to be a rule for me. This does not seem to be the case with the rule of recognition. An anarchist judge is still bound by it, even if she does not endorse it anymore. Secondly, the rule of recognition seems to entail a degree of responsiveness between the agents that endorse it that is also not explained by the internal point of view, since legal officers make their moves in the legal practice taking into account what other players might do and are themselves reacting to moves made by others. To give a more concrete example of this, when judges make decisions within the legal practice, they do so taking into account how other practitioners will react to that decision.[82] The general point behind both problems seems to be that the rule of recognition has a more complex social nature than what the Hartian account suggested.

According to Coleman, such troubles can be addressed if we see the rule of recognition as an instance of a 'shared cooperative activity'. Coleman borrows this concept from Michael Bratman, and it essentially means an activity that has a few peculiar traits. A shared cooperative activity has a degree of 'mutual responsiveness', that is, agents engaged in it are concerned about what other engaged agents are doing within that practice and respond to that. A shared cooperative activity is also characterised by a 'commitment to the joint activity'. The agents engaged with the practice are all committed to its success, but not necessarily because of the same reasons. Finally, such activities present a degree of 'commitment to mutual support': agents engaged with them are committed to supporting other agents so that the activity can be successful.[83] If the rule of recognition is understood as a shared cooperative activity, we can explain the degree of responsiveness we see in legal actors. Judges and others make their moves in legal practice, considering how other actors have behaved and how they might respond to it now. It also explains how rules of recognition can still bind the agent even if she does not accept them anymore, since 'a justified set of expectations (…) can give rise to obligations'.[84] Take Coleman's example of singing a duet. If you and I are engaged in this shared cooperative activity, and halfway through the song you decide you do not want to sing anymore, we can all understand the nature of the reproach you will suffer.[85]

There are two difficulties with this first argument. Firstly, in a sense this is too demanding. The argument presupposes three things about the agents engaged in the activity: (1) that they have a high degree of rationality; (2) that

[82] Coleman, *The Practice of Principle* (2001) 95–96.
[83] ibid 96.
[84] ibid 98. Here Coleman is quoting KE Himma, 'Inclusive Legal Positivism' in J Coleman and S Shapiro (eds), *The Oxford Handbook of Jurisprudence and Legal Philosophy* (Oxford, Oxford University Press, 2001).
[85] Coleman, *The Practice of Principle* (2001) 97–98.

they have goodwill towards the shared cooperative activity; and (3) that they are well informed so that they can be adequately responsive to others. Absent those things, there will be much difficulty for agents to display the mutual responsiveness, commitment to the joint activity and commitment to support other agents that characterise social cooperative activities. Such demandingness, per se, does not prove Coleman wrong, but adds to the implausibility of the model.

The second and most important difficulty with the first remedy is this. Coleman mentions that there is no need for a legal theory to explain how shared cooperative activities generate obligations, for it can rest content with the fact that they do.[86] This might be true, but it is also an unnecessary restriction to the scope of jurisprudence. If legal theorists were to bite the bullet and engage with the more substantive matters of moral and social philosophy, they might end up with more interesting accounts. As it stands, Coleman's account says something like this: 'shared cooperative activities can generate obligations, and the rule of recognition is one such activity shared by legal officers'. To this someone can ask: 'but how those activities generate such obligations?' Coleman will probably reply: 'Oh, that's not my field of inquiry.'

This is an important point, connected to the claim that the law is part of a broader narrative of political rule, that law purports to demand respect from its subjects. The idea of a shared cooperative activity fails to capture this characteristic aspect of law's reason-giving character because it is in a sense too thin. By itself, the idea of a shared cooperative activity does not provide us with resources to explain what distinguishes law – the use of state power – from chess or other activity of this sort, and yet there is a difference. If we are interested in knowing *how* the law can provide one with reasons for action, we need more than analysis in terms of a shared activity, and in this sense Coleman's argument suffers from a similar limitation to Hart's. Naturally, this does not mean that Coleman's first remedy is wrong, but it means that it cannot account for central aspects of the reason-giving character of the law.

In attempting to explain how his brand of inclusive positivism is compatible with the 'practical difference thesis', Coleman introduces a second remedy to Hart's theory, one that might be used to tackle the complaint made against Hart's original account as well. The 'practical difference thesis' states that for something to be law and perform law's function of guidance, this something must be able to affect the practical deliberation of agents, that is, it must influence our reasoning about what we ought to do. This effect must also be caused by law *qua* law, not by law *qua* morality or something like that; otherwise law would not play a function of guidance, since this other element (eg, morality) would be the real guide.[87] Taken as just this, the practical difference thesis seems to play against Coleman's and Hart's inclusive legal positivism, since this kind of positivism allows for moral criteria to play a role in the rule of recognition.

[86] ibid 98.
[87] ibid 134–35.

To conciliate the practical difference thesis with inclusive positivism, Coleman draws from Scott Shapiro's distinction between motivational and epistemic guidance and from Kenneth Himma's use of this distinction. A person is guided in the motivational sense when she accepts a legal rule as the criteria for assessment of conduct. This pretty much captures what it means to accept a rule through the internal point of view. Epistemic guidance, on the other hand, is a more modest phenomenon. To say that the law guides someone epistemically is to say that it brands some patterns of behaviour as the ones endorsed by the law. Epistemic guidance labels some of our obligations as legal, for instance, but does not motivate us to necessarily follow those. In a nutshell, motivational guidance motivates the agent to do X; epistemic guidance highlights to the agent that he should do X.[88]

Following Himma, Coleman claims that the original formulation of the practical difference thesis obscures the distinction between the two kinds of guidance and also ignores the fact that different rules have different audiences. If we take those things into account, then we can have the following picture: the rule of recognition provides motivational guidance to legal officers, but the rules recognised by it provide epistemic guidance to the law subjects.[89] This is how Coleman puts the point:

> A rule of recognition does two things. First, it makes determinate which rules bear the mark of legality. Second, it creates a duty for a certain class of individuals – officials – to evaluate conduct under the set of primary rules that bear that mark. (…) This is the sense in which the rule of recognition is addressed to judges, and not to ordinary folk. It imposes a duty on officials, but not on the rest of us.[90]

The idea here is to present a subtler picture that allows inclusive positivism to explain the practical difference thesis.[91] Nonetheless, this argument has difficulties of its own if taken as an account of the reason-giving character of the law. Place yourself once more in the position of an agent engaged in practical deliberation. If you are an officer, then you are motivated to accept the rule of recognition for whatever reason, and you obey the law because of that. This is probably not wrong, although it might be incomplete. Now, the more serious problem that arises is once again regarding the law subjects. Epistemic guidance, as described by Coleman, is not enough for the law to make a difference in practical deliberation. I am in doubt about what I ought to do, and then the law brands some obligations as legal. So what? I need to have some motivation to abide by the law if the law is to have any weight in my deliberation.

A different example helps us to see the limitation. I have a best friend who is a traditional catholic. We usually engage in quite long conversations about ethics,

[88] ibid 134–35.
[89] ibid 139–40.
[90] ibid 139.
[91] Delacroix summarises Coleman's point in a similar way. See Delacroix, *Legal Norms and Normativity – An Essay in Genealogy* (2006) 169.

and in a talk about the ethics of family relationships, he once presented to me a series of obligations towards relatives whose fulfilment he takes to be mandatory for a good catholic, for instance, the obligation to be faithful to one's partner. Now, the fact that my friend has marked fidelity as a catholic obligation is not enough to provide a reason for action towards fidelity for me. This can only be the case if I am somehow disposed to accept Catholicism as a source of reasons for action. As I am an atheist, the qualifier catholic plays no role in my engagement with reasons. This does not mean, of course, that I cannot have other reasons in favour of fidelity, reasons derived from a sense of respect for my partner, for instance.

The same thing goes with the law. Unless I am already disposed to regard law as something valuable, the fact that the law presents some obligations as legal will be of no difference in my reasoning. Even if it is true that the law marks some obligations as *legal*, it is not true that this is enough for them to actually have a role in our practical deliberation. In a nutshell, the epistemic guidance provided by the law is not enough to explain the reason-giving character of the law. It can be *part* of that answer, but the substantial argument for people's disposition to respect the law must come from elsewhere. I do not think that Coleman himself would have any problem with my claim, but I do think that he would add, 'Yeah, but that was not my problem to begin with.'

In principle, there is nothing wrong with Coleman's strategy, but one should notice what it entails. It entails not only a lack of concern regarding the motivations and dispositions that concrete agents have when they engage in practical deliberation, but also a lack of interest in what really matters about law and its place in our lives, that is, how law plays a role in a narrative of political rule. A satisfactory account of the reason-giving character of the law must say something about those matters; otherwise it will be incomplete in the same sense as Hart's. To use Rodriguez-Blanco's expression, there is a broader story to be told.

B. The Planning Theory of the Law and the Circumstances of Legality

Scott Shapiro's 'Planning Theory of Law' is a more recent attempt to remedy the problems of Hart's original account. To do so, Shapiro – like Coleman – draws insight from Michael Bratman's philosophy, especially his idea of *plans*. This is how Shapiro explains the law: 'legal systems are *institutions of social planning* and their fundamental aim is to compensate for the deficiencies of alternative forms of planning in the *circumstances of legality*.'[92]

Let us begin our unpacking of this quotation with the idea of a plan. For Shapiro, a plan is a kind of norm, something that can be used to assess an agent's

[92] Shapiro, *Legality* (2011) 171. My emphasis.

behaviour and to give her guidance about what she should do.[93] Plans stand apart from other norms, however, because they have a few peculiar features. Firstly, they are 'purposive'; that is, when someone comes up with a plan, she does so with the intent of having something to guide her behaviour.[94] Secondly, plans can have a quite sophisticated structure. Shapiro points out that they can be 'partial', because I can leave the details of a plan unspecified until the convenient time for specification comes, and 'nested' when a more complex plan contains smaller plans within it.[95] The more important feature of a plan, however, is this: a plan has some principles of rationality attached to it. For instance, plans would make no sense if agents were to reconsider constantly what they ought to do, so plans have some resistance to second-guessing. Plans also demand some degree of consistency with the information we have about the world (a plan totally disconnected from reality is no plan at all) and also some degree of consistency with other plans we might have (having plans whose implementation would be mutually exclusive would defeat the purpose of having them).[96]

The next element we must unpack is the idea of 'circumstances of legality', and it is at this point that Shapiro's account introduces a fictional genealogy and a functional view of the law.[97] Imagine a group of people that moves to a desert island that Shapiro calls 'Cooks Island' with the intent of living together. The island is rich in natural resources, and this enables the islanders to live comfortably through most of the year, but the scarcity of resources during winter, however, makes them realise that they need to cultivate their food and stock it if they intend to survive. To move from a mere extractive society to one in which there is agriculture, the islanders must engage in social planning. It is through social planning, says Shapiro, that they will develop some form of property rights that will in turn enable them to develop agriculture and similar practices (A will have this piece of land, B will have this, and so on). The introduction of property rights, however, brings the need for ways of settling disagreements about those same rights, and then the planning gets more complex. Once we introduce ways to settle those disagreements, it is plausible to assume that this society will grow in numbers and complexity; it will develop a market, for instance. This in turn will put pressure for more sophisticated mechanisms of guidance. After some time, what we will have in this society is a master plan with many sub-plans and plan-like norms.[98] At this point, says Shapiro, we get a legal system.[99]

[93] ibid 127.
[94] ibid 128.
[95] ibid 120–22.
[96] ibid 122–24.
[97] For Shapiro, the State of Nature is a 'thought experiment' that helps us to see 'various reasons for creating a legal system'. His argument unfolds pretty much like Hart's but, instead of focusing on the appearance of secondary rules, it focuses on the emergence of more sophisticated plans. See Shapiro, *Legality* (2011) 155–56.
[98] Shapiro, *Legality* (2011) 156–68.
[99] There are some important remarks made by Shapiro that are pertinent here. Plans are characterised by their purposive nature, that is, they are supposed to provide guidance about what one ought

'Circumstances of legality' are, therefore, the 'social conditions that render sophisticated forms of social planning desirable'.[100] Those sophisticated forms of social planning are what we call law. Shapiro's theory also presents a function for law, as the following excerpt makes it clear: 'the law is first and foremost a social planning mechanism whose aim is to rectify the moral deficiencies of the circumstances of legality'.[101] This is Shapiro's theory, in a nutshell:

> Legal institutions plan for the communities over which they claim authority, both by telling members what they may or may not do, and by identifying those who are entitled to affect what others may or may not do. Following this claim, legal rules are themselves generalized plans, or planlike norms, issued by those who are authorized to plan for others. And adjudication involves the application of these plans, or planlike norms, to those to whom they apply. In this way, the law organizes individual and collective behavior so that members of the community can bring about moral goods that could not have been achieved, or achieved as well, otherwise.[102]

What would amount to an answer to the question of the reason-giving character of the law that draws from Shapiro's resources? I believe that there are three different, albeit compatible, arguments that could be made here. A first answer is this: because of their very nature, once we have accepted plans, they will place rational constraints over us. It would be irrational to accept a plan and then ignore what the plan tells us to do. This is something that we have seen already, as the following example makes clear. If I have a plan to lose weight and this plan includes not eating fried food, it would be irrational to order fried food for dinner. The same thing goes for law: if I have accepted law's plan, then it would be irrational to ignore it; to not treat law as normative would defeat the purpose of having law in the first place.

Unfortunately for Shapiro, the 'inner rationality of law'[103] is not enough as an explanation. This is so because the rationality of plans can place constraints only on agents that are already inclined to accept the plan, in this case, on agents already

to do. This means that for a given norm to be a plan, acceptance by the relevant party is required. The upshot of this is that those subject to law's plans must have a 'disposition' to accept them. Shapiro does not explain what he means by 'disposition', but adds two clarifications. The first one is that there is no need for general acceptance across the board. For law to discharge its planning function, it suffices that enough people are motivated to abide by the plans most of the time. The second point he adds is that appeal to intimidation can also dispose people to abide by the plans of law. There is no need for its acceptance to be moral or anything like that. See Shapiro, *Legality* (2011) 179–80. Those remarks are, in a sense, a development over Hart's own views about the Janus-faced structure of the law, and they face the same difficulties, as I intend to demonstrate in a moment.

[100] Shapiro, *Legality* (2011) 170.

[101] ibid 172. See too 181–88. The use of the term 'moral' in the quotation should not mislead us, however. Shapiro is quite explicit that a legal system can be morally abhorrent. The circumstances of legality are shot with moral problems, but the fact that the law is supposed to offer solutions to those problems is not enough for it to be necessarily morally legitimate. The mention of a moral function is a quite strange move in Shapiro's text and sounds incoherent. Because this will not affect my arguments, I will not spend any more time discussing this point.

[102] ibid 155.

[103] ibid 183.

inclined to accept the law as normative. In this sense, it is question-begging. This can be seen in a comparison that Michael Bratman himself deploys. He invites us to think about the case of Donald Davidson's 'inner rationality of mind'. When it comes to this rationality, we have no choice but to accept its constraints, for there is no way we can opt to not have a mind at all. This is not the case with the 'inner rationality of law': the law is not something that necessarily has a rational demand on us in the same way as our minds; that is, we can wonder why we should care about the law. We are not stuck with the law in the same way we are stuck with our minds. As Bratman himself says, to not conform with the law is always an option we can entertain, and even when in practical terms this is impossible, it is something thinkable.[104]

It is at this point that a second answer might come to help. Shapiro might want to say that the law can be reason-giving for agents because of its guiding function. This function, the argument goes, enables people to achieve goals they deem valuable. This is analogous to Hart's functional answer and therefore faces the same problem. There is a need to say something about those goals or about the value of guidance or a combination of those things. About those, Shapiro is silent and indeed does not believe it necessary to say anything. Regarding officials, he even claims that 'As long as most officials accept the plan, play their part in it, and resolve their disputes peacefully and openly, and all this is common knowledge, it does not matter why they are doing so.'[105] Now, as Michael Bratman points out, it makes sense to wonder if there are any reasons that justify or motivate one's endorsement of the law.[106] Once again, the first claim of the Introduction, about agents and their motivations and dispositions, appears as a challenge for a positivistic account of the reason-giving character of the law. To make good on that claim, we must look beyond the resources of the planning theory. Once again, there is a broader story to be told.

C. The Argument from the Legal Point of View

A third argument we can extract from Shapiro comes from the so-called 'legal point of view'. Because this argument is somewhat independent of his planning theory and because different authors have presented something similar under the same label, it is worth having a sub-section only for it. I will start with the most influential account of the legal point of view, namely, Joseph Raz's. As we will see, this account bears strong resemblance to Hart's treatment of the internal point of

[104] M Bratman, 'Reflections on Law, Normativity and Plans' in S Bertea and G Pavlakos (eds), *New Essays on the Normativity of Law* (Oxford, Hart Publishing, 2011) 75.

[105] Shapiro, *Legality* (2011) 190.

[106] Bratman, 'Reflections on Law, Normativity and Plans'. Bratman uses the language of justifying or normative reasons. I am not convinced by that language, but his criticism can be accepted, nonetheless.

view and will share its incompleteness. Something similar happens to Shapiro's version of the argument, to which I shall turn later.

According to Joseph Raz, 'The problem of the normativity of law is the problem of explaining the use of normative language in describing the law or legal institutions.'[107] It is very important to notice that Raz's worry, at least in *Practical Reason and Norms*, is with the normative *language*, not with the reason-giving character of law per se.[108] This is different in other bits of his work, as Raz's 'service conception of authority' amounts to an account of how legal directives can provide reasons for action when emitted by a legitimate authority. I will have more to say about Raz's views on authority in the next chapter, but here I want to focus on what he says about normative language in *Practical Reason and Norms*.

For Raz, the legal point of view is the point of view of the 'law-abiding citizen', who in turn is someone that takes the legal directives as 'exclusionary reasons' for him.[109] The term 'exclusionary reason' is a term of art in Razian theory, and it roughly means a reason that excludes other reasons from deliberation. As he says in later writing, it pre-empts deliberation based on other reasons. Under a legal system, says Raz, judges and other officers are supposed to adopt the legal point of view in the assessment of the conduct of the law's subjects, but this does not mean that those subject to the law should necessarily adopt it as well.[110] When you take a reason from the legal point of view as an exclusionary reason, this means that you disregard other reasons as valid reasons that could bear on the action. This is why Raz sometimes refers to the legal point of view as the evaluations that are internal to a point of view.[111]

For Raz, statements that are internal to a point of view are not the same thing as conditional statements. A conditional statement would be something like this: 'If you want to learn Greek, then you ought to practice.' A statement from the legal point of view, says Raz, does not have this structure; that is, it does not have an 'if' clause that makes the 'ought' valid. According to him, statements from the legal point of view 'state what is the case from the point of view of the theory or on the assumption of the theory'.[112] The normative language of law can be thus explained. It is not very different, for Raz, from the situation in which a meat-eating person tells her vegetarian friend to not eat some dish because it has meat. The meat-eating person, says Raz, has no reason to not eat meat, and when she utters the proposition 'you shouldn't eat that, it has meat in it', she does not announce any reason for her whatsoever, but a reason from a vegetarian point of view that she

[107] J Raz, *Practical Reason and Norms* (Oxford, Clarendon Press, 1990) 170.
[108] See, too, Giudice, *The Normativity of Law* (2024) 1–2.
[109] Raz, *Practical Reason and Norms* (1990) 171.
[110] ibid 171.
[111] ibid 139, 142–44. See also J Raz, 'The Institutional Nature of Law' in J Raz, *The Authority of Law* (Oxford, Oxford University Press, 2009) 112–13; J Raz, 'Kelsen's Theory of the Basic Norm' in Raz, *The Authority of Law* (2009) 140–43.
[112] Raz, *Practical Reason and Norms* (1990) 175.

knows her friend happens to endorse.[113] As I understand him, Raz is claiming that statements from the legal point of view are through-and-through internal, they are born from that point of view, and they do not need the support of anything external to it to make sense.

Since Raz's concern was merely with the explanation of the normative language of law, he can make the following move. It suffices that enough people (mostly legal officials) act according to the legal point of view. If enough people do that, then others might have an indirect reason to also make statements from that point of view as well. For instance, people might have reason to avoid the enforcement of law by its officers, or they might care about how their relationship with others will be impaired if they don't abide by the law. People might then acquire reasons to use the same kind of statements as those that actually accept the legal point of view. Those that do not accept the legal point of view might 'have a practical interest in what is required by law'.[114] Thus, we have an explanation of why people use the normative language of law.

Raz's argument in *Practical Reason and Norms* tells us how people came to use normative *language*, but in itself this does not tell us why people have *reason to act* in one way or another. This is a difference in the scope of the theory that shows itself in two different ways. On the one hand, we are still in the dark about the reasons legal officers might have to adopt the legal point of view. On the other, from the fact that legal officers accept it, it does not follow without further argument that the law can be reason-giving for other people. Those two ways are, in a sense, derivations of my two starting claims in this chapter: that agents have motivations and dispositions that must figure in a satisfactory account of the reason-giving character of the law, and that the law is part of a broader story of political rule and that this is characteristic of it.

It seems to me that Raz's argument about the legal point of view has the same kind of incompleteness as Hart's when it comes to a full account of the reason-giving character of the law. If this is the same kind of incompleteness we saw in Hart's original account, the same thing I said about that also applies to Raz. If Hart was concerned with the intelligibility of rule-based practices, Raz (at least in *Practical Reason and Norms*) was concerned with the use of the normative language of law. Those accounts by themselves cannot provide an explanation of the reason-giving character of the law, nor were they primarily concerned with that. I will come back to Raz in the next chapter, as there is more to be said about his arguments regarding the reason-giving character of the law.

For Shapiro, in turn, the legal point of view consists in 'a theory that holds that the norms of that [legal] system are morally legitimate and obligating'.[115] It has what Shapiro calls a 'distancing function', that is, the legal point of view enables

[113] ibid 175–76.
[114] ibid 177.
[115] Shapiro, *Legality* (2011) 186. It is worth pointing out that Shapiro sees his own argument as inspired by Raz's. ibid 422.

us to make moral propositions from a standpoint that we do not necessarily accept (this is quite similar to Raz's). Think about the following example: I can say that 'from the legal point of view, the use of cannabis for leisure is wrong'. This proposition means only that *the law holds it* to be morally wrong, not that the use of cannabis is *really* morally wrong.[116] So, this answer means that under the moral theory according to which legal norms are morally legitimate, I ought to obey the law.

If the legal point of view is taken as an account of the reason-giving character of the law for agents, it will fail in a similar fashion to Coleman's argument about epistemic guidance. Reasons for action have a *practical* aspect to them, and as Veronica Rodriguez-Blanco convincingly points out, the legal point of view is *theoretical*, by which she means that it cannot explain action.[117] Consider for a moment what it would mean for someone to say, regarding a given action, that 'this is what I ought to do, from the legal point of view'. In a way analogous to what we did earlier regarding Hart's and Coleman's arguments, we can press this person: 'but why should you accept the legal point of view?' In order to answer this second question, the agent will need to appeal to things beyond the fact that, according to the law, this is what she ought to do. For Shapiro, the legal point of view is a peculiar moral theory, but he offers no reason why one should adopt it.[118] Statements made from the legal point of view are like statements made from a catholic point of view. An atheist can say things like 'from the point of view of the Church, I should not sin' without being disposed in any way to not sin. What is lacking in Shapiro's picture is an account of the reasons that could dispose someone to accept the legal point of view. Rodriguez-Blanco's own take on this will be to claim that legal authority is ultimately tracked into good-making characteristics that can be offered as answers to GEM Anscombe's 'why' question,[119] but we do not need to follow her on that to accept the soundness of her criticism of Shapiro's legal point of view.[120]

IV. Two Mismatches Regarding Practical Reason

Let us take stock. For Coleman, the practical difference thesis – and a fortiori the law's function of social guidance – can be addressed through the distinction between motivational and epistemic guidance. This distinction enabled him to

[116] ibid 185–88.

[117] V Rodriguez-Blanco, 'The Moral Puzzle of Legitimate Authority' in S Bertea and G Pavlakos (eds), *New Essays on the Normativity of Law* (Oxford, Hart Publishing, 2011).

[118] It is important to add that Shapiro could avail himself of an answer like the one suggested by Coleman: that was not his aim anyway. Still, we can learn by putting this kind of pressure on his theory.

[119] We have discussed Anscombe's question in the previous chapter.

[120] For a good summary of her criticisms, see G Pavlakos and S Bertea, 'Introduction' in S Bertea and G Pavlakos (eds), *New Essays on the Normativity of Law* (Oxford, Hart Publishing, 2011) 4–5.

maintain that officers were guided motivationally by the rule of recognition, whereas subjects were only guided epistemically by the primary rules recognised by the rule of recognition. Epistemic guidance marked some obligations as legal so subjects could know what the law required. Shapiro, on the other hand, endorsed the idea of a legal point of view, that is, the idea that there is a theory or standpoint from which the legal directives are taken as legitimate. If you are making propositions from the legal point of view, then you are taking legal directives as legitimate.

Both ideas, epistemic guidance and the legal point of view, are instances of what Rodriguez-Blanco has called the theoretical point of view. Recall the example of the catholic friend discussing the ethics of family relationships. The fact that some obligations are labelled as legal or catholic (epistemic guidance) or that there is a point of view that takes some of those obligations to be legitimate (that would be the catholic/legal point of view) does not tell me *why* I respect the law or catholic rules unless I am already committed to the law or to Catholicism. It is worth recalling too that both Coleman and Shapiro presented arguments intended to explain the normativity of law *within* the legal practice. The normative structure of shared cooperative activities and the inner rationality of planning are attempts to explain why – once someone is already engaged with the law – this person has reason to follow certain rules, but as Bratman himself pointed out, those reasons only apply for those already within that practice.

What is lacking in the positivist account that would enable it to account for the reason-giving character of the law (assuming that the positivist is interested in such an account)? This is my hypothesis: *what is lacking is a richer account of the agent engaged in practical deliberation and of how law comes to play a role in the life of such an agent*. The positivist accounts started with the Hartian fictional genealogy but didn't move beyond that, so the agent they presented was the same agent of the fictional narrative. In the fictional genealogies presented, we have this basic scenario in which tribe-like societies face difficulties and create something like law that can alleviate those problems, but we do not have a concrete picture of the agent deciding what to do *now*. This causes, as I will explain below, *mismatches* between the positivist account and us, more concrete agents. At this point, it is important to recall Williams' quote from earlier: 'If you stop at the schematic picture, you may be left with the idea that truthfulness is a merely functional quality, and then be puzzled by the fact that it manifestly is not.'[121]

To present the mismatches, I want to start with another, related, question: why is the view of the agent implicit in positivism so *thin*? Since positivists are concerned about the internal point of view, and about how to explain the practical difference made by the law, there can be no doubt that there *is* an agent underlying the positivist accounts of law, but it is an agent that is depicted in the thinnest possible way. To see this, let us look back at the positivist fictional genealogy presented by Hart. The move from a pre-legal situation to a legal one happens either because agents

[121] Williams, 'Why Philosophy needs History' 408.

accept rules as reasons for action (or engage in shared cooperative activities or shared plans). This move in the positivist narrative implies that the agents can reason about what they should do. They are rational agents capable of assessing two or more situations and picking one of those. Those agents are also good-willed. In Coleman's story, the agents are responsive to each other and committed to mutual support in the shared activity (it is important to notice that this does not necessarily entail support in other activities). They are also willing to abide by the obligations that the shared cooperative activity gives rise to. In Shapiro's story, the disagreements that foster law's appearance are all in good faith, and the agents that later are responsible for the plan are also committed to its success.

Because those stories are supposed to be as schematic and as general as they could be, those agents are not supposed to belong to any specific culture or to have any specific set of values beyond the constraints of rationality. They are stripped-down to a bare conception of the self. The narrative presents the agents with difficulties (the problems that secondary rules solve, for instance); then law is understood in functional terms, as a solution to those difficulties; finally, agents can recognise this shift towards law as an improvement. That is all that the story tells us. So, here is the agent underlying the positivist account: she is a rational, good-willed agent, but she has no concrete moral values, personal motivations, projects, and the rest. I think that we can borrow a term from Williams and refer to this agent as being 'characterless'.[122] In what follows, I will claim that there are two mismatches between this characterless agent and more concrete agents that are closer to reality.

Recall that in the fictional genealogy, the agents were in a State of Nature without the law, and the emergence of law solved problems they had in a way they can recognise the existence of law as an achievement. For this agent, there was a time T1 in which there was no law, and a time T2 in which there was law. This is an important point, because it sets the thin agent apart from the more concrete ones that are already immersed in law since T1. A good illustration of this is provided by Shapiro's account. The inhabitants of Cooks Island came up with the law as a way to solve the problems they had prior to the law. This makes the law's function quite transparent for them. Agents like us are very different from this scenario, because we were brought up in a world in which the law was already there, and in a context in which it is far from clear that social control or guidance are the only functions of law. This is not to say that the law was not assuring social control in a sense, but to say that this is not straightforwardly obvious for agents as we know them.[123] This is the *first mismatch*. Even if law indeed has a function of social control, that might not be the reason that explains

[122] B Williams, *Shame and Necessity* (Los Angeles, University of California Press, 1993).

[123] It is worth mentioning that it is possible for the functional value to disappear for good. It is possible for a certain practice to start with a certain functional value that explains how we got to that practice, but as time goes by, another value or role came to be associated with it while the practice became less and less suitable to fulfil its original function. At the end of the day, the original functional value drops out of the picture completely, whereas a different value explains or justifies the practice.

why people obey the law, especially if this is offered as a general reason that applies to all relevant agents.

More importantly, concrete agents belong to social worlds.[124] Agents have a sense of identity or character (I am using those two terms in a deliberately vague way in this chapter, but in the next one they will be refined). This sense of identity or character is a complex bundle of their own use of reasoning and imagination, their immediate influences – like parents and friends – and more diffuse social influences, such as their position in society and religious views. Those elements shape in a greater or lesser degree the values, attitudes and dispositions of the individual. They are part of agents' subjective motivational sets, and they are the basic elements from which agents can engage in practical reasoning, as we have discussed in the previous chapter. This sounds like a platitude, but it is important and often overlooked in jurisprudence.

To see why this realisation is important, think about the contrast between Victor Hugo's characters, Jean Valjean and Inspector Javert. There is no denying that both are honourable men and that they inhabit a context in which the law is either straightforwardly oppressive or morally ambiguous. Yet they have different relationships with the law. Valjean has a sense of respect for the law, but breaking it to save people is something he was willing to do, whereas Javert's respect was closer to blind reverence and total identification with the law, to a point where breaking it also meant a major identity crisis for him; indeed, he ends up claiming that 'there is no way to go on'[125] before throwing himself in the waters of the Seine.[126]

We can make sense of the difference between them by paying attention to the different kinds of relationships that concrete agents have with the law, and such relationships are at least partly informed by the social world inhabited by the agents and by their dispositions, motivations, projects, values, and so on. Concrete agents engage with the law from the kinds of persons that they are and not from a standpoint abstracted from their identities. To borrow Deigh's expression, individuals have 'emotional bonds' with the law that explain why (and when) they recognise the reasons for action provided by law.[127] Those bonds are individualistic in the sense that they belong to specific individuals and relate to their relationship with the law. Because of that, they are also contingent; not everyone will have them (a point already adumbrated at the end of the previous chapter).

[124] The idea that individuals inhabit social worlds plays a key role in many of Williams' texts. See, for instance, B Williams, 'Saint Just's Illusion' in B Williams, *Making Sense of Humanity* (Cambridge, Cambridge University Press, 1995).

[125] This is connected to our discussion in the previous chapter about practical necessity.

[126] My narrative here is based on the musical version of Victor Hugo's *Les Misérables*, composed by Claude-Michel Schönberg, Alain Boublil and Jean-Marc Natel. English lyrics were written by Herbert Kretzmer. It is worth noticing that Javert even claims 'I am the law' in his last piece, 'Javert's Suicide'. The piece depicts the identity crisis he faces when his belief in the law falls apart.

[127] Deigh, 'Emotion and the Authority of Law'. It is worth pointing out again that Deigh was originally talking in terms of legal authority.

The 'characterless' agent, on the other hand, has nothing of that, and therefore the way she engages in practical reasoning ends up being very different from the agent that has a character. In order to decide what one ought to do, the concrete individual must tap on her values, motives, dispositions, projects and so on. Those are the materials that will enable us to formulate a better account of the reason-giving character of the law, but those resources are precisely what the 'characterless' agent presupposed by positivism does not have. Practical questions, and the deliberation they demand, are radically first-personal, as Williams says.[128] Here we have a *second mismatch*: the reasons that the thin agent of positivism presents as the result of her deliberation are not the ones that necessarily follow from the deliberation of real, localised agents, because they are based on a different set of motivations.

This mismatch is important because it highlights something that demands further explanation. Recall the claim that the law characteristically demands respect. This is a demand that moves from the law towards the subjects. Let us grant that this claim is true. We still need to understand what respect is and how and when people recognise the law's claim; that is, there must be considerations in the other direction as well: considerations that start from the first-personal point of view of the agent and move towards the law. The main suggestion of the second mismatch is that there can be no such considerations if our starting point is something like the characterless agent. When it comes to a richer account of the reason-giving character of the law, such an account will tell us not only about how law purports to engage with the agents' practical reasoning, but also about how the agents themselves make sense of the demands of law.

V. Genealogy and the Civic Engagement View

As I have mentioned earlier, Sylvie Delacroix presents an account of legal normativity in her excellent book, *Legal Norms and Normativity*.[129] She ingeniously combines Williams' genealogical method with Korsgaard's general account of normativity to present an original account of legal normativity, and, given the resources she mobilises, it is fruitful to pause and analyse her arguments in this chapter, even if she is not a legal positivist.

Delacroix contrasts her view on legal normativity with the more static, 'downstream' accounts of Montaigne, Kelsen, and Hart. In her view, those authors were committed to two problematic ideas that frustrated their attempts to get a full account of legal normativity. Those authors were, firstly, committed to an explanation of legal normativity that was as independent as possible from

[128] B Williams, 'Formal and Substantial Individualism' in B Williams, *Making Sense of Humanity* (Cambridge, Cambridge University Press, 1995) 125; B Williams, *Ethics and the Limits of Philosophy* (London, Routledge, 2011) 74.

[129] Delacroix, *Legal Norms and Normativity – An Essay in Genealogy* (2006).

the 'context of social interaction giving rise to law'. Secondly, they were suspicious of moral objectivity. Once the old narratives of divine authority were out of the game, there was no way to ground legal normativity in anything more certain, unless one were committed to moral realism. Because moral realism is a difficult position to defend, those authors ended up being sceptical about the objectivity of morality.[130]

Delacroix's own views are meant to challenge both ideas. She believes that through genealogy we can get an account of legal normativity that is simultaneously closer to the social fabric in which law is inserted and morally objective. This is how she summarises her position:

> I think legal normativity is best understood as a dynamic process which feeds itself out of the daily confrontation between legal requirements and other types of demands, including those of morality and prudence.[131]

A bit further she adds that:

> One cannot explain law's normativity, its capacity to bind us, without including an account of practical deliberation, without referring to the possibility, and indeed the responsibility we all have, of assessing law's claim to bind us. This assessment, in turn, requires us to consider what we want law for: the values or purposes which are meant to warrant law's claim to impose some non-optional course of conduct upon us.[132]

Genealogy tells us how we ended up having something such as law, but it also tells us, in Delacroix's view, why law is normative.[133] For law to play the roles we want it to play, it must be capable of providing reasons for action. Every time we engage practically with the law, we engage in an exercise of judgement about the law and about how the law is faring considering the roles it plays in our life. This is the reason why I believe that the expression *civic engagement view* is fitting for Delacroix's account. Delacroix takes seriously the twin claims I've been insisting on: that we need a subtler account of the agent and that law is part of a political narrative. Nonetheless, there are points of contention worth emphasising. For instance, I find her claim that genealogy 'carries an intrinsic commitment to a constructivist meta-ethics'[134] too strong, but that is not the point I want to dwell upon.

Delacroix captures something important when she emphasises that we bring about legal normativity every time we engage practically with the law. From this, she seems to infer that it is possible that for many people the law acquires special significance because it is *their* law; it is the law they are the authors of. However, this view cannot be generalised. As Dan Priel rightly points out, Delacroix's account relies heavily on notions like 'civic responsibility' and on our

[130] ibid xxiv.
[131] ibid 165.
[132] ibid 177.
[133] ibid 182.
[134] ibid 105.

'responsibility as lawmakers'.[135] Those notions are localised; they essentially belong to western modernity and reliance on them comes at a cost. Not every context in which there is something we can recognise as law has those notions, so to make an account of legal normativity dependent on them either restricts the scope of the account (ie, to modern legal systems in western countries) or distorts the phenomenon explained by the account (ie, trying to understand ancient Chinese law with those categories). Of course, Delacroix's account is not wrong because it uses local notions, but it ends up being a local account of legal normativity.[136]

If Delacroix was concerned – as most legal theorists are not – with history and context, how are we to explain the limitations of her account? I believe that she is led astray by what she calls the 'programmatic element' of legal normativity, the goals that the law ought to serve. Delacroix places the deliberation about this programmatic element at the centre of her account of legal normativity, as we can see from her quotation above. Because for us, in our circumstances of modernity, ideals of civic responsibility are valuable, we can be easily misled into thinking that those ideals must figure in an account of legal normativity, as parts of the programme law ought to serve. However, when an agent engages practically with the law, all that is required is that the law somehow resonates with things that the person values, respects, and so on (this was already suggested in the previous chapters but will be further developed in the next one). There is no need for this to take the shape of an evaluation of the programmatic element,[137] still less of an evaluation of the law taking into account ideals of civic responsibility. The upshot here is not that Delacroix is wrong, but that the account she presents is actually a particular case of the more encompassing account that I will present in further detail in the next chapter.

VI. Conclusions

Let me repeat something I have mentioned in the Introduction. To say that positivism is ill equipped to explain the reason-giving character of the law is not to say that positivism as a whole is wrong. Indeed, Hart and his followers might even be right in their fictional genealogy. In addition to that, I do not think that anything I have said is necessarily incompatible with the main claims of legal positivism. On the contrary, I think that if legal positivists were to embrace a richer view of the practical agent, they would be honouring their commitment to realism and unromanticism in their theories. What the arguments developed in this chapter

[135] Those terms appear many times in Delacroix's book. See, for instance, Delacroix, *Legal Norms and Normativity – An Essay in Genealogy* (2006) xiv, 128, 152, 153, 196, 197.

[136] D Priel, 'Legal Norms and Normativity: An Essay in Genealogy, by Sylvie Delacroix' (book review) (2007) 27(4) *Legal Studies* 750, 754–55.

[137] One might wonder if even framing the question in terms of a programmatic element of the law is not a typically modern way to frame it.

do mean, however, is that a priori conceptual analysis cannot help us to explain how the law affects our practical reasoning. It is worth bringing in another quote by Williams:

> Philosophy has to learn the lesson that conceptual description (or, more specifically, analysis) is not self-sufficient; and that such projects as deriving our concepts a priori form universal conditions of human life, though they indeed have a place (a greater place in some areas of philosophy than others), are likely to leave unexplained many features that provoke philosophical enquiry.[138]

There is more to the reason-giving character of the law than what we can grasp through the use of conceptual analysis. In the next chapter, we will move beyond 'conceptual description' and present a more substantive view on legal normativity. As Deigh remarked, there is more to legal normativity than just the recognition that law is a rule-guided practice. There can be no doubt that understanding what it means for an activity to be rule-guided is important, but rule-guidance is not what is characteristic about law's normativity, as many other activities, like chess or etiquette, are also rule-guided.[139] As part of a broader narrative of political rule, law seems to demand the respect of those subject to it, so an account of how it can do that must be part of an account of the reason-giving character of the law.

[138] B Williams, 'Philosophy as a Humanistic Discipline' in B Williams, *Philosophy as a Humanistic Discipline* (AW Moore ed, Princeton, Princeton University Press, 2006) 192.

[139] Deigh, 'Emotion and the Authority of Law' 144–47. Deigh's own approach will be to argue 'that the law's authority is conditioned on an emotional bond between the law and its subjects'. ibid 141. This bond, in turn, is built upon the more basic emotional bond between parents and children that grounds parental authority. ibid 147–49.

4

Character, Respect, and Legal Normativity

I. Athena's Speech

ATHENA
Neither anarchy nor tyranny, my people.
Worship the Mean, I urge you,
shore it up with reverence and never
banish terror from the gates, not outright.
Where is the righteous man who knows no fear?
The stronger your fear, your reverence for the just,
the stronger your country's wall and city's safety,
stronger by far than all men else possess
in Scythia's rugged steppes of Pelops' level plain.
Untouched by lust for spoil, this court of law
majestic, swift to fury, rising above you
as you sleep, our night watch always wakeful,
guardian of our land – I found it here and now.[1]

The lines above are from the conclusion of Aeschylus' *The Eumenides*. In them, Athena resolves the conflict between Orestes and the Furies and creates a court of law to adjudicate disputes in Athens. The most important lines are those: 'Where is the righteous man who knows no fear? The stronger your fear, your reverence for the just, the stronger your country's wall and city's safety.' There is something here that is similar to what we have seen in the debate between Antigone and Kreon in the first chapter. There seems to be a notion of respect for the law that is doing much work in their speeches.

In Sophocles' *Ajax*, too, we encounter this appeal to respect for the law as something valuable. In his exchange with Teukros, Menelaos (who is, if anything, the antagonist of Sophocles' *Ajax*, at least from the point of Ajax's suicide onwards)

[1] Aeschylus, 'The Eumenides' in *The Oresteia*, trans Robert Fagles (New York, Penguin, 1979) lines 695–705. It is worth noticing that in Herbert Smyth's translation, Athena refers to the tribunal as 'worthy of reverence' and the original Greek line uses the vocabulary of *aidos* (shame) in it. See Aeschylus, 'The Eumenides' in *Aeschylus*, trans Herbert Weir Smyth (Cambridge, MA, Harvard University Press, 1926).

claims that 'What city can thrive where there's no fear of the law? (...) No, the man who lives in fear and shame is safe. But in a city of no respect, just insolence and wilfulness, though it enjoy awhile a following wind, one day it will go under. Fear is in order.'[2] The vocabulary of fear, shame, and respect is used in an imprecise way by the characters in the plays (Aeschylus and Sophocles were not, obviously, working on treatises of analytical philosophy), but, I contend, they were pointing out something that is central to our understanding of legal normativity.

What those speeches do in an imprecise but insightful way is to bring about the idea that the law is something that demands our respect, and that respecting the law is central if we are to have any sort of societal order. Moreover, the speeches also seem to connect respect for the law with notions of character. Both Athena and Menelaos, in different ways, emphasise the individual and how her own prosperity in society depends on respect for law. In this chapter, I will build upon those insights to present an account of the reason-giving character of the law.

In the third chapter, we analysed accounts of the reason-giving character of the law that could be extracted from positivists. Regarding those, the main issues were that they didn't take into account law's role in a broader narrative of political rule and that the picture of the agent underlying those accounts was too thin and detached from concrete agents as we know them. In the next chapter we will analyse the moralised views of Dworkin and Finnis. Regarding the moralised views, the main issue will be that they overemphasise the importance of moral considerations in a way that could be distortive of the reason-giving character of the law; hence, they should be rejected (or even better, adjusted) in favour of the view I will present in this chapter. I will try to avoid the mentioned issues in my account by putting the agent and her considerations at the centre of my analysis and by connecting the reason-giving character of the law with broader considerations of political rule, an idea that appeared several times in the previous chapter but that was not sufficiently developed there.

If the view of the agent that was discussed in the third chapter is too thin, and, as I will explain in the next chapter, the richer view presupposed by the moralised accounts of Dworkin and Finnis is too distorted, the view that I intend to develop in this chapter will have what it takes for us to make sense of the reason-giving character of the law. This will be done as follows. Starting in the next section, I will recapitulate some of the discussion on genealogies, and I will introduce Bernard Williams' discussion of the 'first political question'. This discussion is here so that we can understand what it means to say that the law is part of a broader narrative of political rule. Once we understand that, we will revisit Hart's internal point of view, taking into account our discussion of reasons internalism in the second chapter. The central idea in my revision of Hart's internal point of view is to recast it as an attitude with a more specific content, namely, the very notion of respect for law.[3]

[2] Sophocles, *Aias*, lines 1070–90. The translation I am quoting is *The Complete Plays of Sophocles – A New Translation*, trans Robert Bagg and James Scully (London, Harper Perennial, 2011).

[3] In my presentation of those claims, I will be relying heavily on John Deigh's work.

The argument about the internal point of view will set the stage for the two main sections of the chapter. In the first of those sections, I will provide some philosophical resources for our understanding of what is entailed by the idea of respect for the law. I am going to look at the notions of character, identity, and respect itself. Equipped with those notions, I will be able to present my account of the reason-giving character of the law. The claim, in very general terms, is the following: we can make sense of the reason-giving character of the law once we understand how individuals can have different relationships with the law, relationships that are connected to notions of character, identity, respect and so on. As we will see, the account I will present has many layers to it. There is a thick case in which the agent identifies herself with the law, a case in which the agent recognises some sort of value or good in the law, thus having at least a reason to not act against the law, and more basic cases in which the agent has at least prudential reasons and other similar considerations. After presenting my account, I will address a number of important objections to it.

II. Genealogy, Political Rule, and the Internal Point of View

A. From Genealogy to Political Rule

I have been claiming for a while that the law is part of a broader story of political rule. What are we to understand by this claim? Let us begin by recalling the idea of a genealogy. In the previous chapter, I have recast the Hartian tale about the origins of the law in terms of a Williamsian fictional genealogy. A genealogy was there defined as a narrative that helps us to understand how a given phenomenon emerged, and such narrative can be either fictional or historical.[4] Fictional genealogies or narratives are useful to us because they can bring forth traits of the phenomenon we are interested in that are buried under the messiness of real life and history.[5] For instance, fictional genealogies are useful for our grasp of the function of a given institution. When doing so, a fictional genealogy does not presuppose that the agents in its narrative intentionally or purposefully created the institution, but merely that once they got to it, they could see it as an achievement of sorts. Their situation is in general better with this institution than without it, and they can grasp that.[6] Sticking only to the fictional genealogy, however, will give us merely the shapes and contours, not the content. This is so because we – as the kinds of beings that we are now, with culture, dispositions and value judgements – are not like the agents in fictional narratives. More specifically, in the case of legal normativity,

[4] B Williams, *Truth and Truthfulness* (Princeton, Princeton University Press, 2002) 20.
[5] ibid 21.
[6] ibid 33–34.

the kinds of accounts we could get from positivism also ignored the fact that it is a characteristic feature of law that it demands respect from its subjects. This is essential if we are to understand what is distinctive about law when compared to other rule-guided practices. Nonetheless, the general point we learn from Williams's discussion on genealogy is that if we want to make sense of ourselves and our practices, we also need to turn our attention to the more local, contingent resources that make much of the stuff of our lives.[7]

I have suggested that Hart's genealogy started with a primitive society that faced problems as it became more and more complex, and that Hart's function for the law was *social control*. In that narrative, the idea of the *internal point of view* was key. It enabled Hart to account for the rule-guided nature of law, an aspect that was overlooked by the legal theories that revolved around sanctions. Hart is not, to my mind, wrong, but his account is incomplete if taken as an account of legal normativity. He lacks a '*comprehensive* explanation of the normativity of law',[8] to use Veronica Rodriguez-Blanco's phrasing. In what follows, I will present a modified version of Hart's genealogy, one that puts law in the broader context of what we might call the social life and that better enables us to understand law's place in a broader story of political rule. This updated genealogy will set the stage for a reinterpretation of the internal point of view.

So, what is this broader story that law is part of? Why do we have politics, or more generally something like the state, of which the law is part? The story I have to tell draws heavily from Williams' *In the Beginning was the Deed*, but with a twist or two. Williams, following a tradition that can be traced back to Hobbes and Thucydides, makes the following claim. There is a 'first political question', and it regards the 'the securing of order, protection, safety, trust, and the conditions of cooperation'.[9] We have politics and something like the state to address the first political question, but, adds Williams, this is not enough for at least two reasons. Firstly, for any community at a given time, there can be more than one possible way to answer the first political question, so there is need for some way to pick an option among those. Secondly, and more importantly, the answer offered to the first political question must be an answer that those living under it can *accept*.[10] This is the crucial excerpt from Williams:

> The situation of one lot of people terrorizing another lot of people is not per se a political situation: it is, rather, the situation which the existence of the political is in the first place supposed to alleviate (replace). If the power of one lot of people over another is to represent a solution to the first political question, and not itself be part of the problem,

[7] ibid 60; B Williams, 'Why Philosophy needs History' in B Williams, *Essays and Reviews 1959-2002* (Princeton, Princeton University Press, 2014) 408.

[8] V Rodriguez-Blanco, *Law and Authority under the Guise of the Good* (Oxford, Hart Publishing, 2014) 77.

[9] B Williams, 'Realism and Moralism in Political Theory' in B Williams, *In the Beginning was the Deed* (G Hawthorn ed, Princeton, Princeton University Press, 2005) 3.

[10] ibid 3–4.

> something has to be said to explain (to the less empowered, to concerned bystanders, to children being educated in this structure, etc.) what the difference is between the solution and the problem, and that cannot simply be an account of successful domination. It has to be something in the mode of justifying explanation or legitimation (…).[11]

This quotation nicely brings together the two elements that I have mentioned. A political state emerges as a solution to the problems of the first political question, but to do so, it must make a claim that those under power can accept; it must present an acceptable narrative. 'The whole point' of politics and the state, Williams says, 'was to save people from terror'.[12] It cannot, therefore, be the mere use of power from one group of people against another group. There is what Williams refers as a 'basic legitimation demand'[13] that must be met for politics and the state to be in place. For the exercise of power to be some sort of political rule, this exercise of power must have something to say in its favour that distinguishes it from mere domination or oppression. Political rule has 'something in the mode of justifying explanation or legitimation', to use Williams' words.

That those under power can accept the story or narrative of political rule is a crucial point and more must be said on this score. The acceptance of those under power is not the same thing as acceptance by *us*. We are ourselves under some form or another of answer to the first political question, but the story of political rule that is offered to us (and that we might accept) is not the only one. Different narratives might appeal to different communities at different times. For instance, the narrative of legitimacy offered by King Arthur in Camelot can be accepted by everyone in that context, but a sword removed from a stone (or given by a lady that lives in a lake) is no narrative of political rule for *us* at all, and something akin to a reversal of this also holds true, a fact that *Monty Python and the Holy Grail* brilliantly plays with. However, we can grasp the meaning it had for *those* people in *that* context. That is, we can make sense of their narrative, and we can evaluate things according to it, even if we do not take that narrative to be reason-giving in any sense for *us*.[14]

This kind of approach is, according to Williams, in contrast to what he calls 'political moralism'. Political moralism takes as its starting point some first moral principles, and then proceeds to elaborate a view on politics based on those principles. Utilitarianism as a political philosophy is a prime example of political moralism, but Rawls' account in *A Theory of Justice* can be taken as another example. Williams names his own view a kind of 'political realism', by which he means that it is a kind of view that does not treat politics as an application of moral

[11] ibid 5.

[12] ibid 4.

[13] ibid 4–8. In his paper, Williams presents his discussion in terms of legitimacy and of the basic legitimation demand. I find the language of legitimacy quite confusing for our purposes, so I will stick with the term 'political rule'.

[14] ibid 11.

principle, but as something that has its own autonomy, as something that in a sense has its own language games.[15] Political moralism, in its overtly idealistic and moralised view on politics, stands contrasted with the view taken by many political scientists, that politics is nothing but a matter of guaranteeing interests of this or that person or group. The rosy lens of political moralism was opposed by the grim lens of political cynicism, and it is no surprise, says Williams, that 'the existence of each helps to explain how anyone could have accepted the other'.[16]

Williams' political realism is not a happy compromise between the moralism of philosophers and the cynicism of political scientists, but an attempt at making sense of politics itself, an attempt that looks at what is 'platitudinously politics'.[17] It looks at what the agents involved in politics – which to a certain extent means everyone – perceive as being politics. To recall a quote from Williams in the first chapter, but now applied in a different context, the 'aim is to *make sense* of social events, and that involves relating them intelligibly to human motivations, and to the ways in which situations appear to agents'.[18] This is the story that we have so far: we need politics so we can overcome the problems raised by the first political question, but we can only do with a politics that can present a narrative of its rule that we deem acceptable. Different groups, however, might accept different takes on the first political question, and with this, different narratives of political rule. We do not bow to King Arthur, but to claim that his rule was illegitimate, besides sounding plainly self-righteous, explains very little.[19]

The story that Williams tells us about politics ties back to the view on practical reasoning that I have elaborated on in the second chapter. Political moralism, insofar as it resembles moral theories, is open to the same kinds of objections we have already seen. If real agents do not have in their subjective motivational sets the kinds of principles that political moralism talks about – or if they have them, but do not assign the importance to them that the theory does – there will be a poor fit between theory and what actually is politics. The claim that political moralism is a full-blooded normative inquiry is always available, however. The price for that claim is that in doing so the political moralist ends up changing the subject. If a political moralist claims that she is engaged in an argument about how politics ought to be according to her preferred moral theory, there is nothing wrong with that, but her view on politics cannot be taken as an attempt to make sense of politics. It is not a theory about politics, but about what politics should be.[20]

On the other hand, the cynicism of the political scientist is undoubtedly grounded on the messiness of the real world, but it can be *too* reductive. It ignores

[15] ibid 1–3.
[16] ibid 12.
[17] ibid 13.
[18] B Williams, *Shame and Necessity* (Los Angeles, University of California Press, 1993) 161.
[19] B Williams, 'In the Beginning was the Deed' in B Williams, *In the Beginning was the Deed* (G Hawthorn ed, Princeton, Princeton University Press, 2005) 26–27.
[20] This point connects back to our discussion of Dworkin's criticism of Williams in the second chapter. I will discuss Dworkin's views further in the next chapter.

that politics also has a dimension of principle, not in the sense that politics necessarily involves moral considerations, but that concrete agents, when engaging in politics, can do so motivated by things they take to be moral principles. Even if it is true that the interest-talk of political science is supposed to cash this out, it is also true that this is a very poor representation of what agents think when they engage in politics. They do not merely weigh their interests against the interests of others in order to compound the political. This is not how they understand their own motivations: just like with political moralism, political cynicism has a poor fit with the ways agents reason about what they ought to do. This is what Williams has to say about political theories, and it is a point that nicely encapsulates what we have been saying:

> Any such theory will seem to make sense, and will to some degree reorganize political thought and action, only by virtue of the historical situation in which it is presented, and its relation to that historical situation cannot fully be theorized or captured in reflection. Those theories and re[f]lections will themselves always be subject to the condition that, to someone who is intelligently and informedly in that situation (and those are not empty conditions), it does or does not seem a sensible way to go on.[21]

The law, or some form of normative system similar to it, is going to be part of a solution to the first political question. This is so because any solution to the first political question will demand ways of organising the society itself and the powers, rights, and duties that people will have in it. To put the same point in different terms, the law will be related to a narrative of political rule, and this in turn entails that there must be something told in favour of its acceptance. For people to accept it, this narrative must be connected to what people care about or recognise as somehow valuable; otherwise, this narrative will make no sense for them (or will not be acceptable, and so on). There is more to be said, however.

The law, as part of a story of political rule, does more than just present reasons in favour of its acceptance. The law characteristically demands *respect*. I will discuss the idea of respect in more detail later in this chapter, but the point I want to emphasise here is that the law does not present itself as a theoretical authority. Theoretical authorities provide agents with reasons for belief; it is the kind of authority that scientists and scholars have in general. The law, on the contrary, presents itself as a practical authority:[22] the law purports to make a difference in people's deliberations, and not only because of its power to coerce (since we are already within the domain of political rule). Differently from theoretical authorities, the law is not in the business of merely offering advice to its subjects about what ought to be done. The law intends to *rule over* its subjects.[23] We are here dealing with a thicker notion of what it means for something to be reason-giving.

[21] Williams, 'In the Beginning was the Deed' 25.

[22] A point emphasised again and again by Joseph Raz. See also J Deigh, 'Emotion and the Authority of Law' in J Deigh, *Emotions, Values and the Law* (Oxford, Oxford University Press, 2008). As I have said already in the previous chapter, I take my project in this book to be congenial to Deigh's.

[23] To use an expression I once heard, 'the law is not your buddy'. It is not your local chess club either.

Understanding this thicker notion will help us to move beyond the picture we could extract from positivism. It will help us, for instance, in making sense of the difference between the law and other rule-guided practices. To do so, we must first revisit Hart's internal point of view.

B. Revisiting the Internal Point of View

HLA Hart's internal point of view was discussed in the previous chapter. There, we have seen that Hart's original claim was interpreted in different ways. The *minimalist interpretation*, espoused by Scott Shapiro and Jeffrey Kaplan,[24] argues that all that the internal point of view does is bestow 'intelligibility' to behaviour guided by rules. There can be no rule-guided behaviour, according to the minimalist interpretation, unless the relevant agents adopt an 'attitude' or 'disposition' to evaluate conduct according to a given standard. On the other hand, the *expressivist interpretation*, defended by Gerald Postema,[25] claimed that Hart's account was problematic because it allowed for a gap between the acceptance of rules via the internal point of view and an obligation to obey the law; that is, from the fact that legal officers accepted the law, it does not follow that those that do not accept the law from the internal point of view have any reason to obey it. Postema's argument is too strong, in the sense that it demands more from Hart than what he originally was offering. Nonetheless, Hart's account is incomplete if, to use once more Rodriguez-Blanco's formulation, 'it is presented as a *comprehensive* explanation of the normativity of law'.[26]

We are now in possession of resources to place Hart's original argument in a broader frame and offer something along the lines of a comprehensive account of the reason-giving character of the law. We should start with what it means for law to be part of a broader narrative of political rule. This narrative must be acceptable and must be able to turn the answer to the first political question into 'a sensible way to go on' for those that assess it. I take it to be uncontroversial that the emergence of law is part of any answer to the first political question. Law is connected to how people can come to accept a political order. If the law is to play this role, it must be more than merely the imposition of prudential reasons on agents; it must be able to maintain the central distinction between 'having an obligation' and 'being obligated'. There is need for an attitude, Hart's internal point of view, although a radically revised version of it. For law to simultaneously maintain the distinction mentioned and be able to fill its role in a narrative of political rule, it must be more than just a collection of advice. That was, indeed, the insight of the tragedians: 'The stronger your fear, your reverence for the just, the stronger your

[24] SJ Shapiro, 'What Is the Internal Point of View' (2006) 75 *Fordham Law Review* 1157; J Kaplan, 'Attitude and the Normativity of Law' (2017) 36 *Law and Philosophy* 469.
[25] G Postema, 'Norms, Reasons, and Law' (1998) 51(1) *Current Legal Problems* 149.
[26] Rodriguez-Blanco, *Law and Authority under the Guise of the Good* (2014) 77.

country's wall and city's safety', as Aeschylus would have it.[27] I believe that John Deigh captures neatly this point in his discussion about the authority of law:

> (…) while the power of government to coerce obedience is conditioned on the subjects' vulnerabilities to harm and capacities for fear, the authority of law must be conditioned on something more. This additional factor, moreover (…) must be the subjects' allegiance to the law, their willingness to be governed by the law apart from their being vulnerable to the punitive sanctions by which it is enforced and capable of fearing those sanctions. It must, in short, be the subjects' willingness to subordinate their own ends to the ends the law sets for them.[28]

My suggestion is that we adopt a thicker notion of the internal point of view in the sense of attributing some content to what was originally described as an attitude. The phenomenon that the tragedians Hart (as I am interpreting him) and Deigh were trying to explain in different ways was the notion of respect for law.[29] This is a richer notion because it allows us to understand the characteristic ways in which the law purports to be reason-giving. As discussed in the third chapter, there is more to law's normativity than just the fact that the law is a rule-guided activity. This notion of respect for the law explains what is distinctive in law as a normative practice that sets it apart from games and etiquette, for instance. The next two sections of this chapter will add much to the notion, but already at this point we can see how we have incorporated Hart's original idea in a broader picture.

Now, are we not back to the *same* problem that Postema identified? Postema claimed that 'Hart's theory of social normativity rests essentially on an expressivist, non-cognitivist metaethics.'[30] This, for him, was a source for the troubles he detected in Hart's original account (if we understand it as a fully-fledged account of legal normativity). In a sense, yes, we are back to the same problem, but only if we restrict ourselves to Hart's original resources. Postema's claim about the grounds of Hart's view on normativity seems accurate, but his conclusion, that the account is problematic because real normativity is moral in nature and that this is incompatible with non-cognitivism, is not warranted. What we need is that people accept a narrative of political rule and have some sense of respect for law, and this has no necessary connection to matters of meta-ethical objectivity. It suffices that those under power recognise it as 'a sensible way to go on'.

What does it mean to accept a narrative of political rule? Surely, it is more than the mere recognition that a narrative makes sense as a narrative of political rule to someone else. Once again, we can understand King Arthur's narrative and why the inhabitants of Camelot accept it. The Knights of the Round Table are not *obligated* by Arthur to do anything; they see themselves under an *obligation* to obey the king. That Arthur is the king chosen by Excalibur is the reason why they recognise

[27] On this point, I believe that my account is close to John Deigh's understanding of Hart's internal point of view. See Deigh, 'Emotion and the Authority of Law' 158.

[28] Deigh, 'Emotion and the Authority of Law' 147.

[29] It should be noted that Deigh himself talks in terms of 'allegiance'. Later I will add Raz to this list.

[30] G Postema, 'Norms, Reasons, and Law' (1998) 51(1) *Current Legal Problems* 149, 158.

him as their *ruler*. Now, when we put ourselves in the position of addressees of a story or narrative, we want the narrative to do something more. That narrative must connect itself to us, to the kinds of persons we are. Here we come to a central point hinted at in the previous sub-section: a narrative can be acceptable to us if and only if it connects to our subjective motivational sets, to the things that we care about. This is the natural unfolding of the discussion about reasons internalism in the second chapter.

As it will become clearer later in this chapter, law's demand for respect, the characteristic way in which the law is reason-giving, will be successful insofar as the law manages to establish certain relationships with its subjects, and this is dependent on law's interactions with the subjects' motivations, values, dispositions, and so on. It is not something that comes from an external source to them, or at least not necessarily so. Because it depends only on who the subjects are, it is also independent of discussions on meta-ethics. Let us say, for instance, that every form of objectivism in ethics is false. From this, it does not follow that law can never be reason-giving, because this depends on the relation between law and the motivational sets of its subjects. Conversely, if there is objectivity in ethics, ethics will play a role in the reason-giving character only insofar as those subject to the law care about ethics in the first place (this was part of my discussion on Dworkin, Korsgaard and Wilson in the second chapter). Again, no difference is made by it.

To the extent that Postema's criticism depends on meta-ethical claims, it can be successfully defused by kinds of reasons for action depicted in an internalist model. Even if external reasons existed, for them to actually bear on individual action, they would need to be connected somehow to the subjective motivational set of the agent. This would make them internal reasons in the relevant sense at the end of the day (this is a corollary of the requirement of explanation that we discussed in the second chapter). Nonetheless, even if external reasons for action indeed existed, nothing I am saying in this chapter would bar them from playing a role in the reason-giving character of the law. The argument I am developing, however, can explain legal normativity without appeal to external reasons.

A final remark I would like to make in this sub-section is about a possible source of complexity. It is true that the law typically features in those broader narratives or stories of political rule. Things, however, become more complicated than that because there are instances in which the law can end up having a narrative of its own that is disconnected from the broader narrative of political rule. A possible instance of this is when people describe the legitimacy of the system of common-law as independent of the political sphere.[31] Another instance, one that I will not be able to discuss in this book, is that it is a hallmark of our modern condition that law and politics are conceived as relatively autonomous, law's legitimacy coming partly from this very fact. The importance

[31] I thank Steve Bero for this example.

of this point is that agents can have different relationships with the state and/or its politics, and with the law. Some further remarks about those distinctions will be presented later.

We now have a better grasp of what it means for law to be part of a broader story of political rule. We also have a better grasp on the idea of an internal point of view as an attitude and its relation to law's demand for respect. On the other hand, how all this works is still obscure. At this stage of the argument, we need to move a bit away from the more jurisprudential discussion we have been developing up to this point in order to make a short detour on some notions that are usually under the heading of ethics or philosophy of action. More specifically, we need to understand what it means for someone to respect something. It is to this matter that I will now turn my attention.

III. Respect, Identity, Character[32]

A. Respect in General

Before we advance in our inquiry about normativity and respect for law, we must grasp what it means to respect someone or something. Respect is a tricky thing to understand because at the same time we experience it in our lives in a rather unmysterious way, it is hard to explain, and even harder to separate it from other attitudes one might have, such as love or reverence.[33] In what follows, I will not attempt any clear conceptual definition of respect, since it does not matter for our purposes where respect ends and love begins, for instance. Still, I will present a working definition of the idea that carves for us some distinctive aspect of our experience. It is important that we can at least distinguish respect from personal identification or personal acceptance of values or institutions on the one hand, and from mere acknowledgement that certain values or institutions are important to a given person on the other.

My suggestion is that we understand respect as an attitude that involves giving some weight to the respected object in our practical deliberations. What do I mean by that? I mean that when respect for a given object is present, such respect will count as a reason for action to abstain from offending or somehow acting contrary to the object of respect. This is what distinguishes respect from

[32] The discussion regarding the ideas of respect, 'loss of power' and the 'imagined other' mentioned by Williams, and the emotion of shame in this chapter draws from my 'There are Many Senses to an Emotion – Loss of Power, Diminishment and the Internalised Other' (2024) 43 *Topoi* 435.

[33] The notion of respect is a quite debatable one. The most influential view on respect nowadays is probably Stephen Darwall's, but the sense I am using the notion is not the same as the one he discusses. See S Darwall, 'Two Kinds of Respect' (1977) 88(1) 1 *Ethics* 36; S Darwall, 'Respect and the Second-Person Standpoint' (2004) 78(2) *Proceedings and Addresses of the American Philosophical Association* 43.

mere acknowledgement. I can acknowledge that religious dogma is valuable for a friend of mine without this necessarily entailing that I regard it as valuable myself. Our capacity to acknowledge value that is not our value is extremely useful, as it enables us to present intelligible accounts of actions done for the sake of values we do not accept. I can make sense of my friend's decision to not skip the Sunday mass because I know something about how he values things. This mode of acknowledgement, I contend, should not be confused with respect.

Respect makes some demands on us, in the sense that it somehow guides or constrains our engagement with the respected object. To better understand respect, let us take a look at the following example: imagine that you do not consider monogamy something valuable for you, but your partner, whom you love very much and respect, does. In this case, the object of your respect is not monogamy, but your partner. Now, if you respect your partner, then your respect for them might provide you with reasons for action in a given direction, namely, that you should respect what they respect. Sometimes your respect might not be in relation to that person (eg, your partner) but in relation to your relationship and to what you have built together. This is arguably the case with some old-fashioned couples that refuse to divorce because they respect their story together (it is important to highlight that I am not saying that this is a good – or bad – thing. I am merely trying to make sense of the idea of respect in practical deliberation).

What is important to keep in mind for what follows in this chapter (and also in the next one) is that respect is a complex idea that can relate itself to different, independent objects. In the previous examples, we can respect a value or institution, a person, our relationship with that person, and so on. As we progress through the argument, I will come back to the notion of respect to add more details to it, but this working definition is enough for our purposes.

B. Identity and Character

There are two other important notions we must grasp in this sub-section, the notions of identity and character. As I will explain, they are related to one another.[34] Let us take as our starting point Williams' definition of a person's character as a 'sense of having projects and categorical desires with which that person is identified'.[35] In this quote, by 'projects and categorical desires', Williams means the materials that give meaning to a person's life. They are what motivate the person in being alive. Now, the quotation also uses the notion of identification, and this demands some explanation that goes beyond Williams' original formulation. Someone *identifies herself with* some desire, project, or value when this desire,

[34] In my discussion of character, I will be drawing mostly from Williams, but I will borrow a page or two from Harry Frankfurt's work as well.

[35] B Williams, 'Persons, Character, and Morality' in B Williams, *Moral Luck* (Cambridge, Cambridge University Press, 1981) 14.

project, or value is part of the person's understanding of herself; that is, the person sees it as being part of what she really is, or as I have it, her character. This is not the same thing as identity in what I will call an *attributive sense.*

Identity in an attributive sense comes in two forms. There is, firstly, the case in which someone can be *socially* identif*ied* through traits or characteristics that are not necessarily the same as the traits or characteristics that the person identifies *herself* with in the sense of those things being part of her character. For instance, third parties can identify someone by her religion or her ethnicity, but there is no reason for those traits to necessarily figure in the person's character. In many cases, of course, they will be part of the person's character, as when a person's sexuality is also a reason for her to feel proud.[36] A person's character, we may say, is what the person identifies herself with, whereas identity in an attributive sense can extend to cover elements that the person does not identify herself with. One can despise an identity that is socially attributed to her and try to separate that from her character, from who she really is.

Secondly, there is a sense in which something is part of someone's attributive identity that is *not* synonymous with identity socially attributed as we have understood the term up to this point, but that is *not* synonymous of character as well. Here is an example of this that I am adapting from Harry Frankfurt. I might feel simultaneously joy and envy towards the achievement of a friend. Both emotions, joy and envy, are in me; they are my emotions. This means that they are part of my identity in the attributive sense; they are emotions identif*ied* as belonging to me, even by myself, but they are not necessarily part of my character, or at least not *yet*. Both emotions can be identified as mine, but for one of them to be part of my character, something else is needed; I need to *identify myself* with one of them. If I identify myself as a good friend, I will put effort into identifying myself with joy and will try to foster that emotion instead of envy. My identification with an emotion does not mean that its rival disappears, but that I am trying to overcome it. In the example, envy is not part of 'what I really am'.[37]

In *Shame and Necessity* Williams refers to the character of a person as her *ethos*, the nature of a given agent;[38] and in 'Identity and Identities' he claims that in the constitution of one's identity – the term here understood as what I am calling character – 'the will may be exercised in coming to coincide with something that I already unchangeably am'.[39] In an array of not-so-helpful terms, we might say that the character of a person refers to her 'spirit', 'way of life', 'style', or to things 'close

[36] See, in general, B Williams, 'Identity and Identities' in B Williams, *Philosophy as a Humanistic Discipline* (AW Moore ed, Princeton, Princeton University Press, 2006).

[37] H Frankfurt, 'Identification and Externality' in H Frankfurt, *The Importance of What we Care About* (Cambridge, Cambridge University Press, 1988) 66–68. It is in this sense that Frankfurt speaks of love (for him, a particular mode of care) as a given 'configuration of the will'. See H Frankfurt, *The Reasons of Love* (Princeton, Princeton University Press, 2004) 16–21.

[38] Williams, *Shame and Necessity* (1993) 72–73, 103.

[39] Williams, 'Identity and Identities' 63–64. This idea is also central to Harry Frankfurt's account of the will and of care. See, for instance, Frankfurt, *The Reasons of Love* (2004).

to her heart'. 'Way of life' and 'style', however, capture something important. As I understand it, the idea of a character has an aspirational aspect insofar as the agent tries to be true to her character or to what she understands that her character should be. This was something already evident in the discussion of Frankfurt's example, that I strive to be what I identify myself with. In this, the character of an individual is an expression of Nietzsche's motto, quoted approvingly by Williams, of you 'becoming what you are'.[40] Character, then, is what I *identify myself with*, and this is not necessarily the same thing as identity in the *attributive sense*. Equipped with those working definitions of respect, identity, and character, let us go back to legal normativity.

IV. Respect for Law and the Reason-Giving Character of Law

A. The Contours of the Account

It is time to put all the pieces together. There is a narrative of political rule that is offered to us. What are we to make of it? If this narrative makes sense to us and we accept it, it becomes an item that interacts with our practical reasoning. The way it becomes an item in this sense, I claim, is connected to the notions of respect, identity, and character I have sketched above. The acceptance of a narrative implies that we recognise value in it, that it highlights or tells us things that we believe are important. Since the law is part of the structure that tackles the first question of politics (and there is also the case of law having its own narrative), and since we accept its narrative of political rule, then we also accept the law as a valid source of reasons. Think about it: we have the problems highlighted by the first question of politics. A political order emerges to deal with them, and as part of this political order we have the law. If we accept the narrative of that political order, then we should accept law as well. To put the same argument in different terms, when we recognise that the law has some good in it, or that the law fosters things we believe valuable, we can see the law as connected to what we care about, and then we can have a route from the law to reasons for action.

Recall that we have recast Hart's original argument of the internal point of view in terms of law's demand for respect. This demand, I contend, is something characteristic of law that sets it apart from other normative practices. Given what we have seen in the previous section, this means that when an agent accepts the narrative of political rule, she *at least* respects it, and in effect the law, therefore having reason to not do things that offend against the political order in question. So, the agent that accepts the narrative has at least this kind of motivation or disposition: she

[40] Williams, 'Identity and Identities' 63.

does not want to go against the political order or the law because she respects those things, and such respect provides her with reasons for action. What we have here is a picture of legal normativity that has two sets of considerations converging. On the one hand, there is the idea of law's demand for respect. This moves from the law in the direction of the agent. On the other, there are the considerations about practical reasoning and of what it means for an agent to respect something. Those look from the agent to the law. Let us unpack all of this.

B. The Thick Case

Think about the following scenario. In a political community that accepts the narrative of political rule, lawmakers pass a Bill that establishes a fare for the use of public transport. People in this society take pride in their politics and in their law and recognise them as valid sources of reasons for them. When a youngster tries to free-ride on their trains and is caught in the act, the other commuters shout things like 'Have you no shame?', 'What would your parents think of you?' or 'I would be mortified if you were my son!' There are some possible reactions from the youngster towards this. A first possibility is that he simply does not care. He does not care about the political order, or about the judgements of others, or even about the fine he will probably need to pay. In this scenario, the law is not reason-giving for him at all, and this was a possibility that I have adumbrated at the end of the second chapter, when I said that the generality of an explanation of legal normativity will depend on the generality of the items in motivational sets. The youngster is a less dramatic version of the 'hard-cases' we saw in that chapter. A second possibility is that – when faced with the reactions of others – the youngster 'wakes up' to reality and realises that what he did was wrong. He then might feel guilty or ashamed. 'I am sorry for what I have done' and 'That's not the kind of person I am', are plausible things for him to say in this case. In this second scenario, there are things *in* the youngster that enable the reactions of others and/or of the law to hook in him.

Let us put the youngster to the side and look instead at the commuters, that is, at the community in this example. They all share a sense of acceptance for the narrative of political rule and the political order it engenders. They have an attitude that I have been referring to as respect for the law. As far as I know, the most well-defined version of respect for law is that of Joseph Raz.[41] As I will explain in a moment, Razian respect for law is a central idea to my account, but an idea that needs further refinement. This is how Raz describes this attitude:

> The government and the law are official or formal organs of the community. If they represent the community or express its will justly and accurately, then an entirely

[41] I have briefly alluded to Razian respect for law in the previous chapter. Here I will discuss it in further detail.

> natural indication of a member's sense of belonging is one's attitude toward the community's organization and laws. I call such an attitude respect for law. It is a belief that one is under an obligation to obey because the law is one's law, and the law of one's country. Obeying it is a way of expressing confidence and trust in its justice. As such, it expresses one's identification with the community. Respect for law does not derive from consent. It grows, as friendships do; it develops, as does one's sense of membership in a community. Nevertheless, respect for law grounds a quasi-voluntary obligation. An obligation to obey the law is in such cases part and parcel of one's attitude toward the community. One feels that one betrays the community if one breaks the law to gain advantage, or out of convenience, or thoughtlessness, and this regardless of whether the violation actually harms anyone, just as one can be disloyal to a friend without harming him or any of his interests, without even offending him.[42]

This is a lengthy quotation, but there is much to learn from it. The key bits, however, are that respect for the law 'is a belief that one is under an obligation to obey because the law is one's law, and the law of one's country' and that 'it expresses one's identification with the community'. This neatly captures the attitudes that the commuters have. The notions of respect and identification are, as we have seen in the previous section, quite obscure, but we can nonetheless grasp the beginnings of what I will call the *thick case*: the situation in which people identify themselves with law and with the political order to which it belongs, and in doing so, they treat the law as reason-giving. Another important aspect highlighted by Raz is the 'sense of belonging'. People recognise that they share roughly similar attitudes and values (this, of course, is a product of history and culture), and this grounds a sense of shared identity among them. In the thick case, the members of the community have a shared attitude of respect towards its political order and the law. In Raz's parlance, 'One feels that one betrays the community if one breaks the law.'

The previous paragraph is roughly right, but there is need for much fine-tuning. The context of Raz's discussion of respect for law is the debate about a general obligation or duty to obey the law. In 'The Obligation to Obey: Revision and Tradition', after dismissing Finnis' view of the duty to obey the law as a 'seamless web', Raz goes on to say that even if we cannot ground a general duty to obey the law that applies across the board, the *attitude of respect for law* can ground such a duty, granted that the agents have such an attitude. To respect the law (in Razian terms) is not in any sense mandatory for individuals, but if they respect it, then such respect can ground a general duty to obey the law.[43] This last point is better developed in an earlier essay, called 'Respect for Law'. In that essay, Raz claims that 'respect is itself a reason for action. Those who respect the law have reasons which others have not. These are expressive reasons. They express their respect for the law in obeying it (…).'[44] A few pages later, he claims that 'respect for law is a

[42] J Raz, 'The Obligation to Obey: Revision and Tradition' in J Raz, *Ethics in the Public Domain: Essays in the Morality of Law and Politics* (Oxford, Clarendon Press, 1995) 354.
[43] ibid 353–354.
[44] J Raz, 'Respect for Law' in J Raz, *The Authority of Law* (Oxford, Oxford University Press, 2009) 259.

somewhat self-satisfied and complacent attitude to the law. It expresses confidence that the law is morally sound'.[45] With those additional bits of information, let us proceed to the fine-tuning.

In the previous section I have suggested that respect means giving something due consideration, the recognition of the value of something, even when we do not identify ourselves with that something. It may be the case that my respect for – let's say, the values that my father has – never comes into question. It may be that because of sheer luck, we never actually confront each other regarding those values. This does not mean that I didn't respect his values, but that as life went on, I never came across the need to confront the respect I had for them. Naturally, to *express* respect is not necessarily the same thing as *abiding by* the values I respect. If my father has conservative values and believes that marriages are only authentic if done in a church, respect does not necessarily entail that I should marry in a church. I can resist and do things my way, but if I really respect his values, they would have had at least some weight in my deliberation, and I will probably have some stain caused by them, a sense of loss or remorse after sticking to my guns. To use Raz's term, I might feel that I somehow betrayed my father.

The example just discussed also helps us to see what is out of tune in the second quotation by Raz, about respect and the moral value of law. From the fact that I respect something, it does not necessarily follow that I am confident about its morality. I may be morally indifferent to it, and maybe be morally opposed to it. Some examples might help here. It is possible, I think, to be morally opposed to the prohibition of abortion yet have an attitude of respect either towards the contrary opinion or towards those that believe that it should be prohibited (that is, there can be different objects of respect). Similarly, I can respect the results of an election, even if I believe that in the age of fake news popular opinion has degraded to mere prejudice, and I could lament if someone elected in this context is stripped from power by a coup, even if the revolutionaries endorsed values similar to the ones I identify myself with. Those hypotheticals add complexity to the picture, and in this we can see one advantage of the apparently cumbersome distinctions that I have made earlier, between character, respect, and different senses of identity.

It is fair to say that Raz's respect for law, insofar as it is an expression of identification with one's community, is actually running together some ideas that I have distinguished. Firstly, there is this sense of respect I have been developing in the last couple of paragraphs. This sense of respect explains why if I stick to my guns and don't get a religious marriage, I can still feel a sense of betrayal or loss. It is not that I *identify myself* with those values, but that I respect them (or, alternatively, respect those that hold those values), and they play a part in my practical reasoning. In his discussion about restrictions to the political value of liberty,

[45] ibid 261.

Williams suggests something along those lines (although we should be careful with the language of identification here):

> A helpful consideration here is the extent to which the person whose liberty is in question is *identified* with the actions that might be felt to restrict or violate that liberty. This idea helps us to explain the case of the citizen who thinks that a certain political decision is both procedurally correct and right in principle, but nevertheless experiences its consequences for himself as a cost in liberty. *The reason that this is possible is that his sense of himself is not entirely that of a person identified with the state's decisions*, however rightful.[46]

Secondly, we have the idea of character, of identifying myself with something. In cases in which I identify myself with the law of a community, the law plays a role as an expression of my character. In a way, the law tells something about me, and vice-versa. This seems to be more or less captured by Raz's talk about obedience to the law as a way to express one's loyalty to the community.

The upshot of this distinction is that it is more profitable to talk about two closely related attitudes contained in Raz's respect for law, attitudes that can nonetheless be distinguished: (strictly speaking) *respect* for law and *identification* with the law. Both attitudes, respect and identification, however, come in different varieties (this was something already foreshadowed before, in the discussion of the possible reactions of the youngster). A community and its law are not the same thing (and indeed, as I will soon add, law and politics might not be the same thing as well), so it is possible to respect or identify yourself with both of them, or with only one of them. This is another nuance that was not clear in Raz's original treatment of respect for law but that has importance, as I will try to show later.

What I take to be the *thick case* of the reason-giving character of the law is, therefore, the one in which there is a common thread running from the narrative or political rule underlying a given political order, the law that emerges from the political order, the identification (not only mere respect) of the community with that law, and the identification (not only mere respect) of the individual with that community. In this situation, the recognition of law as reason-giving will be part of the individual's character. If obedience to the law is something that I identify as being part of who I am, to break it would be tantamount to distancing myself from my own character, to feeling let down by myself. I am calling this the thick case because it is the strongest possible case, in which all the parts – the political order, the law, the community, the individual – are harmonious with each other

[46] B Williams, 'From Freedom to Liberty: The Construction of a Political Value' in B Williams, *In the Beginning was the Deed* (G Hawthorn ed, Princeton, Princeton University Press, 2005) 88, first emphasis by the author, second emphasis is mine. I am grateful to Damian Cueni for pointing out this paragraph to me. As Cueni pointed out to me in conversation, in 'From Freedom to Liberty' Williams seems to be calling attention to differences in how individuals can recognise legitimate exercises of authority in terms of principle, procedure, and identification. Strictly speaking, this is not the same thing as the differences I am trying to draw in this chapter, but they point out to the same phenomenon: the multi-layered structure of the reason-giving character of the law.

and mutually reinforcing. Notice that this is not the same thing as the morally best situation as well; indeed, the thick case is ecumenical regarding morality, since the actual content of the law does not matter, as long as the law is *taken by its subjects* as justified by some narrative political rule that they can identify themselves with. The case is the strongest possible because there is full identification from the individual with all levels of the analysis, so it is possible for law to have a practical weight that is unmatched in all the other scenarios. Also, given that this is the strongest case, we can 'peel it off' to the weaker, thinner cases. This makes this case the ideal one to start our analysis.

C. The Case of (Only) Respect for Law and Raz's 'Feeling of Unease'

The thick case is one in which we have a common thread from the narratives of political rule to the law and to the character of the individual. This, obviously enough, is not the only way in which legal normativity presents itself to us. One of the advantages of the account I am presenting is that it allows us to make sense of the plurality of ways in which law can be reason-giving. Besides the thick case of identification, another case that was lumped together in Raz's idea of respect for law is the case of (only) respect for law. As we have seen, someone can respect something, even when this something does not form part of the person's character.

Think about the following situations involving agents and the law. An agent can have a flatly hostile attitude towards the law; she does not identify herself with it, nor respect it. This is not the only possible stance, however. We can have a protester that believes the law to be unfair and misguided; she protests for its change, but she also respects the legal and political order. It is the case of someone that is doing what she thinks is right but that recognises that something of value might be lost in the process. This protester does not feel like she went out of character by protesting against the law, and in this we have a key difference with the thick case.[47] Indeed, we can even have a criminal that breaks the law and has an attitude of respect towards it. A figure like Jean Valjean from *Les Misérables* is something like that. Arguably, Valjean respects the law but believes that there were powerful reasons for breaking it. Javert, on the other hand, would most likely be a case of a person that fully identifies himself with the law.

The point is that in the case of (only respect for law), people might sometimes disapprove of the law in the same sense I can disapprove of the conservative values of a relative. People can, nonetheless, abide by the law. They see the law as making a claim on them that has enough weight in their practical deliberation to guide

[47] As Hrafn Asgeirsson pointed out to me, civil disobedience might be another good example of this. In many cases of civil disobedience, the person that is challenging the law also accepts the legal implications of her acts.

their action in one way or another. When I say that it is characteristic of law that it demands respect from those subject to it, I mean that the law demands *at least* this sense of respect. This is what sets the law apart from other normative practices and what I think was underlying the speeches in Aeschylus and Sophocles. There is this distinctive experience of seeing oneself as being a subject of law. Indeed, even the practical difference thesis we analysed in the third chapter could be seen as pointing out this aspect of our engagement with the law.

At this stage of the argument, I believe that it might be fruitful to discuss a specific picture of the relationship between law and practical deliberation, Joseph Raz's theory of exclusionary reasons,[48] and how my account of the reason-giving character of the law relates to it. Raz' classical example for his theory is the command given to a soldier.[49] When a commander tells a soldier to seize a vehicle, this command is a protected reason in the sense that it combines what Raz calls a first-order reason (to seize the vehicle) with a second-order reason (that you ought to act on the first-order reason that compounds the command and not on other reasons). Technical language notwithstanding, Raz is onto something important. When someone confronts the soldier, asking him why he did what he did, the soldier appeals *to* the command. When he does so, this appeal is in the sense that he was under an obligation to do as he did; that is, he is not appealing to the possible soundness of the command.[50] Raz is capturing something relevant about how we experience the force of some reasons in our practical deliberations. Raz's point is, I think, phenomenological.[51]

To this distinction between different levels of reasons (first-order reasons and second-order reasons), Raz adds two conceptual points. The first point is that the law claims legitimate authority (I will say more about Raz's view on authority at a later moment in this chapter); the second point is that legitimate authorities operate by issuing directives that work as protected reasons.[52] Razian legal normativity can thus be explained: law by its nature claims legitimate authority, and when law has that authority (Raz is clear in saying that it can fail to do so), law will provide directives to agents that are protected reasons. Agents are not supposed to act on their own balance of reasons, but on the balance of reasons provided by the authoritative directive. The Razian account has quite a pedigree. In a sense, it is

[48] Raz's canonical explanation of his theory is *Practical Reason and Norms* (Oxford, Clarendon Press, 1990) especially the first chapter, but see also the first three chapters of *The Authority of Law* (Oxford, Oxford University Press, 2009) and the second part of *Ethics in the Public Domain: Essays in the Morality of Law and Politics* (Oxford, Clarendon Press, 1995). The first three chapters of *The Morality of Freedom* (Oxford, Clarendon Press, 1986) are also relevant.

[49] The example appears in Raz, *Practical Reason and Norms* (1990) 38–39.

[50] See, in general Raz, *Practical Reason and Norms* (1990) 38–45.

[51] In this way of framing the point, I am borrowing from Roger Shiner's reading of Raz. See R Shiner, 'Exclusionary Reasons and the Explanation of Behaviour' (1992) 5(1) *Ratio Juris* 1–22, 7.

[52] See, for instance, J Raz, 'The Claims of Law' in J Raz, *The Authority of Law* (Oxford, Oxford University Press, 2009) 30; and J Raz, 'Authority, Law, and Morality' in J Raz, *Ethics in the Public Domain: Essays in the Morality of Law and Politics* (Oxford, Clarendon Press, 1995) 214.

a more refined version of Hobbes' distinction between command and counsel.[53] It has also attracted a number of criticisms.[54] What I am going to do now is to argue, firstly, that there is no necessary incompatibility between my account and Raz's; and secondly, that my account can capture the phenomenon Raz is talking about without the need to appeal to his distinction between two levels of practical reasoning.

Regarding the first point, notice first that a protected reason demands that its addressee not *act* on other reasons, but it does not, and cannot, demand that the addressee refrain from *deliberation* about the merits of the protected reason.[55] When a judge, for instance, says that a given agent is under obligation to do X, this agent can evaluate the judge's claim. She can conclude that, morally speaking, the judge is wrong, but that she ought to obey him because this is the law. When someone asks her why she did X, she can say, 'I did X because that was the law', and the person will get what she meant. Nothing bars us, however, from asking her why she cares about the law or why she respects it, for instance. Once we have made questions like those, the agent's reasoning shifts to broader concerns. 'Well, I care about the law because I wouldn't be able to live as a lawbreaker' and 'Oh, I respect the law because of its importance in society' are two possible answers. We move towards the kind of account I have developed previously in this section. Razian-protected reasons do not demand that the agents be (deliberately) passive regarding them. That demand, indeed, would be senseless given that as agents we necessarily engage in practical reasoning and act.[56]

Regarding the second point, Raz claims that there is a 'peculiar feeling of unease' that emerges when an agent disregards a protected reason; let's say the soldier above does not do X. There was a command; the command was really bad, so the agent decides to not obey it based on his balance of first-order reasons. The balance of first-order reasons in the case pointed against the protected reason. There seem to be, says

[53] For a discussion on Hobbes' account, see Korsgaard's analysis in the first chapter of C Korsgaard, *The Sources of Normativity* (Oxford, Oxford University Press, 1996).

[54] See, for instance, C Gans, 'Mandatory Rules and Exclusionary Reasons' (1986) 15 *Philosophia* 373; N Gur, 'Legal Directives in the Realm of Practical Reason: A Challenge to the Pre-emption Thesis' (2007) 52 *The American Journal of Jurisprudence* 159; H Hurd, 'Challenging Authority' (1991) 100 *Yale Law Journal* 1611; E Miam, 'The Curious Case of Exclusionary Reasons' (2002) 15 *Canadian Journal of Law and Jurisprudence* 99.

[55] Even though Raz is not always clear on this point. Sometimes he does suggest that protected reasons exclude not only action but deliberation as well. See Raz, *The Morality of Freedom* (1986) 47–48. For the interpretation I am adopting, see Raz, *The Morality of Freedom* (1986) 39. A powerful criticism of the reading that protected reasons exclude deliberation is H Hurd, 'Challenging Authority' (1991) 100 *Yale Law Journal* 1611, 1628.

[56] In a later essay, Raz makes his account clearer by explaining that protected reasons exclude only reasons that oppose the directive, granted that the directive is backed by Raz's account of legitimate authority, the normal justification thesis. This gives even more leeway for deliberation on the merits of the directive, and moves Raz a bit further from the original Hobbesian take on commands. See J Raz, 'The Problem of Authority: Revisiting the Service Conception' in J Raz, *Between Authority and Interpretation – On the Theory of Law and Practical Reason* (Oxford, Oxford University Press, 2009) 144–45. I thank Kenneth Ehrenberg for pointing this out to me.

Raz, 'two incompatible assessments of what ought to be done', the command and the balance of first-order reasons.[57] In such a case, the agent has this 'feeling of unease' described by Raz. For Raz, we need something like the distinction between first- and second-order reasons because this distinction enables us to see that practical reasoning is not unidimensional. The protected reason operates at a different level from the first-order reasons, so the conflict between them on what one ought to do is not actually solved. The protected reason does not lose its force because the soldier in the example decides to disobey the command.[58]

The feeling that Raz describes is certainly real; indeed, it seems to be in the vicinity of what I am describing as respect for law (and one should notice that on this very idea I was also drawing from Raz). Many critics, however, have claimed that the feeling does not vindicate the existence of Razian protected reasons. Chaim Gans, for instance, has pointed out that the feeling of unease is not enough to prove the existence of exclusionary reasons because the feeling also appears in cases of conflicts between what would be two powerful first-order reasons, like the case of Sartre's conflicted patriot that does not know if he should stay home and take care of his mother or if he should leave it and join the resistance against the Nazis (to stick to Gans' own example). On the other hand, there are also cases in which we would have an exclusionary reason, but not the accompanying feeling of unease. This is the case Gans uses to illustrate this: assuming that rules of etiquette are exclusionary, no one would feel uneasiness by breaking rules of etiquette if that would allow one to save the life of another person in danger. The combination of the two examples shows why, at least for Gans, the feeling that Raz identifies is not enough to prove the existence of exclusionary reasons. There are situations in which the feeling appears that does not correspond to a conflict between exclusionary reasons and first-order reasons, and situations in which the fear appears in which there would be an exclusionary reason being violated.[59]

Independently of the cogency of those criticisms against Raz, I believe that the feeling he identifies can be explained without appeal to a second order of reasons, in the sense that I do not need to engage with their possibility of existence or not. To see this, think about what it means to respect someone or something. When an agent respects the law, she sees something of value in it, but this does not preclude the possibility of conflicts between the law and other things that she values. If the agent is a judge or a legal officer, she might end up following the law to the detriment of those other values she has, or she might end up breaking the law for the sake of those values. My point is that in either case, Raz's 'peculiar feeling of unease' is a plausible reaction. The agent feels 'torn', to use another of Raz's terms to describe the feeling, because she is going against what she respects either way (the previous talk about feelings of betrayal should come to mind here). A similar, but more extreme, feeling might also appear when we bring character into the

[57] Raz, *Practical Reason and Norms* (1990) 41.
[58] ibid 40–48.
[59] Gans, 'Mandatory Rules and Exclusionary Reasons' 387–89.

discussion. *Les Misérables*' Javert is illuminating here. When Javert finally breaks the law to do what he believes is right, the feeling of being torn becomes unbearable to him because it becomes a crack in his own understanding of himself.

A summary of the discussion in the preceding paragraphs might be useful. In the case of (only) respect for law, the agent recognises that the law has a claim over them, that it exercises influence in their practical deliberation, but this is not as deep as in the thick case, since we are not dealing with matters of character. This case invited a comparison with Raz's account of exclusionary reasons, and I agreed with Raz that there is a feeling of uneasiness or of being torn that appears when we go against things that we respect. There is, however, no need for this feeling to ground the existence of second-order reasons. Even if it does, this does not mean that we cannot explain the feeling using the resources I have been developing throughout the book. As I have said before, my account is not incompatible with Raz's, but it does not depend on it either.

D. Prudential Reasons and Loss of Power

We can move even further away from the thick case. Sometimes people will only have prudential reasons to treat the law as reason-giving. In cases like that, the person simply does not care about the law or its claim to respect; she obeys it merely because she wants to avoid punishment. The less an agent cares about the law, the more likely it will be that the only reasons she has to obey it are of a prudential nature. If all we have going on for law are prudential reasons, then it makes sense to say, depending on what we want to know about that agent and about the law, that for her the law is no different from the gunman situation. This is the thinnest possible sense of the reason-giving character of the law.

It would be naïve to underestimate how common this sense of the reason-giving character of the law is, but there are other relatively thin possibilities as well. In what follows, I want to build on a fairly unknown discussion (at least among legal theorists) of Williams' endnotes to *Shame and Necessity*.[60] In the first endnote, Williams raises the possibility that the emotion of shame could have its beginnings in what he refers to as a perception of 'loss of power'. The argument has a bit of a Nietzschean flavour, but it is quite intuitive, as it builds on some very basic aspects related to how we experience the emotion. In general, we do not want to feel ourselves diminished in relation to other people (and even in relation to what we take to be our best selves). When an event or an action triggers this feeling of losing power, the agent senses that she is somehow ranking lower than others, somehow inadequate to occupy the space she is occupying. Williams describes this feeling of losing power as feeling disadvantaged or unprotected towards others.[61]

[60] Williams, *Shame and Necessity* (1993) 219–23.
[61] ibid 221.

What is interesting about this experience of losing power is that it does not demand a real audience to appear, and in this lies its power to develop into subtler, more complex forms of shame that might have value for ethical reflection.[62] How can it appear without a real audience, however? There are cases in which an 'imagined other'[63] is enough for the emotion to be triggered. Think about the following example: you write a love letter to someone. After writing it, you read it aloud and realise that the letter is extremely embarrassing. There is no need for a real audience here for you to feel ashamed; it suffices that you imagine someone reading the letter for you to want to run away. You feel yourself unprotected, exposed, even without others around you. The idea here is that this is what is needed for one to feel shame. As this figure of the imagined other starts to gain substance, it can embody our values, as well as people and institutions that we respect. In this sense, it can become a point of reference for our emotion of shame that has an ethical import, although that is not our topic.

What role can this idea of 'loss of power' have in our account of the reason-giving character of the law? Let's go back to the case of the youngster in the public transport. Assuming that he simply doesn't care at all about the law and the opinions of the community, he might still be liable to the feeling of loss of power. He fears being seen as less valuable, to be seen in a disadvantageous position. Because of that, the law can provide reasons for action for him, something like the following: 'if you don't want to feel diminished in relation to others, you should comply with the law'. In this primitive case of treating the law as providing reasons, the agent is mostly concerned with not being seen as a lawbreaker by others (and those might be imaginary others). In this, we are already at some distance for the case of mere prudential reasons in the sense we discussed them.

There are some nuances that are worth highlighting here. Firstly, the person must recognise that being seen as a lawbreaker is a bad thing independently of her opinions on the law and on the community; that is, she must perceive the loss of power independently of her judgement on the audience. This is important because it enables us to make sense of people that feel shame – broadly speaking – even if they despise the audience (real or imaginary). After all, someone that breaks laws as a form of protest, for instance, through refusal to wear a given set of clothes demanded by law, can still feel shame when those she criticises pass judgement on her; this is a very human reaction. Furthermore, there is no necessary connection, although there might be contingent ones, between the perceived loss of power and the realisation that being seen by others as a lawbreaker might impair the agent's relationship with those people. The importance of noticing this is connected to this same example: our protester might have no interest at all in being in any kind of relationship with those she deems oppressive. In this aspect, there are no necessary connections to instrumental reasons to abide by the law.

[62] I present further discussion about the emotion of shame and Williams' thought in Murata, 'There are Many Senses to an Emotion – Loss of Power, Diminishment and the Internalised Other'.

[63] Williams, *Shame and Necessity* (1993) 82.

It might be the case that at the end of the day those considerations regarding the feeling of loss of power are just a species of the more general prudential reasons. I have no opinion on that. The term 'prudential reasons' is usually employed to highlight reasons that arise from the fear of sanctions or punishment, and although loss of power can be seen as a sanction of sorts, this does not help much. The term 'prudential reasons' is also usually deployed in contrast with 'moral reasons', and as we have seen in the second chapter, I am somewhat sceptical about the latter. At any case, no harm follows from understanding the reasons provided by law in the basic case as prudential, or from understanding them as something else. Our interest here is in making sense of the phenomenon of the reason-giving character of the law, not in presenting an air-tight conceptual analysis of it.

So, this is what we have so far. We have a thick case in which there is a continuum between the narrative of political rule, law's demand for respect, and character of the individual. We also have the case of (only) respect for law, in which the agent recognises something of importance in law that is enough to provide at least reasons to not act against it, but this recognition does not connect the law with the agent's character. Finally, we have the more primitive cases in which there is no continuum, that is, the cases of prudential reasons and of the fear of loss of power. The account I am proposing here elaborates on the two main claims that I've been arguing for since the beginning of the book, namely, that agents as we know them have dispositions, values and so on and that those elements occupy a central role in practical reason; and that it is a characteristic feature of the law that it demands respect from those subject to it. When compared to the accounts we have analysed earlier, we can see that the account I am proposing moves beyond the bare contents of the positivistic accounts since it provides a substantive view on respect and how that relates to agents. At the same time, my account does not moralise agents nor the law and avoids the blunt dichotomy between prudential and moral reasons. More must be said for this account to be plausible, however.

E. Conflicting Stances: Fleshing Out the Account

Let us go back to the case of (only) respect for law. A judge that has respect for law in this sense can also believe that the law is misguided or wrong in a given case. She can have liberal views on abortion, but the law in her state is of conservative content and prohibits abortion in all circumstances. When the case of a woman that aborted because she was raped appears in her court, we can explain the way the judge feels torn through the distinction between character and respect. To declare the woman guilty goes against the values the judge identifies herself with, but it is the decision demanded by the legal order she respects. Indeed, the judge can even question the kind of person she is when she applies the law she believes is unfair. 'What I am doing with my life?' and 'How am I supposed to live with myself after this?' are two questions that might very well pop into her mind. If the model I am sketching is roughly correct, we can make sense of those conflicts people have without the need to appeal to anything but to some materials that make up an agent: the components of one's character, and the things one respects.

There are other conflicts that my model can explain as well. As I have indicated previously, it is possible for someone to identify herself with (therefore relating to character) the law and/or the community, and the same thing goes for respect. In the thick case, everything went on harmoniously, so we had a unified picture of the reason-giving character of the law in that case. Those items, however, can come apart. In what follows, I will present those scenarios and explain how they account for important cases of our relationship with the law. Many of those further cases appear because both identification and respect can have different objects.

A first situation is this: an agent that does not identify herself with the law nor respect it can identify herself with a community that does not identify itself with the law nor respect it. Think about the stance that a revolutionary fighter would have regarding the law of a tyrannical state. If this agent or other members of the community were to see law as reason-giving, this would be in the shape of the primitive cases I have explained. From this first situation, we can have a more complicated one, in which an agent respects the law but also identifies herself with a community that does not care two straws about the law. The son of a gangster could be in this situation. For some reason (maybe school) he has learned to take law's demand for respect seriously, but he identifies himself with a community that has a different attitude to it. Another situation would be the already mentioned case of Javert. Javert identifies himself with the law, not in the sense that a despot would see himself as the law, but in the sense that for Javert, nothing is more defining of who he is than obedience to the law. This is a case of someone that does not have any ties with the community, but that, in a sense, lives in and for the law.

A case like Javert's might introduce a further possibility of conflict, for as I have anticipated, there might be cases in which the political order and the law have different narratives underlying them and the agent can identify with both, just one of them, or neither. On a certain interpretation, we can say that Javert identifies himself only with the law (whatever the law is), and not with the whole of the political order. This means that where I have originally mapped three items – the political order (containing the law), the community, and the individual – we can have four items, for the political order and the law can be separated. The senses of respect and identification of the agent can, therefore, connect themselves with those items in many different combinations. So, one can identify herself with the political order but not with the law, or with the law but not with the political order; or she can identify herself with the political order and just respect the law, and so on. For much of this chapter, this bifurcation between the law and the political order will not be important, but it is important to highlight its possibility, especially because, as mentioned earlier, in our modern condition there is an important sense in which the law and the political are not conceived as the same thing.

I have no doubts that there are many other cases as well, but for the rest of this sub-section I would like to focus on a particularly complicated case based on the possible distinction between the law as a whole and specific pieces of law. As pointed out by Joseph Raz, it may be the case that the talk about a *general duty to obey the law* is nonsense.[64] Raz argues that 'the extent of the duty to obey the law in a relatively just country varies from person to person and from one range of cases to another'.[65] This view is the natural offspring of Raz's account of authority, but even if one disagrees with Raz on authority, his insight about the duty to obey the law seems to be valid nonetheless. Think about the following examples, adapted from real cases. In some places like China, India, or Brazil, citizens have a relationship with the law that is not adequately described in terms of a duty to obey the law as a whole. Conventional property law and criminal law often have high percentages of compliance, but intellectual property law in Brazil and China and traffic law in India, on the other hand, have extremely low percentages of compliance. People tend to disregard those branches of law in those countries; they don't feel themselves as bound by them, and at the same time no Brazilian in her right mind would see herself as a criminal for downloading an unauthorised copy of a movie.[66]

There seems to be a tension here. Previously, we have seen that for Raz, respect for law can ground a duty to obey, and I have myself argued that respect for law grounds at least reasons to not act against the law. At the same time, however, people do not see the law as a closed deal. In most cases, people approach the law in a 'piecemeal'[67] manner, that is, they can engage with bits of the law without necessarily understanding that their engagement with those bits implicates anything regarding their engagement with the law as a whole. Something similar seems to be the case with civil disobedience. Usually, civil disobedience movements do not refuse the whole of law, but certain pieces of it, like discriminatory laws or unjustified restrictions to liberties. This is one of the ways in which civil dissenters differ from fully-fledged revolutionaries. Whereas revolutionaries flatly reject the whole of the law, civil dissenters accept most of it, or at least the most important parts of it, like basic constitutional arrangements and so on.

Those cases can be contrasted with the case of the judge we saw earlier. The judge respected the law and thus felt its weight in her practical deliberation even though she disagreed with its content. How can we make sense of this mess? Here is my suggestion: at this point, we need to look back at the contents of the first claim of this book, that concrete agents have dispositions, motivations, values and so on, that is, what Williams has called subjective motivational sets. Law

[64] See, for instance, Raz, 'The Obligation to Obey: Revision and Tradition' and J Raz, 'The Obligation to Obey the Law' in J Raz, *The Authority of Law* (Oxford, Oxford University Press, 2009).

[65] Raz, 'The Obligation to Obey' 350.

[66] Of course, we can have nasty cases, as when family law is supposed to tackle gender inequality and communities simply disregard it.

[67] I am borrowing the term from Noam Gur's depiction of Raz's theory. See Gur, 'Legal Directives in the Realm of Practical Reason: A Challenge to the Pre-emption Thesis'.

characteristically demands respect (that was the second claim), and this means respect for the whole legal system. This does not mean that this demand will be recognised as such by every person under the law. For a person to respect something or someone, this potential object of respect needs to somehow connect to things that the person cares about. Respect, we have seen, entails that the people recognise something valuable or good in the object of respect, and this in turn provides at least a reason to not act against such an object. In some cultures, people might indeed have an attitude of respect for the law as a whole that would render them vulnerable to the law's demands even in situations that others would find it difficult to understand. For instance, it is said that in some countries people do stop the car at the red sign even if there is absolutely no one around, nor any sort of supervision. True enough, they might do that due to habit, but when asked why they did that, pointing out to habit is only part of a broader answer.

In the vicinity of those cases, we can have situations in which the agent actually disagrees with the content of this or that legal directive, but because she respects the law as a whole, she respects that directive as well (this was, arguably, the case of our judge). This is not as mysterious as it looks and is a common feature in our lives. We sometimes abide by rules we do not agree with because we respect those that have promulgated the rule. For example, a teenager might refrain from taking her partner to her parents' home because they said they don't want it and she respects them, even if she thinks that their rule is nonsensical. We can say somewhat loosely that in cases like those the respect for the 'whole thing' is transferred to this specific rule or directive.[68]

Finally, there might be cases of some rules or directives that the agent perceives as being so detached from whatever value the law has that the agent does not see noncompliance with those rules or directives as an expression of disrespect towards the law. This is likely the case of a person that downloads an unauthorised copy of a movie in a country with low compliance rates regarding intellectual property law. It makes sense for this person to not regard herself as a lawbreaker because she perceives herself as compliant with all the important legal rules. There is no contradiction between her breaking of intellectual property law and her sense of respect for law. To summarise, because of the differences between subjective motivational sets of agents, agents will express their respect for law in different ways even though law's demand is for respect for law as a whole.

The resulting picture is a fairly complex one. There are considerations coming from two directions: there is law's demand for respect on the one hand and the considerations about how and when a person might respect the law on the other. On the side of the agent, there are also the subtleties due to the differences between the cases in which a person identifies herself with the law, the cases in which there is (only) respect for the law, and the cases in which there are only prudential reasons or the fear of loss of power. There are also the ideas of political rule, law,

[68] I am thankful to Steve Bero for suggesting the expression 'transfer' in this context.

and community, and those can come apart depending on the scenario. Finally, there is the insight about the differences in the way that agents will engage with law's demand for respect. The combination of all those items, and their relation to the subjective motivational sets of the individual, are the components of my account of the reason-giving character of the law.

V. Four Objections

The previous sections presented my account of the reason-giving character of the law. In this section, I intend to address four objections that can be made against it. In the following section, I will compare my own account with Raz's view on legitimate authority. It is worth pointing out that much of what I will say in this section, especially about the third and fourth objections, anticipates the analysis of moralised legal normativity that I will offer in the final chapter of this book. As presented in this section, however, the objections are understandable on their own terms, and it is beneficial to have them analysed and rebutted in the context of the full presentation of my account of the reason-giving character of the law.

A first objection is that the account is too messy and too obscure; that is, it has too many items in it, and that therefore makes for a poor philosophical argument. I grant the first part of the objection: my account is messy, obscure and has too many items. However, I resist the second bit, that it is a poor account. Everything being equal, a simpler account is preferable to a complicated one, but our practical engagement with the law is a complex phenomenon that has many subtleties. Any account that ignores the messiness of real agents engaging with the law will face problems in the sense that it will overemphasise some aspects of our practical engagement with the law and downplay others. This was the case with overly minimal accounts, like the ones we derived from legal positivism in the third chapter, but something similar can be said about accounts that put too much emphasis on the moral reasons one might have, as we will see in the next chapter.

In the next chapter we will discuss and ultimately refuse the claim that all genuine obligations are moral obligations. According to that claim, the only actual, reason-giving, obligations are those that are demanded or licensed by morality. This is a clear, neat, account of obligations, but one that fails to do justice to the phenomenology of obligations. As we will see, it makes sense for people to feel bound by promises they made, even if those promises have immoral content. In those cases, the content of the promise is taken by the promisor as morally repugnant, and yet they feel the sting of the promise's normativity. The same goes for the discussion about respect for the law in this chapter. A claim in the sense that only morally just law can provide reasons fails to capture the 'feeling of unease' that someone that disagrees with the law but respects it feels. There is more to our engagement with the law than just morality.

This first objection is fuelled, I think, by a powerful temptation in philosophy, that we might have too many ideas around us, and that truth will bring those ideas together in coherent wholes or purge some of them. In either case, the temptation is to see philosophy as an activity that simplifies reality through theorisation.[69] This is not the place to discuss this temptation, but we can see how it impacts our understanding of legal normativity. Instead of looking at who we are, with all our nuances, we are tempted to look for a unified, simple, account that could explain all relevant cases and exclude the non-relevant ones as deviations.[70] In modern moral philosophy this temptation comes in pair with the allure of the morality system, of treating moral considerations as supreme or of overriding importance, a topic we touched on in the second chapter and that will appear again in a slightly different form in the next.[71] The rest of the story follows naturally. If we are looking for a simpler account, and we also believe that morality has supreme importance, it would follow that only moral reasons are the real deal. As we have seen throughout this book, we should be wary of such a view.[72]

There is a second possible objection that in a sense is opposite to the objection of messiness. Someone might complain that my account is merely a formal structure, that my account only presents the frame for the real action. We have narratives of political rule, subjective motivational sets, the ideas of character and respect, the legal and political order duo, and so on. All those items are combined to present the structure of the reason-giving character of the law, but in themselves they do not present any content. There are no concrete reasons offered, only the information that such reasons must be connected to the subjective motivational sets. The objection tells us that this is not enough, that we are still far from an account of legal normativity. I believe that this critic is onto something important, but something that I cannot provide in this book. All I have done here is to explain *how* the law can be reason-giving. This *how* is filled in much greater detail by the history, traditions, and shared judgements of communities. Through their forms of life, they fill the structure I have presented, so what can be reason-giving in classic Athens will not be reason-giving in modern London. For any given individual or community, the account I offer must be supplemented by history, arts, psychology, economics, and so on, a point already adumbrated in our first chapter, when we discussed philosophy as a humanistic discipline.

Nothing that I have said precludes one important possibility. Recall our discussion about Korsgaard in the second chapter. Korsgaard argued that Kantian pure practical reason is not incompatible with Williams-style internalism. Her claim was that it was not proven that there are no recurrent elements in people's

[69] B Williams, *Ethics and the Limits of Philosophy* (London, Routledge, 2011) 103–32.

[70] Recall, too, our discussion about philosophy as an attempt to make sense of ourselves and the absolute conception of the world in the first chapter.

[71] Williams, *Ethics and the Limits of Philosophy* (2011) 193–218.

[72] To quote Giudice somewhat out of context: 'The normativity of law is interesting, important, and significant for several reasons; its theoretical and practical study, to be apt, must also to be multifaceted.' M Giudice, *The Normativity of Law* (Cambridge, Cambridge University Press, 2024).

subjective motivational sets that can ground Kantian morality in every agent's motivations. If we could ground pure practical reason in every person's motivational set, then we would have a genuinely universal account of Kantian morality that was also internalist.[73] Someone might argue that this kind of Korsgaardian move is also available in jurisprudence. An argument of this sort would look like this: 'there is an item that is present in every subjective motivational set, and this item explains how law can be normative for every rational agent'. I do not deny that such an argument might be possible, but it is certainly hard to make.

A more modest argument, however, seems more plausible (and I see no reason to deny it). Someone might claim that as long as agents have any preferences against living in the State of Nature, they will have at least instrumental reasons to comply with the law. Those very basic instrumental reasons do not demand that the agents have any view on the law whatsoever, and they are also very general. Presumably, almost everyone but the extreme anarchist would prefer to live in society rather than in the State of Nature. This seems to me true, but there are two important caveats here. The first one is that even though this claim is very general, the reasons it talks about are not present for every rational agent, as we can have cases like the extreme anarchist (so this argument does not deliver what the original Korsgaardian move purported to). The second, and most important caveat, is that this claim tells us very little about how agents engage with the law. All that it tells us is that most people most of the time have reasons to comply with society's regulations because they do not want to live in a State of Nature. This claim fails to capture aspects that are distinctive of our practical engagement with the law, the kind of experience that Aeschylus, Raz and Deigh were pointing out in different ways. In turn, this means that the truth of this very general claim does not exhaust an account of the reason-giving character of the law. There is need for the kind of account I am proposing in this book, and indeed, this very general claim – that most people most of the time prefer to live in a political community rather than in the State of Nature – sits quite comfortably at the side of our discussion about prudential reasons and loss of power as thin cases of the reason-giving character of the law, so it may even be considered another variation of the thin case.[74]

Let us move to the third objection, namely, that the account I have sketched leaves no space for morality. Like many counterarguments in this chapter, this one is also a variation of an objection already tackled previously in the book. My account does leave space for morality, but it is the space that morality can meaningfully occupy in practical deliberation of concrete agents. Recall the discussion of Dworkin, Korsgaard and Wilson in the second chapter and its application to the case of Aphrodite in Euripides' *Hippolytus*. There, I have argued that morality is indeed a source of reasons for action for individuals, but only insofar as morality

[73] C Korsgaard, 'Skepticism About Practical Reason' in C Korsgaard, *Creating the Kingdom of Ends* (Cambridge, Cambridge University Press, 1996).

[74] I am grateful to Hrafn Asgeirsson for putting pressure on this point.

is connected to the motivational sets of the agents. In addition to that, the power that moral considerations can exert in deliberation is not supreme. Moral reasons can be beaten in deliberation without this meaning that the action that the agent concludes in favour of is irrational.

The account of legal normativity elaborated in this chapter is in tandem with the conclusions just recalled. Because reasons for action on my account have their normativity dependent on aspects like character and respect, they do not need to be committed to morality. The many examples we have been discussing illustrate the advantage of doing so. Now, to be sure, I am *not* saying that there are no moral obligations or anything of that sort. All that I am saying is that moral obligations – when they exist – will only be normative for agents if they can connect to what they care about. Equally important, the account I am proposing is not mutually exclusive with moral accounts of legal normativity. It is only incompatible with views that either exclude nonmoral sources of normativity or establish the supremacy of morality in every case, a point that will be further developed in the next chapter.

Closely connected to the previous objections, there is a fourth one. Someone might complain that different accounts of normativity have different concerns, that they intend to illuminate different phenomena. Borrowing a couple of ideas from Dworkin, for instance, an objector might retort that her account is supposed to explain how law can justify coercion. 'An account of legal normativity', this critic says, 'is supposed to lay down the conditions that must be met for law to be justified in its use of force. Because of that, such an account will necessarily be about moral reasons. An account based on the subjective motivations of agents surely has psychological value, but *it cannot justify law*.'

To phrase this a bit differently, if we understand that agents, in their engagement with the law, are looking for some form of value or the goodness in law, or for law's justification, there is a mismatch in my own account similar to the ones we identified in legal positivism in the third chapter.

A satisfactory account of legal normativity looks at it through a first-person perspective; my own account – or so the objection goes – is looking at legal normativity from a third-person perspective. This seems to me a mistake because it fails to account for what it means for something to be justified *for someone*. Evaluation is always dependent on the subjective motivational set of individuals, even when such evaluation presents itself as external to them (and, indeed, even if there are external reasons). It is true that the critic is tracking something relevant in her claim about how from the first-person perspective the agent is looking for a justification, but, as I have been arguing in this book, to see something as justified is a matter of acceptance of narratives of political rule, and such acceptance is dependent on the relationship of the narrative with what individuals care about. There can be no narrative of legitimacy or justification that free-floats from the subjective motivational sets of individuals.

Another thing that the objector might mean is that her theory is prescriptive or ideal, that it sets *the* conditions of *real* justification, independently of what concrete agents think about it. This approach converts the objector's theory into a fully blooded normative political theory. There is nothing wrong with this approach, which draws from some of the things we discussed in the second chapter about the possibility of external reasons, and we will discuss a version of it, again based on Dworkin's theory, in the next chapter (although it is worth mentioning that such a move is not Dworkin's own). Recast as a prescriptive theory, the account offered by the objector would have different burdens, as it would occupy a different space than my own account. Among those burdens are the ones that we have identified in the previous objection, that such an account is committed to controversial assumptions like the supremacy of morality. In any case, understood as a prescriptive theory, the objector's account would indeed be concerned with different matters than my own. What I am most fundamentally concerned with is the explanation of action in general and how we can make sense of a complex phenomenon like legal normativity without compromising the richness of practical reasoning as we find it in the world.

VI. Legal Normativity and Authority

Finally, the comparison with Raz's theory. Strictly speaking, I have not discussed authority in this book, but something must be said about Raz's theory of authority. As I understand Raz's 'service conception of authority', there are two sets of claims. Firstly, we have a set of claims about what makes an authority legitimate. For Raz, those are claims about what makes the authority capable of providing reasons for action for those that are subject to it. Secondly, we have a set of claims about how authoritative directives play their part in the agents' practical deliberation.[75] This second set of claims was already discussed in this chapter when I analysed Raz's exclusionary reasons. According to Raz, authoritative directives provide agents with protected reasons to do or not to do something (protected reasons, in turn, are complex reasons that combine a first-order reason to do or not to do that something with a second-order reason that excludes acting based on other reasons that are not the protected one). As we have seen, my own arguments are compatible with but independent from Raz's view on practical deliberation. What about his claims about legitimate authorities?

Raz's account of legitimate authority is made up of two interconnected theses. The first one is the 'dependence thesis', according to which 'all authoritative directives should be based on reasons which already independently apply to the subjects of the directives and are relevant to their action in the circumstances covered by the directive'.[76] This thesis is intuitively appealing: an authority that

[75] Raz's theory of authority is detailed in the third chapter of Raz, *The Morality of Freedom* (1986). Other relevant texts are Raz, 'Authority, Law, and Morality' and Raz, 'The Problem of Authority: Revisiting the Service Conception'.

[76] Raz, *The Morality of Freedom* (1986) 47.

imposes directives that are far too removed from whatever reasons the agents might have will not be recognised as legitimate and therefore will not be able to provide any reasons for action at all, save for prudential ones. Notice too that the dependence thesis is neutral regarding the existence of external reasons. All it says is that directives should be grounded on reasons that apply to the agents. The thesis does have a nice fit, however, with reasons internalism, something that is also suggested by the second and presumably more distinctive thesis. The second thesis is the 'normal justification thesis'. According to it:

> [T]he normal way to establish that a person has authority over another person involves showing that the alleged subject is likely better to comply with reasons which apply to him (other than the alleged authoritative directives) if he accepts the directives of the alleged authority as authoritatively binding and tries to follow them, rather than by trying to follow the reasons which apply to him directly.[77]

The normal justification thesis basically claims that legitimate authorities help agents to act according to the reasons that they already have. For Raz, the dependence thesis and the normal justification thesis are 'mutually reinforcing'.[78] The way I understand this mutual reinforcement is the following: the dependence thesis explains the constraints for an authority to be recognised as such by those under it. If a purported authority emits directives that have no bearing at all regarding the reasons agents have, agents will not see this exercise as an exercise of authority over them. On the other hand, the normal justification thesis explains what it takes for an exercise of authority to be justified. This exercise of authority *must be in the service of its subjects*, helping them to conform to the reasons that they already had. The normal justification thesis also explains why, for Raz, the authority of law is piecemeal. The law will have legitimate authority over an agent if and only if the law is better than the agent at putting the agent in the course of acting for the reasons that apply to her. If in a given case the agent 'knows better' than the law, then the law will not have legitimate authority (according to the normal justification thesis) over that agent.[79]

Some people have argued that Raz's theory of authority is too thin, too general to make sense of the phenomenon it purports to explain,[80] but this is not quite right. According to Raz, a general theory of authority like his own only needs to 'establish what it takes for there to be legitimate authority, rather than that it should show who has authority over whom and regarding what'.[81] The aim of Raz's theory, it seems to me, is merely to provide us with an account of the conditions for an authority to be legitimate. In that sense, the overly general features of his

[77] ibid 53.

[78] ibid 55.

[79] I am somewhat simplifying the picture. In *The Morality of Freedom*, Raz discusses a number of ways of extending the scope of authority that are secondary to the normal justification thesis.

[80] See, for instance, C Orrego, 'Joseph Raz's Service Conception of Authority and Natural Law Theory' (2005) 50 *The American Journal of Jurisprudence* 317.

[81] Raz, 'The Problem of Authority: Revisiting the Service Conception' 136.

theory are not an issue since the theory is supposed to cover all kinds of (practical) legitimate authority, from parental authority to the law.[82]

Nonetheless, Raz provides a more robust account of what are possible grounds for legitimate authority. According to him, there are at least two possible grounds within the service conception of authority. Firstly, we have considerations of *expertise*: in many cases the purported authority will have a better grasp on the reasons that apply to agents, and therefore agents will be better off by following the authority. Secondly, there are considerations of *coordination*: there are situations in which there is need for action to be coordinated, and having an authority capable of issuing directives can be perceived by agents as a way of attaining coordination. For instance, there are some goods, purposes or values that can only be instantiated through large-scale coordination, and insofar as agents have reasons to pursue those things, they will have reason to recognise authorities capable of coordinating their behaviour.[83] In the case of coordination, agents have reasons to pursue a given value (for example), and the way they can pursue that value is not by acting according to their own balance of reasons regarding how to pursue that value, but by deferring to what the authority says, since the instantiation of that value depends on coordination between different agents.

Both grounds play a role in the explanation of law's authority. The law is supposed to do a better job than individual agents regarding many of the reasons that apply to them (eg, think about regulations about pharmaceuticals or nuclear materials). The law also enables people to pursue goods or values that would be unattainable without coordination (eg, systems of distributive justice).

With all those arguments in place, how does my account of the reason-giving character of the law compare with Raz's theory of authority? There are two things I want to say. Firstly, it seems to me that much of what Raz's theory of authority tries to explain can be accounted for by the arguments I have developed in this chapter and elsewhere in the book. Connected to that, it seems to me that if this is the case, then we have good reasons to prefer my view since it explains important insights of Raz's account and the more general idea of respect in a single, unified account. Secondly, my account has an advantage when compared to Raz's since it can explain the same things without the need to appeal to a second order of reasons; that is, it can deliver the same insights but with fewer resources.

Let us begin with the first point. To see what I mean by it, think firstly about the dependence thesis. According to the dependence thesis, if the directives emitted by the purported authority are not based on the reasons that agents have, those directives will not be authoritative. Recall the picture of practical reason that I've

[82] I have presented a more detailed engagement with Orrego's criticism of Raz in the dissertation I have written in the Masters programme at the University of Sao Paulo (Brazil). This paragraph summarises my argument in that text.

[83] See, in general, Raz, *Practical Reason and Norms* (1990) 194–95; Raz, *The Morality of Freedom* (1986) 70–105; J Raz, 'Facing Up: A Reply' (1989) 62 *Southern California Law Review* 1153, 1179–97.

presented in the second chapter. In that chapter, I have argued that an agent has a given reason for action only if this reason can somehow be derived from her subjective motivational set through a sound deliberative route. The combination of the dependence thesis with my view on practical reason means that if the directives emitted by a purported authority are not based on the agent's subjective motivational set, then this directive will fail to be authoritative, since the directive will not be reason-giving (except in a prudential sense). In a nutshell, to say that authoritative directives must be dependent means, roughly, that they depend on the subjective motivational sets of individuals under the purported authority.

Let us now take a look at the normal justification thesis. This thesis might be too narrow *if* it is taken as a condition for law to be reason-giving. I have no doubt that if an authority has a better grasp on the reasons that apply to me, then I have good reason to abide by the authority, since by doing so I will be helping myself to follow my own reasons (but as I will explain in a moment, I might not be aware of that reason). This is why, indeed, the normal justification thesis and the dependence thesis are connected, since if the reasons grounding the directive are not the ones that apply to me, then this directive cannot be authoritative for me (so we can say that X is an authority regarding English poetry, but from that we cannot infer that X has any authority over me). This is also the reason why Raz believes that expertise alone is usually not enough to ground all relevant kinds of practical authority: I might be more knowledgeable about certain policy issues than anyone else in my political community, but since some issues might require coordinated action at a large scale rather than expertise, I would not be a legitimate authority regarding these issues. If the law of the state can coordinate behaviour regarding those policy matters, I might have reasons to defer to its directives, even if I think that I could have done a better job in its place.[84] In Raz's words, it is essential that a purported authority has 'the ability to co-ordinate the actions of members of the society in cases in which they have reason to co-ordinate their actions, and the ability to do so better than they can'.[85]

Two things to notice about what I have just said before we continue. Firstly, notice that those conclusions would remain true even if external reasons existed, since those reasons would only be reasons *for action* if they could explain why an agent does X (or could have done X), and if that is the case, then those reasons must be somehow connected to what motivates (or could motivate) that agent. Secondly, notice that there is no need for the agent herself to be aware of those reasons. Reasons internalism only requires reasons for action to be connected to the subjective motivational sets of agents, there is no need for the agent herself to be *aware* of them. This can be seen in Frankfurt's example of the agent living in a radioactive place we discussed in the second chapter. If an agent lives in such a place and she cares about her health, she has reasons for action to move from that

[84] See, for instance, Raz, *The Morality of Freedom* (1986) 73–76.
[85] ibid 76.

place even if she is not aware of that. Reasons internalism, as we have seen, allow for corrections of fact and reasoning. That is why we could say that the person had no reason to drink from the glass that contained petrol when she was thirsty. This observation is important because Raz makes no demands regarding awareness on the part of the agent when it comes to the satisfaction of the service conception of authority. Since reasons internalism makes no demands in this sense as well, it can account for Raz's thesis.

The internalist model I defended in this book is compatible with Raz's insights regarding expertise and coordination. Furthermore, much of Raz's insights can be explained nicely through the idea of respect for law I've been developing in this chapter. Recall that according to my view, an agent respects something if she sees some sort of value or good in the object of respect that entails at least reasons to not act against that object. As I've said before, respect differs from mere acknowledgement because it makes some requirements on us through reasons for action. When we have the law coordinating behaviour, an agent can have the attitude of respect for law when she sees that the coordination provided by law helps to attain something she deems valuable. This can be the case even when she thinks that she could have done better: 'The regulations regarding X are far from what I take to be ideal, but they do serve valuable goals, so I better respect them' is a thought that such an agent could have. Expertise is also explainable in terms of respect. Think about what it means for an agent to recognise the law as more knowledgeable than she is regarding reasons that she has. In this scenario, it is not far-fetched to say that the agent would respect the law if the law were providing her with assistance in following the reasons that she already has: the agent sees that the law has value (in helping her to follow her reasons), and this can ground the attitude of respect for law.

There is a further observation that must be made at this point. As I understand it, Raz's own discussion of respect for law is presented as an autonomous argument in relation to his service conception of authority. Sometimes Raz writes as if his argument about respect for law is a secondary or ad hoc way of grounding law's authority. As I have tried to show, my own account can explain Raz's views on coordination and expertise in terms of respect, so an advantage that my account can claim is that it places much of Raz's discussions under the umbrella of respect for law (at least insofar as we are dealing with agents that have this attitude). In more general terms, as we saw a moment ago, Raz's key insights are compatible with the internalist model. This means that there are good reasons to prefer my approach, since it can explain much that Raz explains, together with the broader idea of respect for law, in a single, unified account.

I hope that the arguments of the previous paragraphs are enough to show that much of Raz's conception of authority can be explained by the general account I've been developing, and that we have at least one reason to prefer my account. Let us move to my second remark regarding the comparison with Raz, the one concerning second-order reasons. This will provide an additional reason to prefer my view, as it can deliver the same insights as Raz's but using fewer resources. As I have explained earlier in this chapter, my arguments are independent from (but not incompatible with) the idea of exclusionary reasons, and it is worth bringing that earlier discussion back. Raz has rightly noticed that when agents break the law (or generally go against some authoritative directive), they will have a feeling of unease or remorse. Assuming that the agent did what she thought that she ought to do, taking into consideration her balance of reasons, Raz would say that the feeling of unease appears because the authoritative directive functions as a protected reason (a second-order reason). When the agent ignores the second-order reason to act on her balance of reasons, this second-order reason is not defeated; it remains in place. Raz has a nice illustration of this in *Practical Reason and Norms*: when a soldier disobeys his command but manages to fulfil his mission in an excellent manner, this soldier can feel this sense of uneasiness even if he believes that he did the right thing, and those at the top of the military hierarchy tend to simultaneously award the soldier and submit him to martial court.[86] This seems to point out this aspect of the second-order reason as undefeated.

The idea of respect for law can explain the feeling of unease without appeal to a second order of reasons, hence its comparative advantage. When an agent respects something, this agent sees some sort of value in the respected object that at least grounds a reason to not act against it. In the case of the soldier, respect would provide at least a reason to not act against the command, and to use an expression from Raz himself, the soldier might feel that he has betrayed his commander when he does as he thinks he ought to do according to his reasons. This also helps us to understand why this soldier could accept the martial trial: he knows that he acted against something he respects. Acceptance of the trial is a way for him to express this acknowledgement. At this point, it is also important to recall our previous discussion about the law as a whole and particular pieces of law. When an agent respects the law as a whole (or relevant bits of the law), this agent might have her respect transferred to particular pieces of law, just like in the case of the teenager whose respect for her parents provided her with reasons to not bring her partner home, even though she thought that her parents' directive was misguided. Respect for the law as a whole can ground the feeling of unease that Raz describes when an agent goes against some particular legal directive that she considers misguided (this is analogous to the soldier scenario), and depending on the case, it might even be enough to make the agent abide by that directive.

Let us summarise the comparison with Raz's theory of authority. Firstly, my account can explain much of what was explained by Raz's, since the service conception of authority covers roughly the same ground as my views on practical reasoning thanks to the dependence thesis. To this first point I have added that not only does my account capture much of what was important in Raz's, but it does so in a unified manner; we have at least one reason to prefer it. Secondly, my account is able to explain the phenomenology of reasons alluded to by Raz (the feeling of unease) without the need to appeal to a second order of reasons, and this is,

[86] Raz, *Practical Reason and Norms* (1990) 42–43.

I think, a further advantage to it. The view that I have been developing in this chapter is not only compatible with Raz's theory but can also deliver many of the same insights through a more unified, minimalist, framework.[87]

VII. Conclusions

This chapter had a quite sinuous path. We have started from more abstract considerations of genealogy and political philosophy, in our discussion of the first question of politics and of the narratives of political rule, and from that we gradually fleshed out the account of the reason-giving character of the law I have promised in the first chapter. We have revisited Hart's internal point of view, supplementing his original account with the resources developed in the second chapter. There was this peculiar experience that Hart, Deigh, Raz, the tragedians and many others were trying to grasp and that I have described as law's demand for respect from its subjects. This idea, I have claimed, was necessary to provide content to Hart's internal point of view in the sense that this was something characteristic of law as we know it. Those were considerations that moved from the law towards the agent.

An account of the reason-giving character of the law would be incomplete without the other side of the coin, considerations that moved from the agent to the law. To get to those, I have started with working definitions of the notions of respect, identity, and character. Equipped with those, I was finally able to present my account of the reason-giving character of the law. There was, first, a thick case, the one in which there is a continuum between the narrative of political rule, the law, the community, and the individual (that identifies herself with the law). The thick case was then 'watered down' into the case of (only) respect for law, in which the individual respects the law but does not identify herself with it. When the law demands respect from its subjects, it demands so at least in this second sense. We also have the most basic scenario in which the agent is merely concerned with loss of power, prudential reasons, or, as suggested during the analysis of the objections, very generic instrumental reasons to not live in the State of Nature.

Regarding objections, I have tried to analyse and refute four: that the account is too obscure, that it was a mere formal structure, that it leaves no space for morality, and that different accounts had different concerns. Against the first objection, I have argued that we should not prefer an account only because it is simpler. Against the second objection, I have said that the account provides what can be demanded from an account of this kind. Against the third objection, I have argued that my account does leave adequate space for moral reasons. Against the fourth objection, I have argued that my account is concerned with our practical

[87] It is worth highlighting that the arguments offered in this section do not prove Raz wrong, far from it. They provide us with a different, and to my mind more fruitful, way to explain the same phenomena.

experience of engagement with the law, not with fully blooded normative theory. I have concluded that section with a brief comment on Raz's theory of authority.

By way of conclusion, I would like to recall that there are two convictions underlying this book. Firstly, that there is more to philosophy than just conceptual analysis, and secondly, that there is more to practical reason than just moral reason. The first conviction was displayed more clearly in the third chapter, about the thin view of the agent presupposed by much legal positivism. The second conviction appeared both in the positive account here presented and in my analysis of the power of moral reasons in the second chapter. It will also appear in the next chapter, through my criticism of the moralised accounts of legal normativity offered by Ronald Dworkin and John Finnis.

My account was mostly offered in this chapter, and what I have tried to do with it was to bring to the light the emotional-conative aspect of legal normativity that is often overlooked by legal philosophers. The account offered presented the reason-giving character of the law in layers that went from full identification of the agent with the law, passing through respect for the law and getting to the mere fear of losing power. The ways in which the law provides reasons for action are complex and often obscure, even (and maybe especially) for the agent herself.

5

Moral Reasons and Legal Normativity: Ronald Dworkin and John Finnis[1]

I. Introduction

This is the final chapter of our analysis of legal normativity and, in a sense, a development of some of the objections we have analysed in the previous one. In this chapter, I intend to analyse two different theories that attempt to explain legal normativity as a kind of moral normativity. The claim I will make is not that those theories are wrong, but rather that they distort the phenomena they purport to explain. Their main insights, nonetheless, can be incorporated in the account I have presented in the previous chapter, as indeed was already suggested when I addressed the possible objections to the account. The chapter is roughly divided into two parts besides this Introduction and the Concluding Remarks. In the first part, I will deploy the Williamsian resources we are already familiar with to discuss the claim made by Ronald Dworkin that legal obligations are, at the end of the day, a particular kind of moral obligation. I am sceptical about Dworkin's claim. To borrow a term from Roger Shiner, when it comes to the normativity of obligations, Dworkin's proposal ends up being 'external', and by that, I mean that it grounds normativity in something external to the agent that engages in practical deliberation about what she ought to do. In doing so, the proposal ends up being an insufficient or distorted account of normativity.[2] Dworkin's view is not enough to explain how the law can provide reasons for action for agents. To make this point, I will revisit some of the arguments deployed in chapters two and four, notably from the discussion on the limits of morality and practical reason. The main point I want to call attention to in the first part of this chapter is that Dworkin fails to capture important elements in his account and that there is more to the story of legal normativity than what he tells us.

Regarding this first part, about Dworkin, this is what I intend to do. I will begin by explaining in reasonable detail Dworkin's argument in favour of legal

[1] This chapter uses materials that originally appeared in DP Murata, 'Obligations Beyond Morality: A Critique of Ronald Dworkin's View on Legal Normativity' (2022) 16(2) *Revista Direito Mackenzie* 1.

[2] I am borrowing the term from Roger Shiner, although I am here using the term in a slightly different way. See R Shiner, 'Law and Its Normativity' in D Patterson (ed), *A Companion to Philosophy of Law and Legal Theory* (London, Wiley-Blackwell, 2010).

obligations as moral obligations. This starts with a picture of the 'moral community' and relies heavily on Dworkin's interpretive method. After this presentation, two sub-sections will follow. In the first of those, I will criticise Dworkin's theory for its excessive reliance on unwarranted claims about practical reasoning and the powers of morality. In the second, I will engage with the reasons that motivated the reductivism of Dworkin's account. The claim I will make is that many reasons are not easily reduced to the moral and that those might play a role in the reason-giving character of the law. The gist of the criticism developed here is that Dworkin endorses an overly moralised view on obligations, a view that ignores that people can genuinely feel obligated by demands that are not moral. My point is that Dworkin's account leaves out something important and that if we only have his account, then we will have a distorted view of legal normativity and obligations in general. Dworkin's account does not pay attention to the dispositions, attachments, and projects that individuals have and that they perceive as being potentially in conflict with moral obligations. To borrow a famous expression by Bernard Williams, Dworkin's account is 'one thought too many' when it comes to the reason-giving character of the law,[3] that is, the Dworkinian account presses on the idea that there must be some ultimate moral reason underlying the reason-giving character of the law.[4]

Before presenting what I want to say about Finnis, it is important to add a cautionary note here. In this chapter I will talk rather loosely about obligations and reasons. I can do so because obligations are reasons for action themselves;[5] obligations figure in our practical reasoning as reasons to do or not to do something.[6] Some of the arguments I will put forward could be made in terms of prima facie obligations and real obligations, or in terms of *pro tanto* reasons and conclusive reasons, and so on. More notable, perhaps, is Raz's view. Joseph Raz, drawing on his arguments we already discussed in this book, refers to obligations as what he calls 'protected reasons', the combination of a directive to do or not to do something

[3] In section II.A I will be discussing mostly Dworkin. However, it does seem fair to say that many legal theorists, positivists and anti-positivists alike, are somehow committed to the claim that if there is normativity in law, this must be moral normativity. This claim arises naturally from the idea that morality is supreme in our practical reason, and as we will see, I will take issue with both the claim and its originating idea. Good examples of authors committed to those claims (it should be noted that such commitment can take different forms) are Scott Hershovitz and Stephen Perry. According to Hershovitz, 'legal obligations just are moral obligations generated by legal practice' See S Hershovitz, 'The End of Jurisprudence' (2015) 124(4) *Yale Law Journal* 1160, 1192. Perry claims that at the end of the day, 'Legal normativity is moral normativity, and the law's claim to authority is a moral claim'. See S Perry, 'Hart on Social Rules and the Foundations of Law: Liberating the Internal Point of View' (2006) 75 *Fordham Law Review* 1171, 1173–74. It goes without saying, however, that my discussion in this chapter cannot be applied without further development to those other authors.

[4] Although, as Stephen Bero suggested to me, maybe the best accusation would be to say that, in fact, the Dworkinian model presupposes 'one thought too few'.

[5] Later I will say something about obligations that are not reason-giving. Those will be called formal obligations and are not proper obligations for the agent.

[6] I am indebted to Kenneth Ehrenberg for calling my attention to the point that obligations are a kind of reasons for action.

with a second-order exclusionary reason not to act based on other reasons.[7] For the purposes of my discussion, we can be agnostic about Raz's proposal. Obligations can be protected reasons or be very weighty first-order reasons or anything in such vicinity. What matters is that there are different kinds of reasons and that some of those reasons present themselves as particularly stringent in a way that they might count as what we ordinarily refer to as obligations. I am *not* in the business of presenting a tight conceptual analysis of the concept of obligation. Rather, I am interested in the phenomenology of obligations, that is, how they appear and make sense for those that first-personally engage with them.

After discussion of Dworkin's proposal, I will move on to discuss John Finnis' approach to the issue of legal normativity.[8] The Finnisian Natural Law account argues that the normativity of law can ultimately be tracked to basic goods that are instantiated through morality. The problem in Finnis' account will be – roughly speaking – the same as Dworkin's: Finnis tries to ground legal normativity in sources that are external to the deliberative agent, and in doing so, he ends up with an account that is, at best, partially correct and, and at worst, distorted. I will open the discussion with a presentation of Finnis' account of the reason-giving character of the law. Such an account is a part of his broader Natural Law theory that has something to say about the intelligibility of action, practical reason, and morality. Finnis starts his argument with the idea that there are basic goods that bestow intelligibility to human action. Every rational action, says Finnis, can somehow be tracked back to those basic goods. Such tracking occurs through the requirements of practical reasonableness. When it comes to the reason-giving character of the law, Finnis' argument is that the law is reason-giving to agents because its requirements can be tracked way back to basic goods. As I interpret him, Finnis is saying that the law is reason-giving because it either fosters, instantiates, or protects basic goods, and that this is something *transparent* to the agent. The agent can, at least potentially, grasp the relationship of law with the basic goods.

After presenting Finnis' account, I will move to my criticism, divided into three parts. I begin my criticism by explaining why Finnis' account of basic goods is too underdetermined. There are difficulties with a list of universal goods, and the idea of human flourishing is not enough to solve the problems at this front. This first part of my criticism is relatively independent from the discussion in the book so far (as it is not, strictly speaking, about practical reason and normativity), but because basic goods occupy such a prominent role in Finnis' theory, we should pause to discuss this before moving to the main claims I want to make. After that, I will move to the main issue in Finnis' views. As I see it, the main issue is that the idea of practical reasonableness (which is roughly equivalent to moral constraints in reasoning for Finnis) cannot vindicate itself; it lacks an argument

[7] J Raz, 'The Obligation to Obey the Law' in J Raz, *The Authority of Law* (Oxford, Oxford University Press, 2009) 233–37. The idea of obligations as protected reasons is pervasive in Raz's work.

[8] It should be noted, then, that by the term 'Natural Law' I will be referring mostly to Finnisian Natural Law.

for its acceptance. Finnis' view on practical reasoning is too narrow because it is committed from the start with implausible assumptions about rationality and agency. Finally, I will bring those points back to the discussion of the reason-giving character of the law in order to claim that the Finnisian account cannot deliver what it promises. If basic goods are radically underdetermined and practical reasonableness cannot vindicate itself, then the claim that the reason-giving character of the law depends on how it fosters, instantiates, or protects basic goods becomes much harder to defend. In addition to that, there seems to be no need for Finnis' requirement of transparency regarding law's function, in the sense that we do not need that sort of transparency in order to get an explanation of the reason-giving character of the law. Some concluding remarks will follow.

II. Dworkin: Legal Obligations and Moral Obligations

A. The Dworkinian Account

To understand Dworkin's account, we must begin with his analysis of associative obligations. The starting point is Dworkin's idea of a 'bare community',[9] that is, a community defined in historical, cultural, or geographical terms. The idea of a bare community captures the descriptive use of the term, and it is a necessary but far from sufficient condition for the existence of obligations among its members. The reason why this is so is clear enough: the existence of a bare community is a matter of fact, whereas obligations – moral, political, legal – are normative matters. To draw an obligation from a matter of fact would be a violation of Hume's principle, or so Dworkin argues.[10] For a community to be able to create obligations for its members, it has to bear the right normative relation to them. When this relation is present, we get what Dworkin calls a 'true community', a *moral community*.[11]

For Dworkin, this right normative relation is made up of four items. The first item claims that the community members recognise themselves as such and that such recognition entails duties and obligations among them. The second item adds that the members recognise those obligations as due to the individual members of the community, not to the community as such. The third item establishes that a moral community is geared toward the well-being of all its members. Finally, the last item claims that in doing so, the community treats all its members with an equal measure of concern. Such equal measure of concern, says Dworkin, is not incompatible with hierarchical structures or assigning different roles to people within that community. It does rule out, however, the idea that some people's lives

[9] R Dworkin, *Law's Empire* (Cambridge, Harvard University Press, 1986) 201.
[10] R Dworkin, *Justice for Hedgehogs* (Cambridge, Harvard University Press, 2011) 302–303.
[11] Dworkin, *Law's Empire* (1986) 201.

in the group have more (or less) worth than the lives of other members in it.[12] This is how Dworkin summarises his view on the moral community: 'The responsibilities a true community deploys are special and individualized and display a pervasive mutual concern that fits a plausible conception of equal concern.'[13]

Why do those items enable a moral community to generate real, 'associative' obligations for its members? When a community abides by the four requirements above, it has the right fit with what Dworkin calls principles of dignity, that people's lives have objective value and that every person is responsible for his or her life.[14] The exegesis of Dworkin's view on dignity is not of importance here, but the general shape of his argument is. This is what his argument looks like: (I) people's lives have objective value, and people are responsible for the success of their lives; and (II) when a community helps people to foster their dignity, it can provide them with real obligations that can be traced back to their very dignity. There is a distinctly Kantian flavour to this argumentative line. The thought seems to be that if the community somehow diminishes the objective value of my life, then this community fails to provide me with real (moral) obligations. I might even think that I have an obligation; after all, it might be the case that I have been brought up in that community and internalised its values and ways, but this does not mean that they can *actually* demand anything from me. This can be clearly seen in excerpts like the following one, which will also be important later:

> Role conventions do not impose genuine associative obligations automatically: the conventions must satisfy independent ethical and moral tests. Sexist or racist practices, or those that define honor among murderers, drug dealers, or thieves, impose no genuine obligation on those they purport to oblige, no matter how thoroughly adherents seem to accept those obligations (…) once we realize that role practices impose genuine obligations only because – and therefore only when – they allow their members more effectively to meet their standing ethical and moral responsibilities, then we also realize that these practices cannot impose obligations when they act as obstacles rather than means to that goal. Social practices create genuine obligations only when they respect the two principles of dignity: only when they are consistent with an equal appreciation of the importance of all human lives and only when they do not license the kind of harm to others that is forbidden by that assumption.[15]

How does this analysis of associative obligations[16] feed back into Dworkin's account of how the law provides reasons for action? This is done through Dworkin's view on what he takes to be the proper methodology for jurisprudence. Dworkin has famously argued, against what he took to be legal positivism, that the law is not an artefact that you can know via facts or institutional pedigree, but that

[12] ibid 199–201.
[13] ibid 201.
[14] Dworkin, *Justice for Hedgehogs* (2011) 203–204.
[15] ibid 315.
[16] There can be, of course, other accounts of associative obligations. In this chapter, the term is used to refer only to Dworkin's account.

it is an 'interpretive concept'.[17] There is no such thing as nature or a conceptual definition of the law, but rival interpretations that purport to present the law in 'its best light'.[18] We find out what the law is, says Dworkin, when we constructively interpret it. According to Dworkin, an interpretation is successful if it meets two dimensions.

Firstly, there is a dimension of 'fit'. The interpretation must duly account for what Dworkin refers to as the 'paradigms' of the interpreted phenomenon.[19] For instance, an interpretation of the genre of epic poetry would be a poor one if it ignored the roles played by honour, duty, and courage in the poems. Those traits are part of what defines that genre. Secondly, there is a dimension of 'justification'. It will often be the case that more than one interpretation succeeds in accounting for the paradigms of practice or concept. This calls for a more straightforwardly evaluative dimension in interpretation. In this second dimension, we search for the most compelling interpretation, taking into account the purpose or point we see in whatever we are interpreting.[20] That is, we interpret something constructively when we attempt to present this something in 'its best light', and with regard to a practice with stakes as important as the law, the 'best light' means the most morally appealing way (taking into account the constraints of fit).[21] When it comes to interpretive practices like law, agents develop an 'interpretive attitude' made of two elements: the participants recognise some purpose or value in the practice, and they also believe that such practice can be reformed in order to better serve this purpose or value.[22] When the interpretive attitude is present, says Dworkin, 'People now try to impose *meaning* on the institution – to see it in its best light – and then to restructure it in the light of that meaning'.[23]

For Dworkin, legal theories 'try to show legal practice as a whole in its best light, to achieve equilibrium between legal practice as they find it and the best justification of that practice'.[24] The theory that delivers this for Dworkin is the idea of 'law as integrity'. At this point the analysis of the moral community connects with matters of legal normativity. For Dworkin, the interpretation that shows law in its best light, the law as integrity, establishes that the contents of the law are what a community of principle, that is, a moral community, would have as its law.[25] This is the schematic narrative he tells us: in order to know what the law is, we must interpret it constructively; to interpret something constructively, we need to

[17] This claim is repeated by Dworkin in a number of texts. The *locus classicus* is Dworkin, *Law's Empire* (1986) 1–113.

[18] Dworkin, *Law's Empire* (1986) 47–90.

[19] ibid 72–73.

[20] The two dimensions of interpretation are discussed mostly in Dworkin, *Law's Empire* (1986) 45–86.

[21] Dworkin, *Law's Empire* (1986) 45–86. See also Dworkin, *Justice for Hedgehogs* (2011) 99–188.

[22] Dworkin, *Law's Empire* (1986) 47.

[23] ibid 47.

[24] ibid 90.

[25] This is somewhat simplified. The dimension of fit entails that there are constraints imposed by the concrete institutional history of a legal system. I will comment on this point below.

portray this something in its best light; the law is shown in its best light when it is understood through the lens of integrity. Law as integrity, says Dworkin, guarantees 'a kind of equality among citizens that makes their community more genuine and improves its moral justification for exercising the political power it does'.[26] For Dworkin, therefore, *what the law is* is the same as *what the law is in its best interpretation*. He denies the classical distinction between finding the law and creating the law since, for him, those are merely two sides of the same coin.[27]

This is the conclusion of the Dworkinian argument:

(1) if the law in its best interpretation is the set of regulations that a community of principle, a moral community, would adopt, and
(2) only a moral community can provide an agent with real associative obligations, obligations that are accepted by the test of morality; then it follows that
(3) law in its best interpretation has the potential to provide subjects with moral obligations, because those would be the obligations demanded by a community of principle.[28]

This interpretation is supported by Dworkin's later writings. In *Justice for Hedgehogs*, he claims that the law is *part* of political morality.[29] What Dworkin is *not* saying is that law will have moral force in every case. There can be cases in which the moral force of the law is not coextensive with the claims of the law, and in more extreme scenarios, the law can fail altogether to have moral force. In those situations, the law would not be reason-giving in the relevant sense.[30] Dworkin's claim does mean that the reason-giving character of the law, however, is of a moral nature. If there is anything capable of providing normativity to law, this must be morality.

Before moving on with the argument, there are some clarifications that I believe are necessary. It might be suggested that my interpretation of Dworkin suffers from two flaws.[31] Firstly, I am missing Dworkin's own framing of the matter. In *Law's Empire*, Dworkin claims that judges need to justify the coercion exercised by the state and that in order to do so, they present constructive interpretations of the law. Being constructive interpretations, they are not only a matter of moral principles since those very principles must be embedded in legal traditions. This is a relevant point that is often overlooked by Dworkin's critics. Nowhere, as far as I know, does Dworkin claim that law is just morality applied to a concrete case. To the contrary, he insists, even in his later writings, that regarding the question of what law is, 'any responsible answer' must take into account 'historical facts about legislation and,

[26] Dworkin, *Law's Empire* (1986) 96.
[27] ibid 225.
[28] Later I will introduce a distinction between moral obligations, strictly speaking, and obligations licensed by morality.
[29] Dworkin, *Justice for Hedgehogs* (2011) 5.
[30] ibid 321–23.
[31] I am thankful to Veronica Rodriguez-Blanco for pressing the point of this paragraph and the next one, demanding further explanations.

perhaps, social convention.'[32] What we must bear in mind, however, is that how we should take into account those materials is itself a matter of interpretation and moral controversy. As Dworkin puts it in *Law's Empire*, 'Interpretation folds back into the practice.'[33]

Keeping those considerations in mind is important to not distort Dworkin's theory, but they are no cause of trouble for my coming arguments. This is so because such justification, subtler and paying attention to the legal traditions in which the justification is offered, will still be of a moral nature, since only when they are of a moral nature will they be able to provide an agent with reasons for action in the Dworkinian model. For Dworkin, 'law is a branch of political morality, which is itself a branch of a more general personal morality, which is, in turn, a branch of a yet more general theory of what it is to live well.'[34] That the justification/interpretation we are talking about must be moral in the Dworkinian model is reinforced by the way he frames it as a justification of state coercion. The point here is similar to the one we saw with Postema's criticisms of Hartian normativity: we need an account of normativity that goes beyond mere 'expressivism' of the opinions of legal officials, that is, we need a moral account of legal obligations. If the law demands our allegiance, then it better be more than just *doxa* from entitled people.

The preceding remark takes us to the second clarification. It might be suggested that Dworkin's account is supposed to capture the point of view of a judge, not of a citizen, and that, therefore, my criticisms regarding Dworkin's view on legal normativity might be misplaced. It is true that Dworkin's emphasis is on the judge, but I do not think that his account begins and ends with it. When talking about political obligation, Dworkin explicitly defends what he calls a 'protestant attitude': 'Political obligation (…) becomes a more protestant idea: fidelity to a scheme of principle each citizen has a responsibility to identify, ultimately for himself, as his community's scheme.'[35] If that is correct, everyone under the law must engage in constructive interpretation in its dealings with the law. For Dworkin, each one of us has a responsibility to actualise the law, and in that sense, being Hercules is not a calling for judges only.

B. The Deficiency of the Account

The claim I will advance in this sub-section is that there are other sources of obligation beyond morality and that those might play a role in the reason-giving character of the law. To start my case, I would like to point out a strange consequence of a view like Dworkin's. Scott Hershovitz, in his discussion about presumptions and obligations, suggests that a person is under no

[32] Dworkin, *Justice for Hedgehogs* (2011) 407.
[33] Dworkin, *Law's Empire* (1986) 48.
[34] Dworkin, *Justice for Hedgehogs* (2011) 5.
[35] Dworkin, *Law's Empire* (1986) 190. See also ibid 413.

moral obligation to love her child if the child turns out to be a 'moral monster'. Hershovitz intended to claim that we can understand the feeling of uneasiness that a mother in this situation would feel by appealing to presumptions in favour of certain obligations, in this case, a presumption that one ought to love one's child (but, in fact, there would be no such obligation, or so he says).[36] It might be sensibly asked if the talk about a moral obligation to love is really the best way to explain the love parents nurture for their children. In the case of a wicked son, a mother can say, 'Yes, he did awful things, but he is my son and God help me, for I cannot stop loving him.' What are we supposed to say to this mother? That she is irrational? That she should stop loving him because she has no obligation to do so, or since her son is a monster, that she has an obligation not to love him? The 'righteous absurdity'[37] of those claims illustrates how love – and other projects and attachments, as seen in the second chapter – can be at odds with the demands made by moral obligations.[38] There are things that are reason-giving for individuals in ways that are not related to the notion of *moral* obligation, and that cannot be reduced to mere prudential worries.

We have seen earlier that for Dworkin 'practices impose genuine obligations only because – and therefore only when – they allow their members more effectively to meet their standing ethical and moral responsibilities'.[39] The problem for Dworkin and others that endorse similar views is that their claims presuppose the *supremacy of morality*,[40] the idea that morality can override any other kinds of considerations an agent might have, but this cannot be taken for granted. For instance, we can easily conceive cases in which an agent will feel obligated to engage in immoral acts because of a promise; that is, cases in which we realise that 'immoral promises' can generate reasons for action.

[36] Hershovitz, 'The End of Jurisprudence' 1189–92.

[37] B Williams, 'Persons, Character and Morality' in B Williams, *Moral Luck* (Cambridge, Cambridge University Press, 1981) 16.

[38] To be fair, Hershovitz claims that 'The upshot is that I construe my role as a parent to impose moral obligations that I do not, strictly speaking, have. But there are overwhelming moral reasons to do so, and we are all better off for it.' See Hershovitz, 'The End of Jurisprudence' 1191. This means that he recognises that we do not think about the limits of our moral obligations all the time, but he still construes parental love in terms of obligation.

[39] Dworkin, *Justice for Hedgehogs* (2011) 315. Hershovitz follows this by saying that 'A promise to murder cannot generate an obligation to murder' and that in believing that it can is 'one of the many ways in which mobsters are morally misguided'. See Hershovitz, 'The End of Jurisprudence' 1180.

[40] A clarificatory remark: by morality, in this context, I am roughly referring to what Bernard Williams calls the 'morality system'. The morality system is a creation of modern moral philosophy, and among its claims we have the idea that moral considerations are of supreme importance and that moral obligations, in their supreme importance, cannot demand mutually exclusive actions from the agents, that is, there is always a morally right answer to moral dilemmas. For Williams, the morality system emerges as a piece of good philosophical news about the unfairness of the world. The promise of the morality system is that, at the end of the day, existence can be fair because morality is accessible to everyone. Both utilitarianism and Kantianism are members of the morality system, but the same cannot be said of virtue ethics. See B Williams, *Ethics and the Limits of Philosophy* (London, Routledge, 2011) 193–218. See too, in general, the discussion in the second chapter of this book.

Consider the following example I am borrowing from Sophocles' *Women of Trakhis*. By the end of the play, Herakles is agonising to death due to poisoning. He makes Hyllos, his son, promise to help him die – something that Hyllos does by carrying Herakles to the place he wants to die and by instructing others to build the funeral pyre (he cannot build the pyre or set it on fire himself, as that would be an unforgivable crime according to Ancient Greek *mores*). Herakles, however, demands a second promise from his son. He commands Hyllos to marry Iole. Iole was meant to be Herakles' new wife, and they had already slept together. Herakles' narcissism makes him believe that only his own blood, Hyllos, could take such a woman as his wife, but the younger man sees this demand as blasphemy. After a short exchange of words, Hyllos ultimately agrees to his father's demands. So, Herakles makes two 'immoral' demands. Hyllos manages to fulfil the first one without engaging in what would be blasphemy to the eyes of the Greeks, but the second one cannot be dodged. His final words on this matter are: 'Can the gods condemn me if I do this out of loyalty to my father?'[41] I believe that the wording Hyllos uses is revealing: he is not saying that marrying Iole is the right thing to do, but that the gods would be in no position to recriminate him as he was a loyal son. There is a conflict between the demands of morality and family, and Hyllos believes that familial duty trumps *mores* in this case.[42]

There are different philosophical claims underlying the discussion and examples in the last couple of paragraphs. We need to disentangle those claims and make their relation to the problems of legal normativity and obligations clearer. There are at least three different claims:

(1) Nonmoral features, like projects and commitments, can be reason-giving for agents.
(2) There can be nonmoral obligations that stand in competition with moral ones in our practical reasoning.
(3) There is no reason why legal obligations must necessarily be moral obligations since we have recognised the possibility of other genuine, nonmoral obligations.

Those claims are distinguishable but share some relation of dependency, for someone can in principle accept (1) and refuse (2) and (3), but the acceptance of (2) entails (3) unless the person presents a further argument for its denial. In addition to that, if one accepts (2), she is also committed to (1), and if she accepts (3), she is automatically committed to (1) and (2) as well.

[41] Sophocles, 'Women of Trakhis' in *The Complete Plays of Sophocles – A New Translation*, trans Robert Bagg and James Scully (London, Harper Perennial, 2011) lines 1143–1278.

[42] An anonymous reviewer has suggested that maybe the case of Hyllos illustrates something a bit different, namely, a conflict between two moralities. This is a fair point. Later I will address it, albeit indirectly, in my discussion of the Dworkinian attempts to refine to the idea of moral obligation, but the gist of the claim is this: if we were to accept the possibility of a conflict of moral obligations, we would end up trivialising the notion of the moral and it would fail to do to the work it was supposed to do.

I do not think there is any need for the Dworkinian to deny (1). It is a truism that people can have reasons for actions that are not moral in nature. The trouble starts at (2). Dworkin seems to believe that the only real obligations are moral in nature; that is the reason why, ultimately, in his view, immoral law is not reason-giving. This is a denial of (2), which means that every time some nonmoral consideration clashes with a moral obligation, this nonmoral consideration should yield to the moral obligation. Now, why should we take that for granted? If people can have a myriad of reasons for action, why presuppose that the moral ones must always triumph in deliberation? People can act for nonmoral reasons to the detriment of moral ones, and this does not entail that the agent is being irrational in doing so (think about the case of Hyllos, or about the choices made by many other characters in literature). The idea I want to develop and that I am borrowing from Williams' work is the following: *the claim that morality overrides everything else is one made within morality itself, and the standpoint of morality itself does not need to coincide with the standpoint of the agent deliberating about what she ought to do.*

We have already discussed versions of this argument earlier, especially in the second chapter, but I believe that the following classic discussion by Williams helps in elucidating what is at stake. A ship is sinking, and there is no way for the lifeguard to save everyone. He might save a couple of children, but if he does so, his own beloved wife will perish, and vice-versa. Now, morality tells you that you should do what is morally right, so a utilitarian would tell you to do whatever action maximises welfare, and a Kantian would tell you to do as told by the categorical imperative. Notice that either the utilitarian or the Kantian might recommend either action, saving the children or the wife. The point is that either way morality tells you to do something because that is the morally right thing to do, but this is not the way most people think about it, nor the way that most people think that they should think about it.[43] Consider for a moment what it would mean for the lifeguard to save his wife because that was his moral duty. There is something off if that was the reason he saved her; there is something almost inhuman in saving your wife from death because that was your moral duty. Consider also what that would mean for the wife. Presumably, what she would like to hear is that she was saved because she was his wife and that he loved her.[44] This is how Williams himself presents this matter regarding the ambitions of morality:[45]

[43] As Williams puts this, regarding utilitarianism, 'The first question for philosophy is not 'do you agree with utilitarianism's answer?' but 'do you agree with utilitarianism's way of looking at the question?''. See B Williams, 'A critique of utilitarianism' in JCC Smart and B Williams, *Utilitarianism – For and Against* (Cambridge, Cambridge University Press, 1973) 78. See too J Deigh, 'Morality and Personal Relations' in J Deigh, *The Sources of Moral Agency – Essays in Moral Psychology and Freudian Theory* (Cambridge, Cambridge University Press, 1996).

[44] See the general discussion in Williams, 'Persons, Character and Morality'. See also Williams, *Ethics and the Limits of Philosophy* (2011) 193–218. I am actually making some slight editions on the example, influenced by Harry Frankfurt's reading of it in *The Reasons of Love* (Princeton, Princeton University Press, 2004). For a somewhat critical take on Williams and an attempt to reconcile Kantian ethics with the idea of personal love, see JD Velleman, 'Love as a Moral Emotion' (1999) 109(2) *Ethics* 338.

[45] For an excellent discussion of the 'one thought too many' argument, see N Smyth, 'Integration and Authority: Rescuing the 'One Thought Too Many' Problem' (2018) 48(6) *Canadian Journal of Philosophy* 812.

> But something more ambitious than this is usually intended, essentially involving the idea that moral principle can legitimate his [the lifeguard's] preference, yielding the conclusion that in situations of this kind it is at least all right (morally permissible) to save one's wife. (…) But this construction provides the agent with one thought too many: it might have been hoped by some (for instance, his wife) that his motivating thought, fully spelled out, would be the thought that it was his wife, not that it was his wife and that in situations of this kind it is permissible to save one's life.[46]

If the preceding thoughts are roughly right, then there is no reason to assume the supremacy of moral considerations without further argument. At this point, someone sympathetic to Dworkin's view has two possible moves.

The first path would be to draw resources from 'reasons externalism' about practical reasons. As we have seen in the second chapter, Williams distinguishes between two views on practical reason. The first one – the view he endorses and that I have somehow defended in this book – he calls reasons internalism. According to reasons internalism, all reasons for action are dependent on the motivations that concrete agents have.[47] To be more precise, reasons must somehow come from the agents' 'subjective motivational sets', which are made by desires, projects, values, and motivations.[48] That is, for internalism, a reason will be a reason for action only insofar as it is connected to the subjective motivational set of the agent,[49] or, as I have preferred to formulate this point, a reason for action can only be understood as such if it somehow connects to the structure of care of that agent. Reasons externalism, on the other hand, holds that there can be reasons for action that are independent of what the concrete agents care about or think. An externalist can hold that in a case like the one of the lifeguard, there might be reasons for action even if the agents involved fail to perceive them. Externalism stands as opposed to reasons internalism, in that externalism claims that reasons for action are independent of what Williams calls the subjective motivational sets of individuals.

An externalist can say in the same breath that there are reasons for action that apply to a given case, and that such reasons are independent of the motivations of the agents involved. It is controversial if Dworkin himself would embrace externalism. In *Justice for Hedgehogs*, Dworkin claims that a person has a reason to do something 'if (but only if) doing that would be *good* for him' (emphasis added),[50] and being good here is something independent of whatever motivations the agent might have. At the same time, Dworkin is sceptical about traditional forms of moral realism and emphasises the role of conviction in interpretation. That being said, let us suppose that a Dworkinian embraces externalism. If moral reasons are

[46] Williams, 'Persons, Character and Morality' 18.

[47] Williams, 'Internal and External Reasons' in B Williams, *Moral Luck* (Cambridge, Cambridge University Press, 1981).

[48] ibid 105.

[49] ibid 102.

[50] Dworkin, *Justice for Hedgehogs* (2011) 50.

external reasons, then perhaps the supremacy of morality can be vindicated? Not quite.

There are two reasons why this is so. Firstly, let us grant that there are reasons for action independent of whatever motivations agents have. From that alone, we cannot infer that moral reasons are external reasons of that sort; that is, the existence of external reasons is not *in itself* an argument for claiming that moral reasons are external reasons. That being said, for the sake of argument, let us grant that moral reasons are external reasons. Notice, however, that, by itself, this claim does not vindicate morality's power over other reasons, either external or internal, because there is still a need for a further argument grounding the purported weight of moral reasons in comparison to other reasons, an argument explaining how those external moral reasons enter into one's deliberation.[51] In a nutshell, there is a need for two further arguments, one claiming that moral reasons are external, and another one establishing the practical weight of those reasons.

There is a second, and to my mind more important, reason why externalism is not enough to deliver what a Dworkinian needs. Think about what it would mean for a reason to be at the same time external and a reason *for action*. External reasons are independent of the motivations of concrete agents, so they can exist even if an agent is not motivated to follow them. The important question is this: if the agent is not motivated to follow a given reason in any sense, how can this reason be a reason for action *for* her?[52] Such a reason is not connected to the agent; it does not ring a bell for her. If that is the case, she will not act for that reason. This is what was encapsulated in the *requirement of explanation* we discussed in the second chapter: 'If something can be a reason for action, then it could be someone's reason for acting on a particular occasion, and it would then figure in the explanation of that action.'[53] To put it bluntly, even if something like platonic moral realism were true, and there were moral facts, those moral facts would not be able to be reasons for action for a concrete agent unless such agent cared about those facts in the first place. The crucial issue, it seems to me, is not that there are no external reasons, but that even if they do exist, they cannot be reasons for action because they cannot explain individual action.

Let us go back to the case of the lifeguard. What would it mean for him to act for an external reason? When the boat is sinking, and water is getting into the lungs of those he must save, he must decide, and his decision will be informed by his motivations, commitments, attachments, values, and dispositions. He has no access, in his deliberation, to reasons that are external to the person he came to be in his life. Notice that this is true even if there are objective (ie, moral realism)

[51] If such an argument is possible is a controversial matter that I cannot address here.

[52] This is a bit of a simplification. As we have seen in the second chapter, reasons internalism is compatible with the idea that agents might come to realise that they do have a given reason for action. For this to happen, however, this reason must be somehow connected to the individual's motivational set. The point is: there is no need for internal reasons to be immediately evident to the agent. Eg, only after an exercise of deliberation the agent realises that she has a reason to do X.

[53] Williams, 'Internal and External Reasons' 106.

moral reasons. Suppose that there are such reasons. An agent will only act for them if she can see those reasons as reasons for action *for her*. Unless such objective reasons speak to her, they will not put her on the track of action. They will be reasons similar to the advice we sometimes get from our grandmothers: we can grasp what they mean, but we just do not care about the values they care about, so their advice fails to get a hold on us (think about grandmotherly advice regarding sexual *mores*).[54] The conclusion, to put it summarily, is that reasons externalism cannot vindicate the denial of (2), that 'there can be nonmoral obligations that stand in competition with moral ones in our practical reasoning'. Nonmoral obligations seem to be as important to life as their moral counterparts.

The second path for the denial of (2) would be to refine the idea of a moral obligation, which in turn can be done in two different ways. Firstly, there could be refinement in the 'moral' qualifier. This is the strategy that seems more congenial to Dworkin's general methodology. The idea is that if we understand morality in a broader way that comprises not only ideals of moral duty or utilitarian considerations of welfare, then we could recast the conflict between a moral obligation and a nonmoral one as a conflict between two moral obligations, therefore treating the whole dilemma as moral.

This argument would look like this: morality is itself an interpretive concept, and our best interpretation of morality – the interpretation that best fits and justifies its practices – is one in which all the richness of human experience is captured. Morality, properly understood, is not just about a narrow group of duties defined by abstract value, but also involves duties that arise from many sources we come across in our lives.

I believe that this kind of argument can be made, but the price one pays in doing so is that the qualifier 'moral' loses its distinctiveness. If I can recast every conflict of obligations that the agent perceives as a conflict between moral obligations, what is the word 'moral' doing? Someone in this track could maintain her denial of (2), but at the cost of triviality, since morality would be so broad a domain that it would not correspond to what is usually understood by it. Pursuing this strategy would reduce the disagreement about the nature of obligations to a verbal quibble.

Secondly, someone could attempt refinement on the idea of 'obligation'. Dworkin mentions that the idea of an obligation entails 'some special responsibility of role or status',[55] but (as far as I know) he does not add much to the definition of an obligation besides that. I think it is fair to say that an obligation for Dworkin is tantamount to a very weighty reason to do something (or not). It is the kind of reason to which we would attach a 'you ought to' or 'you must' statement. In any case, a more accurate reading of Dworkin would insist not that every real obligation must be a moral obligation, but, in a weaker claim, that every real obligation

[54] See the discussion in C Wilson, 'Moral Authority and the Limits of Philosophy' in SG Chappell and MV Ackeren (eds), *Ethics Beyond the Limits* (London, Routledge, 2018).

[55] Dworkin, *Justice for Hedgehogs* (2011) 182.

must be acceptable by the appropriate moral tests. Besides being a more accurate reading of Dworkin's claims, this reading means the existence of two kinds of obligations: those that are themselves moral obligations *required* by morality and those that are nonmoral obligations *licensed* by morality. Still, that will not do the trick.

To see why this is so, think about how the conflict between a moral obligation and a nonmoral obligation licensed by morality could actually take place. If *there is* conflict, then this nonmoral obligation would not be licensed by morality to begin with; it would not pass the tests imposed by morality (unless, that is, we assume that morality can present agents with mutually exclusive demands, but this would be a denial of the maxim that 'ought' implies 'can'). However, suppose that it is possible to maintain both claims, that there is conflict, and that the obligation is licensed by morality. Even if this situation were possible, it would not exhaust the possibilities of conflict between obligations. The whole discussion up to this point was meant to emphasise that people do experience obligations that might run *against* morality. The introduction of a more nuanced view on moral obligations is a welcome refinement but does not explain all that there is. The Dworkinian denial of (2) remains hard to sustain.

This is what we have: to deny (2), someone defending the Dworkinian view must insist that obligations are necessarily dependent on morality. Since this flies in the face of the phenomenology of obligations, we have explored some alternatives a Dworkinian could adopt. She could insist that at the end of the day, what really counts is morality, but as we have seen, even if reasons externalism were true, it would not be enough to ground morality's empire. Alternatively, she could refine the notion of moral obligations, but both attempts fail. If we try to widen the notion of the moral, then we end up trivialising the notion. If, on the other hand, we try to refine the notion of obligation, we make just a little progress because that is not enough to account for the cases of conflict agents perceive. An important conclusion follows from this: if there is no way to deny (2), then one is also disposed to accept (3), namely, that there is no reason why legal obligations must necessarily be moral obligations.

C. Further Remarks on the Appeal of Dworkin's View

Once we accept that there can be obligations – weighty reasons to do or not to do something – that are not moral in nature, we ought to revisit the Dworkinian claim that only a moral community can provide its members with genuine obligations. Once nonmoral obligations have their existence recognised, there is no need for a community to be in the right normative relation to its members for it to provide obligations.[56] We can see this if we analyse Dworkin's discussion of an unequal society in *Law's*

[56] Which is not the same as saying that there are no moral obligations in the case of a moral community. This will become clearer later, in my discussion of Dworkin's method in more general terms.

Empire in a bit more detail. Dworkin discusses the case of a community in which daughters have no right to choose their husbands since this is taken as a prerogative of their fathers. According to Dworkin, this community can only provide real obligations to the daughters to abide by their fathers' wishes if and only if it bears the right normative relation to them. Obviously enough, that is not the case in many real-life sexist communities, and the conclusion Dworkin would draw regarding those is that they are not capable of generating proper obligations.[57]

Now, think about what it means to be not a philosopher studying associative obligations, but *the daughter* in the example.[58] Given that you belong to that community's social world, their life forms inform your engagement in practical deliberation. Nothing blocks the possibility that you recognise a sort of obligation even when the right normative relation between you and the community is missing. You might have a sense of gratitude, or duty, towards your family. Those are things that might figure in your subjective motivational set, and they can ground reasons for action that are strong enough to count as obligations. Indeed, as we have already discussed in the second and fourth chapters, some of them can even have the form of practical necessities in which no other course of action seems possible to you.[59] The case of Hyllos is illustrative: he gave his word to his father, but at the same time, he believes that what was being asked of him was morally abhorrent. The feeling of unease he has occurs precisely because he recognises the promise as binding on him; otherwise, there would be no conflict.

As we have seen in the previous chapter, we can think of at least two distinct relationships between the law and its subjects. Those were marshalled together under what Joseph Raz has called an attitude of 'respect for law'.[60] Firstly, people can have a more specific sense of respect. In this sense, agents recognise the law as something that has value, and this gives them a reason to recognise the reasons provided by law as reasons for action. This specific sense of respect can be motivated, in turn, by things like gratitude or a sense of duty. Raz illustrates this nicely with the case of a person who feels part of their community. One of the ways in which this person can express this sense of identification is through an attitude of respect towards the law, an attitude in turn manifested by certain actions on their part (ie, compliance with legal rules).[61] Raz explains this through the idea

[57] Dworkin, *Law's Empire* (1986) 204–206.

[58] Veronica Rodriguez-Blanco deploys a similar strategy in her criticisms of Dworkin in V Rodriguez-Blanco, *Law and Authority under the Guise of the Good* (Oxford, Hart Publishing, 2014). See also V Rodriguez-Blanco, 'Action in Law's Empire: Judging in the Deliberative Mode' (2016) 29(2) 2 *Canadian Journal of Law & Jurisprudence* 431.

[59] See the discussion in B Williams, 'Practical Necessity' in B Williams, *Moral Luck* (Cambridge, Cambridge University Press, 1981) and B Williams, 'Moral Incapacity' in B Williams, *Making Sense of Humanity* (Cambridge, Cambridge University Press, 1995).

[60] See, in general, J Raz, 'The Obligation to Obey' in J Raz, *Ethics in the Public Domain: Essays in the Morality of Law and Politics* (Oxford, Clarendon Press, 1995) and J Raz, 'Respect for Law' in J Raz, *The Authority of Law* (Oxford, Oxford University Press, 2009). As we have seen in the previous chapter, however, I believe that Raz's views need some refinements.

[61] Raz, 'Respect for Law' 255–60.

of 'expressive reasons': 'Expressive reasons are so called because the actions they require express the relationship or attitude involved.'[62] The account of how law can provide reasons for action that I presented in the previous chapter, I contend, leaves room precisely for those relationships and attitudes. Secondly, there is also a deeper sense of identification with the law, a sense that is related to notions of self-understanding. When an agent identifies herself with the law in this deeper sense, she sees the law as part of who she is, as part of her *character*. This was the *thick case* we explored in the previous chapter. For an agent that has this kind of identification with the law, breaking it is something unthinkable, not in the sense that she cannot entertain the idea, but in the sense that this idea fails to have any hold on her.

The general point I am making is phenomenological: the agent does not understand herself as engaged only with moral reasons. An attempt to recast this agent within the frame of the Dworkinian model would cause this agent to have something like Williams' 'one thought too many': where the agent sees only (or mainly) considerations of respect or character, the Dworkinian would insist that ultimately there are underlying moral reasons grounding the obligation. This does not mean that the kind of moral reasons Dworkin talks about never appear, only that they do not exhaust the possibilities of normativity.[63] Now, if we want to understand the reason-giving character of the law, we must understand what is entailed by the idea of respect. At this juncture, I have claimed that there is a more specific attitude of respect agents might have towards the law, an attitude based in things like gratitude or duty, and a deeper sense of identification with the law. Both forms of respect (broadly speaking) are not reducible to moral considerations.

The above remarks connect nicely the discussion in this chapter with the arguments developed previously in this book, but at this stage a question that naturally emerges at this point is this: what could have motivated the limited understanding of obligations, and henceforth of the reason-giving character of law on the part of Dworkin and many others? I believe that there are two motivations behind this, and we must address those in order to consolidate the appeal of my own account.

Firstly, there is a methodological motivation. The Dworkinian account was fundamentally concerned with the conditions that could *justify* the imposition of an obligation over an individual. This has the shape of an inquiry in normative political philosophy. Now, if all the account attempted to do was engage in normative political philosophy, then my criticism would be misguided from the start. Dworkin could claim that he is not describing anything but postulating how things ought to be. This, however, cannot be the case because Dworkin treats justification and description as essentially the same thing. Given Dworkin's interpretive methodology, we cannot describe a complex social practice like law without engaging

[62] ibid 255.

[63] For a similar view, that there can be other grounds for obligations, see for instance, T Honoré, 'Must We Obey? Necessity as a Ground of Obligation' (1981) 67(1) *Virginia Law Review* 39. Honoré's view on necessity is underdeveloped, but I think that is on to something correct.

in a justificatory enterprise. That was captured by the twin aspects of constructive interpretation, fit and justification. Indeed, Dworkin himself refuses Hart's somewhat conciliatory proposal that they were engaged in different enterprises, namely, that Hart was trying to describe legal practices, and that Dworkin was trying to justify them.[64]

This means that the status of the Dworkinian view as descriptive or normative is quite slippery, as he offers his view in a way that deliberately conflates description and evaluation. I do not want to present an argument against Dworkin's conflation per se, and indeed I am sceptical about any sort of strict and universal cleavage between description and evaluation. However, I do want to emphasise that his strategy makes it untenable to hold his account as an *ideal* account of the reason-giving character of the law, that is, an account that can depart considerably from the concrete experience of agents. But then we get to one of the points I am emphasising throughout the book, the claim that if we want to understand how anything can affect practical reasoning, we should take as our starting point the agent that deliberates. This is the reason why I suggested earlier that we should adopt the daughter's standpoint and not the philosopher's.

This is connected to two further remarks about the idea of justification. A first preliminary point is a corollary of the discussion so far. From the agent's perspective, moral considerations enjoy no priority by themselves because they must be connected to the motivational sets of the agents somehow if they are to have some bearing on action. An attempt to ground the reason-giving character of the law exclusively on morality, it seems, will not suffice. The second point is a consequence of the first. When we talk about justification, we must pay attention to whom our addressee is. To whom are we justifying the practice? For a justification to be recognised as such, it must make sense to the addressee; it must, that is, be connected to things that the addressee recognises as important. There can be no justification *for someone* that does not ring a bell for that person.

At this stage, another venue opens for the Dworkinian. Maybe we could understand justification as having a different audience, as being a justification of the practice not to the person that is being coerced, but to us, to the community already predisposed to accept it. In this second case, the justification has no relation to the first-personal practical deliberation of the person being coerced, but with our communal values.[65] This second kind of justification suffers pressure from two different directions. On the one hand, there is something off with the idea of a justification of coercion that needs no acceptance or at least some sort of recognition from the one being coerced. In general, we do not want wrongdoers to suffer merely; we want them to understand *that* they are being punished and *why* they are being punished (which should not be confused with the more

[64] R Dworkin, 'Hart's Postscript and the Point of Political Philosophy' in R Dworkin, *Justice in Robes* (Cambridge, Harvard University Press, 2006). For Hart's proposal, see HLA Hart, *The Concept of Law*, 2nd edn (Oxford, Oxford University Press, 1994), especially the Postscript to the second edition.
[65] Williams, *Ethics and the Limits of Philosophy* (2011) 30–33.

ambitious claim that people want wrongdoers to *repent*).[66] On the other hand, we can wonder about the possibility of a justification general enough to be accepted by the whole of a political community. It is probably the case that our contemporary communities are too pluralistic in terms of values for them to be able to accept a single justification for coercion. It might be that it does not matter how hard we try; our attempts at justification will always sound illegitimate to this or that subgroup in our communities.[67]

We can say that the first kind of pressure is internal to the idea of justification in the sense that it is about the point of justification, whereas the second one is external in the sense that it is about the context of justification. There are other aspects under which the idea of justification comes under pressure, and here I will just mention one of them. Connected to the contextual pressure, under the circumstances of Modernity, we live with the fact (and knowledge) of pluralism, that different people in different places and epochs lived differently. This reflexivity that is typical of our modern condition is at tension with the demand we make that law's enforcement be justified. This is so because the acceptance of justification depends on it being seen as somehow tracking the truth. Claiming that a given justification for coercion is true, however, is no easy task, as many forms of justification collapse under reflection in the conditions of pluralism.[68] Such remarks about the justification of coercion are not new in political philosophy, and they have far-reaching consequences in jurisprudence.

Let us now move to the second motivation underlying Dworkin's view, a motivation that is, I think, phenomenological. If it is true that from the standpoint of the phenomenology of obligations, we recognise obligations that are not moral, it is also true that we use the language of obligations towards (or against) people that do not recognise this or that obligation. To see this, think once more about the case of Hyllos. Let us suppose that after Herakles' death, Hyllos has second thoughts and decides not to marry Iole, given how repugnant that prospect is for him. In such a situation, a former advisor to his father, let us say Philoctetes, could then confront him: 'You have made a promise, you have an obligation to fulfil it.' The same thing goes for law: we use the language of obligations (and of reasons more generally) against those that deny the existence of an obligation or reason to abide by the law.

It seems to me, however, that we need to distinguish between different senses of obligation and that the failure to do so is the cause of much confusion in our understanding of obligations. We can distinguish between the following senses of obligations. On the one hand, we have genuine, reason-giving obligations; on the

[66] A point that can be inferred from Williams' more political texts, such as *In the Beginning was the Deed* (G Hawthorn ed, Princeton, Princeton University Press, 2005).

[67] See, in general, Williams, *In the Beginning was the Deed* (2005).

[68] I develop this point at greater length, drawing from both Williams and Dworkin, in DP Murata, 'Justification, Coercion and Political Responsibility: Remarks on Ethical Environmentalism' (2025) 16(2) *Jurisprudence* 352.

other, we have formal obligations. Genuine obligations are the ones that an agent can (at least potentially) recognise as binding on her because they are created by reasons for action she can (at least potentially) recognise as hers. They come in two flavours: they might be necessary obligations, that is, obligations entailed by necessities of character that present themselves as unavoidable to the agent, or they might be defeasible obligations, obligations an agent can recognise as impinging on her, but that can be overridden by other obligations. Formal obligations, in turn, are obligations that other people believe that she has but that do not bear on her reasons for action. She can, nonetheless, understand the speech of those pressing that obligation on her, and that is why she can talk the language of obligations with them. In the example, Philoctetes would believe that there is a genuine obligation, whereas Hyllos would only see a formal one. In their disagreement, what Philoctetes tries to do is to convince Hyllos that he was indeed under a genuine obligation. It is an attempt at recruitment: Philoctetes is trying to show Hyllos why he should be concerned about certain things, why he is in the wrong frame of mind, and so on.[69]

We have seen, then, two motivations underlying Dworkin's moralised understanding of obligations, one methodological and one phenomenological. I believe that both motivations can be traced back to a single, more fundamental claim: the Dworkinian view has tried to find the origin of obligations in something *external* to the agents, and in doing so, it has lost track of the possibility of obligations that arise from elements *internal* to agents. The Dworkinian intends to provide a justification based on moral principles, and the concern she has is with the justification of obligations that an agent might refuse to accept. The Dworkinian is anxious to grasp some leverage that could be used to show to an agent why the obligations imposed are real and justified for her, even if she refuses to see that. Reasons for externalism and the supremacy of moral considerations appeared as natural for this task.

Nonetheless, agents have reasons for action that are not tracked in morality, like attachments and commitments of a personal sort, and those elements must play a role in an account of the reason-giving character of the law. There can be reasons for action derived from a multitude of resources, like the two kinds of relationship (respect in a more specific sense and identification) we have discussed in this chapter and in the previous one. An account of the reason-giving character of the law that focuses solely on the moral justification of obligation is bound to ignore or distort important parts of our practical engagement with the law. This is why Dworkin's account of legal normativity can be 'one thought too many'. The conclusion I want to draw here is that Dworkin (and others with similar views) can at best explain *some* aspects of the reason-giving character of the law. The alternative view developed in the previous chapter, however, pays due account to

[69] See in general B Williams, 'Internal Reasons and the Obscurity of Blame' in B Williams, *Making Sense of Humanity* (Cambridge, Cambridge University Press, 1995) and the second chapter of this book.

the dispositions, attachments, and projects of agents. It fares better because it does justice to both ourselves and the law.

III. Finnis: Legal Normativity and Natural Law

A. The Finnisian Account

The previous section discussed Dworkin's account of legal obligations as moral obligations. Having completed that stage of the argument, let us begin with the explanation of the reason-giving character of the law according to the tradition of Natural Law.[70] This sub-section will be quite explanatory, as I will try to present Finnis' argument in what I take to be its best light.

According to Finnis, legal philosophy has its starting point precisely in matters of practical reason. This is what Finnis says:

> Why have the sort of thing or things that get called the law and legal system, legal institutions, and processes and arrangements that we call the law of our time and town? 'Why have it?' is of course elliptical for 'Why, if at all, should we have it?' The enquiry is nakedly about whether and if so why I, the reflecting person doing the inquiring, should want there to be this sort of thing, and be willing to do what I can and should to support and comply with it (if I should). It arises in the course of reflection, deliberative reflection, on what I should really do, here and now, and with my life as far as I can envisage it.[71]

This sort of inquiry is carried on by Finnis in his magnum opus, *Natural Law and Natural Rights*.[72] It would be misleading, however, to read Finnis' book as 'merely' a shot at jurisprudence. It is part of his view (and of Aquinas', or so Finnis argues) that our understanding of the law must be part of a broader understanding of what it is to have a good or flourishing life, which in turn is connected to the rights and duties we have in a community oriented towards the common good.

Natural Law and Natural Rights starts with a couple of chapters that directly engage with the mainstream methodological debates in jurisprudence, and in those, what interests me more is how he presents his own view as a corrective of sorts to Hart's internal point of view. I believe it is fair to say that Finnis' question in the first chapter of his book is 'how we identify the law?'. The author's suggestion, following Aristotle, is that we should look for the central case of law, that is, a case that best illustrates what we take to be paradigmatic, 'focal',

[70] For concise summaries of the Natural Law doctrine, see B Bix, 'Natural Law Theory' in D Patterson (ed), *A Companion to Philosophy of Law and Legal Theory* (London, Wiley-Blackwell, 2010), and J Finnis, 'Natural Law Theories' in N Zalta (ed), *The Stanford Encyclopedia of Philosophy* (Winter 2016 Edition), available at plato.stanford.edu/archives/win2016/entries/natural-law-theories/, accessed 30 April 2020.

[71] J Finnis, 'Law and What I Truly Should Decide' (2003) 48 *American Journal of Jurisprudence* 107, 108.

[72] J Finnis, *Natural Law and Natural Rights*, 2nd edn (Oxford, Oxford University Press, 2011).

of our object of inquiry. The favoured example for this is friendship. Following Aristotle, Finnis claims that there are 'central cases' of friendship that display what we take to be important or constitutive of it, and 'peripheral cases', like the kind of friendship you have with a fun but not very trustworthy colleague.[73] This naturally brings the following question, one that Finnis addresses immediately after presenting the idea of a central case: how are we supposed to identify the central case of something?

Finnis begins his case with a complaint that Hart's 'internal point of view' and Raz's 'legal point of view' are 'unstable and unsatisfactory'.[74] It is not very clear why he uses those words as criticism, but as I understand him, he means two things. By claiming that Hart's (and Raz's) accounts are unsatisfactory, he intends to say that those authors didn't completely develop their own commitments to a practical point of view. Both Hart and Raz claim that law is a normative practice, one that provides or taps into reasons for action. According to Finnis, however, their explanations are not enough to provide us with a standpoint from which we can identify the central case of the law because – as Hart emphasises – there are many different reasons that can explain why someone adopts the Hartian internal point of view.[75] An agent might do that because she believes that the law is legitimate, but she might also take the internal point of view because she wants to be a judge, or because she is not a very reflexive person and is just following what others are doing. That's why, for Finnis, Hart's argument (and Raz's) is not enough to provide us with the central case of the law.[76]

What about the instability of the argument? The point is not that the Hartian argument in itself is unstable, but that if this argument were all that there is regarding the proper attitude to law, then no legal system would be possible. Something like the Hartian internal point of view is important for a legal system to maintain itself, but Finnis says that for a legal system to emerge, *more* is needed. The claim is that the move from a pre-legal to a legal situation requires that the relevant agents adopt an attitude towards the law that has more specific content. The relevant agents must see a value or purpose that is served by the law that justifies its existence.[77] What is needed, says Finnis, is the point of view of someone that has practical reasonableness, that is, the point of view of someone that deliberates and acts for the right reasons.[78] So, this is how the argument has unfolded up to this point: Finnis claims that, the value of Hart's contribution notwithstanding, more is needed if we want to have a picture of the central case of the law. What is

[73] ibid 9–11.

[74] ibid 13.

[75] See, for instance, what Hart says in Hart, *The Concept of Law* (1994) 203.

[76] Finnis, *Natural Law and Natural Rights* (2011) 13–14.

[77] For a different understanding of Finnis's criticism regarding instability, see V Rodriguez-Blanco, 'Tracing Finnis's criticism of Hart's Internal Point of View: Instability and the 'Point' of Human Action in Law' in T Spaak and P Mindus (eds), *The Cambridge Companion to Legal Positivism* (Cambridge, Cambridge University Press, 2021) 695–719.

[78] Finnis, *Natural Law and Natural Rights* (2011) 14–16.

needed is the point of view of someone that can pierce through the complexities and grasp law's purpose or value. This point of view, of the one endorsed with practical reasonableness, is the one that can present law's central case.[79]

This takes us to a next question, namely, what are we to understand by practical reasonableness? For Finnis practical reasonableness is a 'basic good', a good that can bestow intelligibility to an action and that is 'self-evident' in the sense that once we get to this basic good, there is no need to keep inquiring why an agent did a given act. Finnis lists seven such goods: 'knowledge', 'life', 'play', 'aesthetic experience', 'sociability (friendship)', 'religion', and 'practical reasonableness'. Every rational action can ultimately be tracked to one or more of those basic goods, but such tracking can be highly complex, as people might have different understandings – some more reasonable, some less, and some downright wrong – about what those goods demand. Christopher Tollefsen, another proponent of Natural Law, summarises this point in the following way: 'all reasons for action are grounded in one way or another on the appeal of one or more basic goods, which are thus themselves the most fundamental reasons for action'.[80] Human flourishing demands all of them in some measure and under some reasonable understanding.[81]

This is why practical reasonableness is a special kind of good, even though Finnis makes it clear that he does not believe that there is any necessary hierarchy between them.[82] Practical reasonableness comprises the 'method' through which we can pursue the basic goods or participate in them. When an agent has practical reasonableness, she deliberates and acts in the right way, so to say. Finnis goes as far as to claim that the practically reasonable agent exhibits Aquinas' '*prudentia*' and corresponds to the Aristotelian '*phronimos*'.[83] Finnis is also at pains to demonstrate that the basic goods, by themselves, do not take us to morality, only to the intelligibility of actions. An action is intelligible because it can be tracked to a basic good (and in this sense, we feel that the inquiry about its sense can come to an end), but this does not mean that this action is moral. *Only when* an act is done in accordance with the requirements of practical reasonableness is this act within the confines of morality.[84] Finnis presents a quite lengthy list with nine requirements of practical reasonableness, among them restrictions to arbitrary distinctions between people and between basic goods, but more important than the precise list of Finnis' requirements is his claim that when an agent falls short of those requirements, her action is 'irrational'.[85] I will discuss the idea of practical

[79] See also Bix, 'Natural Law Theory' 217–18.

[80] C Tollefsen, 'Natural Law, Basic Goods and Practical Reason' in G Duke and RP George (eds), *The Cambridge Companion to Natural Law Jurisprudence* (Cambridge, Cambridge University Press, 2017) 134.

[81] Finnis, *Natural Law and Natural Rights* (2011) 81–85.

[82] ibid 92–95.

[83] ibid 88–89, 100–103.

[84] ibid 30–31, 103, 126–27.

[85] ibid 102.

reasonableness in more detail later in this chapter, as it is in it that I believe that the Finnisian model will face more problems.

We can see from what I have explained in the preceding paragraphs that Natural Law theory has a clear and substantial view on action and agency. This view, at least in Finnis' case, is strongly influenced by the Aristotelian tradition, and has the two sets of values or principles we have discussed. Borrowing an expression from Brian Bix, we can say that those two sets correspond to the first two levels of Finnis' Natural Law theory. The first level comprises the basic goods that render an action intelligible; the second level comprises the requirements of practical reasonableness that render an action moral. Law, in turn, appears at the third level of his theory.[86] This takes us back to Finnis' quotation at the beginning of this section: 'Why have the sort of thing or things that get called the law … ?'.[87]

Here is Finnis' answer: we have the law because it fosters, protects, or instantiates the basic goods in a diversity of ways. Sometimes the law is required for people to participate in a given good because it creates the conditions for people to do so; on other occasions, law functions negatively, providing a warrant for people in the sense that they can pursue that good without fear of intervention by third parties.[88] Because the law fosters, protects or instantiates basic goods, it bears on our practical reasoning. It is worth quoting Finnis in this regard:

> Purely positive law that is legally valid is (presumptively and defeasibly) valid and binding morally – has the moral form or meaning of *legal obligatoriness* – when and because it takes its place in a scheme of practical reasoning whose proximate starting point is the moral need for justice and peace, and whose more foundational starting-point is the range of basic ways in which human wellbeing can be promoted and protected, the way picked out in practical reason's first principles.[89]

There is much to unpack here. Firstly, there are some cases in which the tracking of a legal directive to a basic good is quite straightforward (e.g., laws against homicide or theft). Secondly, there are also some cases in which this is not so direct. In some contexts, the basic good is fostered, protected, or instantiated by the law via *determinatio*, that is, through a process of picking and choosing that makes the law a more concrete thing that fosters, protects, or instantiates the basic good in a given way. There is, according to Finnis, an important margin of freedom in the process of *determinatio*. It makes the law an expression of the basic good in a way that is congenial to the context of the law.[90] Thirdly – and in partial agreement

[86] Bix, 'Natural Law Theory' 216. Finnis uses the distinction of levels in his theory in the Postscript to *Natural Law and Natural Rights*, see Finnis, *Natural Law and Natural Rights* (2011).

[87] Finnis, 'Law and What I Truly Should Decide' 108.

[88] Finnis, *Natural Law and Natural Rights* (2011) 289–90; Finnis, 'Natural Law Theories' sections 1.4 and 1.5.

[89] Finnis, 'Natural Law Theories' section 1.5. See also Finnis, *Natural Law and Natural Rights* (2011) 289–90.

[90] Finnis, *Natural Law and Natural Rights* (2011) 281–90.

with Raz – legal directives are usually taken as pre-emptive reasons, since law's very capacity to deliver what it promises (the fostering, protection, or instantiation of basic goods) depends on people's conformity with it.[91] Fourthly, Finnis speaks in terms of law's defeasible or presumed obligatoriness. This means that there can be cases in which law's preemptiveness can be put aside. Law can be tracked to basic goods via practical reasoning, and when this is not the case, that law is not obligatory. How this is spelt out in detail in concrete cases is, of course, a contentious matter.

We are now in position to grasp Natural Law's account of the reason-giving character of the law. Starting with a view of practical reasonableness that connects action to basic goods that render action intelligible, we move to a view of law as a way to foster, protect, or instantiate those basic goods. In its central case, law is reason-giving because it can be tracked to basic goods that are part of human flourishing. This can have quite complex structures, thanks to the diversity of goods and of ways of instantiating those goods, a diversity that is in part accounted for by law through the idea of *determinatio*. Finnis' account, like Dworkin's, is a heavily moralised one, their differences on morality itself notwithstanding.

For Finnis, there is more to the law than just social control, and in this we are already moving away from the narratives presented by legal positivism in the third chapter. He attributes a much more 'extravagant' (to use Leslie Green's term)[92] function to law. Law's function regards the fostering, protection, or instantiation of basic goods; and more importantly, this can (or should) be possible to track via practical reasoning. This function that Finnis attributes to law is *transparent* to agents should they want to inquire about law's normativity.[93] This transparency seems to be related to the fact that the law has its reason to be ultimately dependent on basic goods (both in its central case and in its peripheral ones). Practical reasoning, according to the Finnisian narrative, would take the agent to the perception of those connections. For Finnis, we move from intelligibility (basic goods) to moral action through reasonable action (requirements of practical reasonableness) and then to the law (that helps to bring forth those goods). It is an account that starts from 'deliberative reflection, on what I should really do, here and now', to use Finnis' quote from before, and takes us to the ultimate point of law.

Finnis' theory is not without problems, however. His theory starts from some things he takes as truisms about human nature and steadily moves towards its more concrete parts and the law. We might say that Finnis' theory looks like a set of interconnected gears. This means that if we dent the first and more abstract gears,

[91] ibid 266–70; Finnis, 'Natural Law Theories' section 1.5.

[92] L Green, 'Legal Obligation and Authority' in N Zalta (ed), *The Stanford Encyclopedia of Philosophy* (Winter 2012 Edition), available at plato.stanford.edu/archives/win2012/entries/legal-obligation/, accessed 15 July 2020.

[93] For a discussion of transparency, see Rodriguez-Blanco, *Law and Authority under the Guise of the Good* (2014) 47–52.

the more concrete ones will suffer as well. I believe that there are three dents in the theory. There is a first, and in a sense preliminary, dent, located at what Bix has called the first level of Finnis' theory, his account of the basic goods. The second and generally more important one is located at the second level, his account of practical reasonableness. The third dent regards the idea of transparency and its role in an account of the reason-giving character of the law. If either of those dents proves to be real, then Finnis' view on the reason-giving character of the law will be in trouble. The general lesson I want to draw from the discussion of Finnis' views is, in a sense, the same as with Dworkin. Both authors advance towards a richer view of the reason-giving character of the law than the one we would extract from positivism, but they end up – for different reasons – overemphasising the role of moral reasons in their accounts. This is not to say, to repeat, that their accounts are wrong, period. But it does mean that they cannot do justice to the complexity of the reason-giving character of the law. Indeed, as I will try to show later, even if we grant much to Finnis, his theory will not suffice to account for the richness of practical reasoning in general.

B. Indeterminacy about Basic Goods

Even though my main concern is with practical reason and normativity, we should take a moment to discuss Finnis' account of basic goods, given its centrality in his argument. Someone might accuse Finnis of being arbitrary on his list of basic goods, so how can he avoid this charge? He attempts to do so by availing himself of two moves. First, he presents a plethora of anthropological references for the choice of his seven goods.[94] He also repeatedly claims that the basic goods are liable to different interpretations (eg, there is more than one way to pursue the good of aesthetic appreciation) and also combined in different ways (eg, the combination of the goods of knowledge and aesthetic appreciation can render the good of culture). Second, Finnis adds a measure of flexibility regarding the items in his list of basic goods. As far as I can tell, he does not hold a strong commitment to *that* specific list; that is, as far as I can tell, he would have no objections to extensions or protractions of the list.[95] Finnis' attempts at flexibilisation in the list of basic goods are proof of his sensitivity to the troubles that people might have with Natural Law. Nonetheless, as I will try to show, they are not enough to deliver what Finnis wants.

A first question that emerges is this: if the whole point was merely the intelligibility of action, why come up with those lists in the first place? To be more accurate, do we need a list of basic goods that are self-evident in order to make sense of action? To better see this point, think about Euripides' Aphrodite

[94] Finnis, *Natural Law and Natural Rights*, 2nd edn (Oxford University Press 2011) 97–98.
[95] ibid 90–91. But see too ibid 448–49.

in *The Hippolytus*, one of our privileged examples in the second chapter. In the play, Aphrodite finds herself offended by the actions of Hippolytus and decides to punish him for that by making Phaedra – his mother-in-law – fall in love with him, with catastrophic consequences. Aphrodite's reaction to the offence of Hippolytus is bound to spill innocent blood, but she sticks to her guns nonetheless, affirming – by doing so – that she finds her honour more important than a human life.[96] The important point for us here is that Aphrodite's actions are fully intelligible for us, even though they are not easily tracked to any of the basic goods in Finnis' list.

Of course, Finnis allows for people to have wrongheaded understandings of the basic goods, and he also adds that there are goods that are combinations or derivations of the more basic ones. However, if we are admitting that much, that people can be misguided or have more complex goods in mind than the basic ones, and that their actions make sense nonetheless, do we really need a list of them at all to understand action? We can explain a case like Aphrodite's (and many others from literature) merely by resorting to what she cares about, to what Williams has called the subjective motivational sets of individuals. It is the subjective motivational set of a person that motivates her to do this or that, that compels her to action. For us to understand those, however, we do not need to appeal to a universal list of goods.[97] Naturally, this does not prove Finnis *wrong* but shows that he might have more than what is needed to make sense of action. A more minimalist account that focuses only on what the agents take to be the good they pursue would probably fare better and cost less.[98]

It is open to a Finnisian to claim that the basic goods do more than just bestow intelligibility to action. They are also necessary for *human flourishing*.[99] This takes us away from the intelligibility or explanation of actions and into the domain of what is a good or worthy life: a good human life is one in which a reasonable proportion of the basic goods in reasonable interpretations is present. At this point, a different problem emerges for the Finnisian account. Recall that Finnis wanted to keep morality at the second level of his theory, the requirements of practical reasonableness. Practical reasonableness is itself a basic good, but its workings occur at the second level, at the deliberative procedures that help the agent to know what she ought to do. However, Finnis needs a point of view from which he can define what counts as human flourishing. If morality is at the second level, he cannot appeal to moral principles to define the contents of the first level. This means that if he attempts to define human flourishing by deploying moral criteria, he will turn the account tautological; that is, he will end up saying that

[96] Euripides, *Hippolytus*, trans D Greene (Chicago, The University of Chicago Press, 1942) lines 46–50.

[97] See, in general, my discussion about reasons internalism and the idea of caring about something in the second chapter.

[98] It is noteworthy that GEM Anscombe, a philosopher with very strong views on the ethical, managed to keep her account of action quite independent from any specific view on morality. See GEM Anscombe, *Intention*, 2nd edn (Cambridge MA, Harvard University Press, 2000) 74–76.

[99] See, for instance, Finnis, *Natural Law and Natural Rights* (2011) 23, 103, among other places.

what human flourishing is depends on morality, and that what morality is depends on human flourishing.

One resource that Finnis deploys that can come to his rescue at this point is the idea that the basic goods are universal.[100] The idea means, roughly, that the pursuit of those goods is a constant across all human cultures that we know. The pursuit of those basic goods is, in a sense, what Bernard Williams has called the 'distinguishing mark of man'.[101] People everywhere take play, aesthetic appreciation, and friendship as goods to be pursued in a worthy life, so it would be safe to assume that those goods are part of *human nature*.[102] If basic human goods are universal in this sense, then there is no need for appeals to morality, and the account does not risk becoming tautological. There is no need to dispute the claim there are some universals of the human condition,[103] but one ought to notice what the claim can imply. As Williams notes, if it is true that acting according to reasons is something that distinguishes humans from other animals, it is also true that we are the only species that can act on the basis of cruelty and deception.[104] The potential for cruelty and deception is as universal as the interest in play or aesthetic appreciation. This raises the question: given that at least some universals of the human condition are as universal as play or aesthetic appreciation, but way less desirable, what criteria could someone have to banish those less attractive but very human traits from a definition of human flourishing?

'Wait a moment', the Finnisian might interject, 'you are ignoring that the basic goods are recognised universally as *goods*. It is true that cruelty and deception are universal as well, but they are recognised universally *as evils*. The Natural Law account does not hold that everything universal is a basic good, but that basic goods are universal'. Fair enough. Still, those items recognised as universal goods are so in a very general sense. Aesthetic appreciation, to take an example, is severely underdetermined by the fact that everyone everywhere sees it as a good. Another item that sometimes figures in those lists, marriage, is equally underdetermined. Some human societies have monogamous marriages, others have polygamous marriages, and so on. We can grant that there are universals recognised as goods, but those will not tell us much about what people value and how they engage with those values. At most, the account will tell us about very general concerns that people have.[105]

There is also a complication, which will be discussed a bit more later, about what can count as a universal judgement for the purposes of the definition of basic goods. Presumably at some time in human history, maybe in Antiquity, honour was taken as a good everywhere in the known world. The unfolding of history has

[100] Finnis, *Natural Law and Natural Rights* (2011) 81–85.

[101] B Williams, *Morality – An Introduction to Ethics* (Cambridge, Cambridge University Press, 1993) 55.

[102] But notice that human nature here is not taken as a metaphysical claim. Finnis adverts caution with the term 'human nature', as can be seen in Finnis, *Natural Law and Natural Rights* (2011) 50–53.

[103] Nor to accept it, but this is not what matters here.

[104] Williams, *Morality – An Introduction to Ethics* (1993) 59–60.

[105] We should also bear in mind that, as some readings of Nietzsche would suggest, can we really claim that cruelty and deception were universally regarded as *evils*?

made honour a less universal concern in two ways. First, those societies in which honour figured as a good went through changes in their values. Second, the world was also 'enlarged' in the sense that throughout history more and more cultures with different values met with each other. How widespread must a value be in order to be universal? In the case of honour, should we say that it once was a basic good and now is no more? Notice that the argument here is conceptual: even if my example is empirically misguided, the need for the natural lawyer to explain when and how a good is a universal good remains.

Merely adding morality as a universal trait of mankind will not suffice to give more content to the claim about universal goods. Let us say that we can accept morality at this stage of the argument, that is, at the first level of the theory or as a universal trait for humans. Someone could then claim that human flourishing is actually *moral* flourishing in all its richness. This does not suffice because even if we accept that it is part of human nature that we live under some understanding of the constraints of morality, this does not entail that we are under the same understanding of the contents of morality. The same problem with the account of the goods reappears, now regarding morality. Even where there are some universally shared rules of morality, like Hart's 'minimal content of natural law', those are too thin, since they do not go beyond some protection of life and some protection of property, for instance. The rules of minimal natural law are plainly compatible with very impoverished lives for everyone but a small elite in a given community.[106] If, on the other hand, we appeal to a specific (richer) view on morality, then we are already running into the tautology mentioned before; we are presupposing a view of flourishing that is not uncontentiously universal.

The argument of the previous paragraphs does not show that a Finnisian account is irredeemable, but that it faces important difficulties that call for further argument. When it comes to human flourishing, I find it difficult to define it. From the fact that there are some universals recognised as goods, we cannot get to more concrete goods, since the universals might ground too little and might leave too much underdetermined. Any attempt to add morality will not do the trick as well, because morality – taken as a universal trait of mankind – is also severely underdetermined, and we cannot appeal to a more specific view on morality without rendering the account tautological. But let us suppose that a Finnisian or a Natural Lawyer can surpass those difficulties. Then, she would need to face the troubles existent at the second level of the account, about practical reasonableness.

C. Indeterminacy about Practical Reasonableness

I take this sub-section to be the most important in my analysis of Finnis since much of the action in his model happens at the level of practical reasonableness.

[106] Hart, *The Concept of Law* (1994).

It is via its requirements that an action brings forth the basic goods it aims for. According to Finnis, practical reasonableness 'express the "natural law method" of working out the (moral) "natural law" from the first (pre-moral) "principles of natural law"'.[107] The fifth chapter of *Natural Law and Natural Rights* is all about explaining those requirements, which can be so listed (the content of each requirement is not so important as the general argument here): that our actions should be more or less within a 'coherent plan of life', that they show 'no arbitrary preferences among values', that they show 'no arbitrary preference among persons', that they strike the right balance between 'detachment and commitment' and the proper concern for efficiency and consequences, that they show as far as possible 'respect for every basic value', attention to the 'common good' and accordance to 'one's conscience'.[108] Now, those various requirements are brought under a single master principle in the postscript of *Natural Law and Natural Rights*, in a lengthy excerpt that is worth quotation:

> Moral thought is simply rational thought at full stretch, integrating emotions and feelings but undeflected by them. (…) Aristotle's phrase *orthos logos*, and his later followers' *recta ratio*, right reason, should simply be understood as 'unfettered reason', reason undeflected by emotions and feelings. And so undeflected reason, and the morally good will, are guided by the first moral principle: that one ought to choose (and otherwise will) those and only those possibilities whose willing is compatible with a will towards the fulfilment of all human persons in all the basic goods, towards the ideal of integral human fulfilment.[109]

A quick preliminary observation. Soon after presenting this master principle, Finnis concedes that emotions might play a more positive role in an agent that has a 'well-ordered psyche',[110] so we should not take him as banishing all emotions from the sphere of practical reason. After all, he does talk about *integration* of emotions into rational thought. Still, this concession is not enough to save the argument. In rough terms, the problem is that Finnis' account conflates rationality and the explanation of action with morality in a way that overemphasises the role of moral considerations in practical reasoning.

By conflating rationality and morality, Finnis ends up in a quest for what Bernard Williams has aptly called an 'Archimedean point': an attempt to ground moral considerations in something external to morality. The general claim of the Archimedean point in ethics or morality is that everyone would be committed to morality because everyone is (or intends to be) *rational*. This is how the argument goes. One of the most recurrent aims of moral philosophy is to justify ethical or

[107] Finnis, *Natural Law and Natural Rights* (2011) 103.

[108] ibid 103–26.

[109] ibid 451. He is quoting J Finnis, 'Natural Law and Legal Reasoning' in RP George (ed), *Natural Law Theory: Contemporary Essays* (Oxford, Oxford University Press, 1992) 215. The idea that moral reasoning and rationality ultimately coincide is pervasive in the text of *Natural Law and Natural Rights*. See Finnis, *Natural Law and Natural Rights* (2011) 23, 102.

[110] Finnis, *Natural Law and Natural Rights* (2011) 452.

moral reasons to every conceivable agent.[111] It goes without saying that not everyone acts morally, and certainly no one acts morally all the time, but the concern of much moral philosophy is in a way deeper than the obvious realisation that people fall short of morality. Suppose that a certain person – following Williams, let us call her the 'amoralist' – simply does not care at all about ethical or moral concerns. When we confront her, we want to say 'you (morally) ought to do this' and the like, but she replies 'well, that's what you think, I simply do not care at all about that'. The search for an Archimedean point is the search for something that we could say *to* her. By attempting to ground morality in something external to it, the moral philosopher can press morality against the amoralist, as long as the amoralist is committed to this external point of leverage. The external point of leverage is taken – by both Kant and Aristotle – to be the very idea of rationality (or so Williams claims). So, here is the trick: if an Archimedean point for morality can be found in rationality, the amoralist can be pressured into morality since she is (or intends to be) rational.[112]

Finnis' strategy bears close resemblance to this. Having identified basic goods that bestow intelligibility to actions, he proceeds to claim that there are requirements of practical reasonableness we must follow if we are to instantiate those goods in our lives, requirements whose offspring is morality.[113] The problem for this argument is that it narrows down the possibilities of reasoning without a plausible reason for doing so, besides that it needs to do so. Here is a first remark on this. Finnis allows emotions and the like to play some role in practical reasonableness, but this role is supposed to be auxiliary only. Now, why would one constrain emotions in this way? As Williams points out, being deeply in love with someone and acting on that is something perfectly rational in the sense that there is a reason (being in love) that is connected to an action through deliberation.[114] If I buy flowers for my partner and someone asks me why, the reply 'Because I love her' is more than enough as an explanation. In a case like that, it makes perfect sense to say that the emotion (eg, love) was the reason that motivated my action.

It is worth mentioning that adding love or any other emotion to the list of basic goods will not do the trick of allowing us to claim that one's action is either rational or irrational. If love were a basic good, we would be able to track the person's action back to it. Suppose we can do that. We would be in a position to see how love could provide reasons for action for an agent. The problem is that seeing that a good can in principle provide reasons for action is not enough to deem a given course of action the rational or the irrational thing to do. Indeed, this is exactly the problem I have just identified. There might be many different

[111] As we have seen already, Williams distinguishes ethics from morality but for our purposes here we do not need to worry ourselves about that.

[112] Williams, *Ethics and the Limits of Philosophy* (2011) 32–33. See also Williams' discussion of the 'amoralist' in Williams, *Morality – An Introduction to Ethics* (1993) 3–13.

[113] Finnis, *Natural Law and Natural Rights* (2011) 126–27.

[114] B Williams, *Morality – An Introduction to Ethics* (1993) 60–61.

items in the first level of the theory, on the list of basic goods. The problem is how to figure out what we ought to do in concrete cases. In the Finnisian model, adding love to the list of basic goods grants *intelligibility* to my action of buying flowers. For Finnis, basic goods bestow intelligibility to an action, but the author discusses the *rationality* of an action as its morality. If love were to be a basic good, it would bestow intelligibility to an action, but not necessarily rationality, since rationality goes hand-in-hand with morality for Finnis.

Leaving Finnis' uses of the terms 'intelligibility' and 'rationality' aside for a moment, we do say things like 'X should have been more rational', but the language of rationality here misguides us. There are contexts in which we use the language of rationality to express that the agent should have been less reckless or something of that sort, that is, there are contexts in which we use the language of rationality to express an ethical evaluation. Something similar happens with statements like 'Medea is not a reasonable person.' We do not mean that she is irrational nor that she does not act on reasons, but that her judgements are somehow ethically off, that she overvalues some things and undervalues others. *If* we take rationality to merely mean to act based on reasons that make sense (that is, as a synonym of what Finnis calls intelligibility), then Medea is *not* irrational, although she might fail some ethical or moral standard. That is to say that one will not find support for the claim that morality and rationality coincide in our language. Careful reflection on what people mean by their utterances shows that our uses of language convey different meanings on this score.[115]

As far as I know, Finnis does not rely on a linguistic claim of that sort, but the problem remains. Among the requirements of practical reasonableness, that is, the 'requirements of *method* in practical reasoning',[116] Finnis attaches items as the restriction to arbitrary preferences among basic goods and a demand for equal treatment of persons. There are obscurities in Finnis' own discussion of those requirements, so for instance, what are we supposed to understand by arbitrary preferences? In the text, he mentions that some preference is arbitrary either if it fails to recognise the value of a basic good as such or if it treats another good that is not basic – like honour or sexual satisfaction – as if it were a basic good.[117] This does not take us far because there are many ways to instantiate Finnis' own seven basic goods, given how indeterminate they can be when it comes to their content. Within a good like life or play, sex can be treated as more important than the fostering of a family, and within goods such as life and sociability/friendship, honour can be treated as more important than equality, without this meaning that an agent that does so is less practically reasonable than anyone else. Worse still, if what I have said earlier, about the flexibility of the list of goods, is true, then there is no content at all to this requirement, since many other things can potentially be basic goods and compete with Finnis' requirements.

[115] A similar point is made elsewhere by Williams regarding the is/ought distinction.
[116] Finnis, *Natural Law and Natural Rights* (2011) 102.
[117] ibid 105–106.

A similar issue can be raised about Finnis' requirement against arbitrary preferences regarding persons. Finnis rightly points out that some basic form of universality applies to reasons. There is a minimum of formal justice regarding reasons, given their very logic.[118] This, however, is radically underdetermined as well. The principle of formal justice – that reasons apply equally to equal situations – is silent on what counts as equality.[119] For instance, Aphrodite's actions can be compatible with the requirement depending on how we understand equality. She could accept that *any goddess* that is offended by a mortal can (and should) do whatever it takes to restore her honour, even if this means trashing innocent people's lives. Sophocles' Kreon, too, can claim that by giving a proper burial to Eteokles and denying it to Polyneikes, he is in accordance with formal justice. It is true that both men died in battle, but their situations were different enough to legitimate the difference in treatment, or so Kreon argues.

Finnis could summon the argument of an impartial observer to assist him, and he indeed does that in *Natural Law and Natural Rights*. The impartial observer could in principle help Finnis' cause since she could rule out arguments like Aphrodite's and Kreon's, that is, arguments heavily based on divine or social status, claiming that those arguments operate under unreasonable biases. Nonetheless, that is not enough to get Finnis' account out of trouble. When it comes to practical reasoning, we are talking about deliberation from a first-personal point of view. The impartial observer can deliberate (supposing that she really can do that, which is already a controversial matter) and come to conclusions, but this deliberation will have a different starting point from the deliberation of more concrete agents, and therefore the conclusions will potentially be different as well. The motivations, dispositions and values of concrete agents would take them to deliberative conclusions that are simply not available for the impartial observer and vice versa.[120] As a reply, one could claim that the complaint is misguided because the impartial observer is a normative ideal, not a descriptive model. The defendant of the model of the impartial observer says: 'that's how someone ought to deliberate'. I will come back to this point in a moment.

What Aphrodite and Kreon have shown is that practical reasoning has no necessary connection to the requirements of practical reasonableness as Finnis conceives them. One can easily find other examples that show that Finnis' requirements are not necessary for an agent to engage in practical reasoning; for instance, Achilles' decision to live a short but glorious life and Ajax's decision to commit suicide after he falls in disgrace. In those cases we can discuss the morality or ethical standing of the decision, but that those were decisions based on reasons

[118] ibid 106–109.

[119] I have discussed this point in further detail in DP Murata, 'Natural Law Archimedianism' (2024) 15(4) *Jurisprudence* 573.

[120] See, in general, B Williams, 'The Human Prejudice' in B Williams, *Philosophy as a Humanistic Discipline* (AW Moore ed, Princeton, Princeton University Press, 2006). About the point of view of the agent engaged in practical reasoning, see the discussion in the second chapter. See, too, the discussion about McDowell and the *phronimos* in that chapter.

and made by rational people is, I think, not something open to discussion, unless we moralise reasoning from the start. It seems to me that, against Finnis, we can hold a more minimalist view on what counts as practical reasonableness: one's practical deliberation should connect, through a sound deliberative route, one's actions to reasons that are derived from what Williams has called the subjective motivational set of the agent. That reasons are connected to action via a sound deliberative route is central. This means, as we have seen in the second chapter, that there can be corrections regarding facts and reasoning (recall the discussion of the glass containing petrol). Equally important, an agent might have reasons for action that point to different and potentially incompatible courses of action. In such situations, the agent will try to figure out what she has the most reason to do, and the things she cares about will bear on this. So, even if an agent has *a* reason to engage in some sort of self-destructive activity, she might have *more* reason to do something else or to simply not engage in that activity, since engagement with it will harm some or most of the things she cares about. The more minimalist view I am endorsing does not mean that everything goes with practical reason.

As a reply to my criticism, someone might make the following suggestion: 'practical reasonableness is not an *account of* practical reasoning, but an *ideal of* it. It comprises not how people actually engage in practical reason, but the requirements that they ought to follow if they want to participate in a basic good'. Notice that against this reading, my arguments in the sense that one can be rational or reasonable without being moral will not hold. In the last paragraphs I was attempting to show that someone can engage in practical reasoning even if this person has little or no regard towards what we call morality, but this new reading is about an ideal. It sets the parameter of desirable reasonableness. This reading is also troublesome, but for other reasons.

The problem is the following one. If we take Finnis' account of practical reasonableness as an ideal or prescriptive theory in the sense that it intends to prescribe the actions we ought to take, we can ask of it the same thing that Williams asks of moral theories in general: '*by what right* does it legislate to the moral sentiments?'[121] Suppose that Finnis' requirements do not have the problems we have been discussing; still, he would need to provide us with a reason as to why people should accept *his* model as *the* ideal for practical reasoning. If people can go on with their lives, engaging in practical reasoning without the need to be constrained by Finnis' requirements, he or someone sympathetic to his view has the burden to say why someone would be doing better by adopting the model.

The obvious route to take on this burden would be to say that there are *moral* reasons in favour of the Finnisian model. This will be of no help since we were looking for a way to bring those *outside* morality *into* it. If an agent does not care about morality, the presentation of moral reasons for her to accept the Finnisian model will be powerless. Once we have decoupled rationality from morality, we

[121] B Williams, 'Preface' in B Williams, *Moral Luck* (Cambridge, Cambridge University Press, 1981) X.

cannot press the Finnisian model as *the* model of rationality. That was the whole point of the discussion about the amoralist. Now, let us revisit the argument of the impartial observer. The impartial observer too is an ideal for practical reasoning, and it is also subject to this same difficulty. Why would someone accept it in the first place? That is, why should an agent that has specific projects, values, motivations, and so on, accept the deliberative conclusion of an agent that has none of this as her own? Unless the agent is already committed to some of the Finnisian requirements, they will have no grasp on her. To put this point in other words, if the Finnisian model of practical reasonableness is presented as an ideal for deliberation, one cannot claim that the model ought to be accepted because it is the best model from the standpoint of the model itself.

At this point, a Finnisian might complain that I am demanding more from the model than what the model purports to offer. The Finnisian can say that the model does not provide external or categorical reasons for agents *outside* morality to join it, but that it provides us – people already *within* morality in one way or another – with guidance about how we ought to deliberate in order to bring about the basic goods. This would be a similar argument to the one Williams attributes to Aristotle in *Ethics and the Limits of Philosophy*.[122] It is a more modest, but more robust, argument. Most people, as we know them, are more or less within morality. The figure of the amoralist is extremely rare, if possible at all, and people, as we know, *do care* about doing the right thing most of the time. It is to those people that the Finnisian requirements of practical reasonableness are given. 'I see that you are concerned about what you ought to do', would say the Finnisian, 'Here are some principles you therefore should use in your deliberation.'

There are problems with this argument as well. If the Finnisian model is taken as a recommendation to those already within morality, there is also need for an argument in the sense of an explanation of why someone should prefer this model rather than others. Notice that there is an important difference compared to the former arguments analysed. Now we are already granting that the agent is within morality and that she is trying to decide what she (morally) ought to do. Yet, once again, the Finnisian account cannot recommend itself. The account can claim that it better helps to participate in the basic goods in a reasonable manner, but by itself this claim is not enough to vindicate the model. Even if we take for granted Finnis' list of basic goods, those goods can be achieved in different ways and intensities in one's life and are not liable to any objective hierarchy. This means that there are no grounds for the claim made by the Finnisian. Basic goods can be achieved by other approaches as well, and without any hierarchy between goods, one would have no reason to not adopt an account that would help her to participate as far as possible in, let's say, aesthetic appreciation to the detriment of sociability or religion.

[122] Williams, *Ethics and the Limits of Philosophy* (2011) 34–59. Much of my discussion regarding this point follows Williams' discussion of Aristotle in *Ethics and the Limits of Philosophy* and elsewhere.

Maybe a Natural Lawyer can try a different route. Following Grisez, Christopher Tollefsen has argued that 'Identifying "practical reasonableness" as a basic good thus seems to require a problematic circularity that should be avoided'.[123] If I understand him correctly, Tollefsen's manoeuvre is to claim that morality is not a basic good in itself, but the unfolding of a truth about basic goods and human flourishing. This is how he explains this:

> Our practical apprehension of the basic goods identifies not merely one good, but a multiplicity of goods; and it identifies them as goods not simply for ourselves, but for all beings relevantly like us. Accordingly, reason's most general deliverance in considering the goods in deliberating about options is that we, as agents, should be *open to all* those goods in *all* their possible instantiations, including their possible instantiations in other persons. The work of practical ethics accordingly is working out the implications of this most general prescription or norm.[124]

The argument resembles an argument for coherence. If I recognise something as a good for me, then I must recognise that this something is a good for everyone else, or as Tollefsen says, 'for all beings relevantly like us'. This is a first step towards morality or practical reasonableness, and it does not presuppose that practical reasonableness is in itself a basic good. If that is the case, then any criticism that depends on the status of practical reasonableness as a basic good will lose its bite.

The main problem for an argument like this is in the expression 'for all beings relevantly like us'. The expression, 'under the spell of morality', takes us smoothly to 'all human beings' or 'all rational beings', or even 'all beings with a soul'. Recall the case of Euripides' Aphrodite. She could recognise honour as a good (for the sake of the example, I will simply assume it as a good), and she could also recognise that it is a good for all gods, without committing herself to any recognition of its importance for humans. Alternatively, she could recognise different kinds of honour to be bestowed on mortals and immortals. She could also recognise honour as a good for every being but be uncommitted to its realisation for everyone in equal measure. That is, she does not assume a standpoint of equality between persons. The question 'Why should I care about them?' can always be posited, and we cannot rule it out by merely appealing to coherence, precisely because depending on how Aphrodite (or anyone) is fleshing out the idea of 'for all beings relevantly like us [her]', she *is* being coherent. The argument for practical reasonableness as a kind of fundamental claim for coherence has the same gap we saw before: that from rationality or intelligibility we cannot jump to morality. At best, we can grasp some claims of formal justice (eg, treating similar cases alike), but what counts as 'similar' and 'alike' is not given by rationality itself, but by the dispositions, values, and motivations that inform concrete, contingent, forms of life.[125]

[123] Tollefsen, 'Natural Law, Basic Goods and Practical Reason' 155.
[124] ibid 150.
[125] I have made a similar criticism regarding Joshua Jowitt's recent attempt to present a robust Natural Law theory of legal normativity based on Alan Gewirth's philosophy. See Murata, 'Natural Law Archimedianism'.

Let us return to Finnis. At the end of the day, it seems to me that the Finnisian account faces a dilemma. Finnis' accounts of basic goods and of practical reasonableness are sensible to the diversity and incommensurability of goods. He is quite resistant to any kind of reductionism about the richness of human flourishing and wants to leave enough space in the model to account for this. However, by opening his model to the richness of human life, he risks collapsing it, for the way we go on with our lives is not easily constrained by any theory. The requirements of practical reasonableness, in this sense, emerge as an attempt to bring some order to the chaos of life, but there is no argument why we should prefer *that* order. Aristotle's original theory was less resistant to reductionism, but this allowed him to 'find' order in his teleological account of the world. In the more traditional (or conservative) readings of the Aristotelian model, there is *a* right way to live, and that is according to human nature as given by the teleological account. Now, as has been pointed out by several authors, we have no reasons to accept the Aristotelian teleology. The presuppositions – biological, cosmological and social – that rendered some plausibility to the teleological account have all been abandoned, and without them the account is arbitrary. In turn, without the teleological account, we are back to the radical indeterminacy of life and of what we ought to do to flourish as humans.[126]

I believe a bit of a summary might help at this point, regarding the discussion of the last two sub-sections. The general lesson is that a Finnisian has many challenges to tackle if she wants to present an adequate account of agency and practical reasoning. First, she must find a way to present a convincing list of basic goods, but she must also provide a convincing, non-tautological way of adding flesh to those goods, since from their universality we cannot move to any specific content in those goods. Second, the Finnisian must either present an argument in favour of the principles of practical reasonableness as necessarily connected to rationality, or that the principles of reasonableness are the correct way to deliberate in prescriptive terms, without appealing to those very principles. Both paths have their own challenges, as I have tried to show. We should now move back to law, to see how the criticisms made in the past two sub-sections affect Finnis' view on legal normativity.

D. Indeterminacy about the Reason-Giving Character of the Law

The whole discussion up to this point feeds back into the Finnisian account of the reason-giving character of the law. To see this, let us recall some important remarks. The Finnisian account offered a substantive view of the function of the law. The law fosters, protects, or instantiates basic goods, and this function

[126] See, for instance, Williams, *Ethics and the Limits of Philosophy* (2011) 48–59.

is one that is transparent to agents; that is, when the agent deliberates, she can perceive or grasp that function.[127] If what I have said in the previous sub-sections is roughly right, then this function is not as enlightening as one would have thought at first glance. There is much obscurity surrounding the idea of basic goods, both about what they are and about how to bring them about in more concrete cases. Secondly, Finnis' account was intended to be tracked on 'deliberative reflection, on what I should really do, here and now', but as we have seen, the Finnisian model of practical reasonableness demands further argument if it is to be vindicated as universal, and if practical reasonableness is offered as a prescriptive model, then it is in need of an argument for its acceptance. The problem is not that Finnis' general claim, that the law provides reasons for agents because it is ultimately tracked in basic goods, is wrong, but that the claim is radically indeterminate. We have no reliable list of goods nor a well-defined understanding of individual goods, and an objective ordering of them is not available. Finnis' attempt to tackle this via a robust account of practical reasonableness fails for the reasons I have been discussing. All of this means that we are in the dark as to when the law is actually tracking goods and therefore providing reasons for action.

Think about the following case. In a very conservative country, many believe (let's say, a majority that is slightly larger than the opposition) that sex before marriage is grossly immoral, that it violates the basic goods of life and religion. A law is duly approved in this country imposing heavy fines on people that have sex before their marriage. For that majority, this law is obviously tracked to basic goods and is therefore reason-giving. On the other hand, things are not like that for the minority. They are also committed to the basic goods of life and religion (they might also be committed to a good external to the list, but this makes no difference for the example), but they do not see pre-marital sex as an offence against those goods. On the contrary, some of them even believe that having happy, non-committed sex is a form of participation in those goods. In their view, this law offends basic goods and therefore gives them no reason for action. The claim that the law provides reasons due to its relation to basic goods is of no help here if one wants to get out of the conflict between the views of the majority and the minority.

'Not so fast', the Finnisian can interject. There are many goods that can only be fostered, protected, or instantiated with the help of the law. Even if one statute or precedent impairs one good in a given case, the law in general is reason-giving, that is, there is a 'seamless' structure to the law that bestows a reason-giving character to the law as whole. There is a general obligation to obey the law, even if one believes that one concrete case is wrong.[128]

[127] For Finnis on transparency, see Finnis, *Natural Law and Natural Rights* (2011) 340–42.

[128] Finnis, *Natural Law and Natural Rights* (2011) chs X and XI, 469–70. See also J Raz, 'The Obligation to Obey: Revision and Tradition' in J Raz, *Ethics in the Public Domain: Essays in the Morality of Law and Politics* (Oxford, Clarendon Press, 1995).

This line of defence is connected to the idea that the law provides pre-emptive reasons for its subjects. Now, no one would claim that this general obligation to obey the law is absolute. If the legal system systematically fails to foster, protect, or instantiate basic goods, it will also fail to generate this kind of obligation. Also, if we have a statute or precedent that is taken as unbearably offensive to a basic good, this statute or precedent will lose its pre-emptive character, and civil disobedience might be around the corner. A general obligation to obey the law is not an absolute-all-things-considered obligation. To borrow a term from Raz's dictionary, it can be said that there are cases that fall beyond the 'scope' covered by the obligation.[129]

So, this is the problem that emerges for Finnis' account: how are we supposed to know when a given statute or precedent is too offensive to a basic good or when a legal system systematically fails to foster, protect, or instantiate basic goods once we are deprived of a more robust account of those goods and of how we participate in them? Of course, there are the easy cases that no one would deny, cases like blatantly racist laws or fascist legal regimes, but apart from those, everything else is pretty much up for grabs. In the example of the prohibition on pre-marital sex, how are we supposed to know if that prohibition is enough to justify disregard for that law? Alternatively, if the whole legal system is full of laws like that, then how are we supposed to know when that is a case of systematic failure in the advancement of basic goods? The problem is complicated by the fact that all parties involved claim that their views track what is good or valuable; that is how they, from their first-personal views, perceive their own positions. From their positions, they are certain about their views, and their detractors seem simply misguided, wrong, or worse.

Values like 'human dignity' and some baseline sense of equality are *just there for us* now, as foundational matters.[130] Any ethical judgement made by us now will pay its due to values such as those. Yet, those notions were not always available (and even when they were, they were subject to different understandings through time).[131] Think about this example given by Williams in a different context. It would be unthinkable for Alexander the Great to give up his adventures to spend the fortune he had on the alleviation of famine or poverty. Unthinkable here means not that Alexander was incapable of doing charity here and there, but that giving up the honour and glory to be generous was a judgement that simply made no sense for him, given the culture and values that were ingrained in him. That would be madness.[132] Some basic goods (or some understandings of basic goods) were

[129] J Raz, *Practical Reason and Norms* (Oxford, Clarendon Press, 1990) 46.

[130] B Williams, 'Philosophy as a Humanistic Discipline' in B Williams, *Philosophy as a Humanistic Discipline* (AW Moore ed, Princeton, Princeton University Press, 2006) 195–97.

[131] Much of this discussion tracks on Williams' 'relativism of distance'. See Williams, *Ethics and the Limits of Philosophy* (2011) 173–92; B Williams, 'The Truth in Relativism' in B Williams, *Moral Luck* (Cambridge, Cambridge University Press, 1981).

[132] Williams, 'Moral Incapacity'. See also B Williams, '*The Last Word, by Thomas Nagel*' in B Williams, *Essays and Reviews 1959-2002* (Princeton, Princeton University Press, 2014).

simply not available to him, yet it would be preposterous to claim he was irrational in preferring conquest rather than charity.

What has been said about Alexander also applies to lawmakers, officers and subjects in ancient times. Their legal systems and legal statutes (granted the proviso that they can be meaningfully grouped together with 'our' legal systems and statutes) tracked goods or understandings of goods that are not available to us and paid no due account to ideas that are just there for us, like dignity or equality. In a meaningful sense we can say that ancient legal systems systematically failed to foster, protect, or instantiate basic goods for us, and that if by some bizarre event we were thrown in Alexander's court, his laws would not be reason-giving for us, except in a prudential sense. This kind of culture-clash inspires equal parcels of drama and comedy in fantastic literature and television, and it is not hard to see why both can spring from it. Now, we have no reason to deny that legal systems of the past can be reason-giving to the communities of the past. If we follow Finnis' own basic claim that the reason-giving character of the law is based on its relation to basic goods and that this is something transparent to agents, we can notice that someone from Alexander's court can see the good that their law fosters, protects and instantiates *for them*. Naturally, this is not the same thing as saying that they perceive such goods as goods only for them. As we have seen in the second chapter, the argument here adumbrated is consistent (and sometimes even demands) that people take their perception of the good as universal.

The answers to the questions asked before – about when a specific statute or precedent or a whole legal system is offensive enough to basic goods so that this offensiveness can justify our disregard for the law – are radically underdetermined. This is a point that we have already seen in our previous discussions and that resurfaces here. Those materials will be reason-giving for those that take them as tracking some good, and not reason-giving for those that deny that. Those two views will depend on who the agent assessing the law is, on what her concerns are and on what she cares about. At the end of the day, unless a Natural Law account like Finnis' is committed to some strong and controversial philosophical assumptions, like Aristotle's teleology, it will fail to provide a complete answer to the reason-giving character of the law.

Nonetheless, the absence of a more concrete answer is not the same thing as a wrong answer. The idea that the reason-giving character of the law is tracked on what people take to be good or valuable is essentially correct, and it grasps an important feature of the phenomenology of our discussion about the good, even if we lack any specific account of what good or valuable is. Indeed, we can grant even more to a Finnisian account. Much of our law can be seen as reason-giving by pretty much everyone. We do not need a specific list of basic goods to know that the protection of life or physical integrity in one way or another is something valuable. Laws against murder or assault can be easily tracked back to that realisation and thus be seen as reason-giving by pretty much everyone, or at least, by pretty much everyone that shares enough in terms of forms of life. Naturally enough, those more modest claims fall short of the ambitions of a book like *Natural Law and Natural Rights*.

Another argument that can be made in support of my claims in this chapter up to this point and that is worth mentioning is in terms of *epistemic indeterminacy*. I can only point out to this argument, however, since an in-depth analysis of it would take us too far from my concerns. To see this argument, notice first that the points made in the previous paragraphs remain even if external reasons, reasons for action that are independent from the subjective motivational sets of the agents, were real. In the previous paragraphs, I have been presenting the argument in terms of certainty and knowledge, that is, that we have no way to know if more concrete instantiations (eg, law) offend basic goods because we have no way to know which goods are basic goods and what they entail in concrete cases. If reasons externalism were true, we could at least have that there are basic goods (even if we fail to know them) and that there are actions that foster or violate those goods (even if we fail to know them). Let us grant, for the sake of the argument, that reasons externalism is true (and, indeed, I do not think that I have said much against the truth of externalism; rather, my arguments were mostly about how a reason could be a reason for action for a concrete agent).

What are the issues here? Firstly, from the existence of external reasons, we cannot infer that we can grasp those reasons; that's the importance of the 'even if we fail to know them' qualifier in the previous paragraph. Secondly, even if we somehow manage to identify the basic goods involved, unless we have a way to determine how to participate in them, we are bound to operate in an essentially indeterminate space, and the only thing that can guide us within it is our own take on what the good entails in concrete cases. Even if there are external reasons that apply to Alexander and to us, we might still be in the dark about what to do. That is why we can talk about epistemic indeterminacy here. As the situation that calls for action approaches, we navigate the world, taking into account our own understanding of the good that is informed by our motivations, dispositions and so on. Now, if by chance those materials in our subjective motivational sets map into external reasons, they would still be *our* materials, and therefore those external reasons 'out there' will become internal reasons for action.[133] At the end of the day, the fact that basic goods exist outside us would make no difference since the goods are too indeterminate in themselves, and practical deliberation is necessarily informed by a plethora of resources that spring from the concrete agents we are.

E. The Requirement of Transparency in Natural Law

Before concluding this chapter, I would like to add a brief discussion about the idea of transparency. Up to this point I have taken for granted that the transparency requirement of the Finnisian model was sound, but there are two

[133] This point is made, in a different context, by SG Chappell and N Smyth, 'Bernard Williams' in N Zalta (ed), *The Stanford Encyclopedia of Philosophy* (Fall 2018 Edition) section 5, available at plato.stanford.edu/archives/fall2018/entries/williams-bernard/, accessed 3 December 2019.

issues with it. The first issue is a corollary of the discussion in the previous subsections and is similar to the first mismatch analysed in the third chapter. The second issue with the idea of transparency, in turn, resembles Dworkin's 'one thought too many' we discussed earlier in this chapter. Let us take a look at each in turn.

Firstly, the issue regarding the mismatch. In the third chapter, I have argued that there is a mismatch between the picture of the agent presupposed by much legal positivism and the concrete agents that we are. For the agent in the positivist picture, the function of law was transparent; that is, she could see it if she thought about that and recognise that having the law was an improvement when compared to the situation prior to law's existence. On the other hand, concrete agents might not have access to the function of the law. This sort of mismatch also appears in Finnis' theory. Think about it: for the function of law to be transparent, agents must be able to reason their way to it, but if what I have said before about the indeterminacy in Natural Theory is true, then this becomes less plausible. Agents might not be able to grasp law's function since the basic goods that law fosters or protects are radically indeterminate, or they will only be able to grasp a very general function that will not have enough in it to bear on practical reasoning. This does not mean that agents cannot see some form of good or value in the law, but that this does not warrant the argument for transparency. An account of the reason-giving character of the law that relies on the idea of transparency might end up not being able to explain when and how the law provides reasons for action.

Secondly, the issue regarding 'one thought too many'. When the law figures in the practical reasoning of concrete agents, they often will only have the considerations I have loosely grouped under the idea of respect for the law. This does not necessarily take the agent to considerations about basic goods and their instantiation. Agents can have different kinds of relationships with the law that will account for the reason-giving character of the law. As we have already seen in the fourth chapter, the notion of respect involves the recognition of a value, and this in a sense that provides the agent with motivation to foster (or at least to not act against) that value. When thinking about what she ought to do, an agent will take the reasons provided by the law as reasons for action if there is some connection between the law and her subjective motivational set. The law characteristically demands respect from its subjects, and for the agent to have such respect for the law, all that is needed is some sort of 'emotional bond', to use Deigh's term, between the agent and the law. Insofar as the Finnisian presses the point that the reason-giving character of the law is ultimately dependent on basic goods, she can be guilty of engaging in 'one thought too many'. In a nutshell, if the first issue pointed towards difficulties in the idea of transparency, the second issue pointed towards ways of accounting for the reason-giving character of the law that do not depend on it.

IV. Concluding Remarks

This chapter analysed in reasonable detail Dworkin's view of legal obligations as moral obligations, and Finnis' Natural Law view on legal normativity. Although in different ways, both authors presented heavily moralised accounts of the reason-giving character of the law. Dworkin's account fails not in the sense that it is wrong full-stop but in the sense that it either explains just one part of the reason-giving character of the law, or that it distorts the whole of it *if* it is taken as an exhaustive explanation. Underlying Dworkin's theory, there are many presuppositions of much modern moral philosophy, presuppositions as the supremacy of moral considerations over all other kinds of reasons an agent might have, the belief in the existence of only moral obligations (or of obligations that do not conflict with morality), and so on that are shared by many others. Once we start to have doubts about those presuppositions, and much of the second chapter was about that, we also start doubting Dworkin's central claims. There are reasons for action that are not well translated into morality, as agents have commitments, attachments, projects, and dispositions that cannot be reduced to moral considerations. The richness of concrete, real-life can very well play a role in the reason-giving character of the law.

Against Finnis' account, I have argued that basic goods are too underdetermined in the sense that it is very hard to pin down a list of them, and that even if we had a list, we would not be able to flesh out the content of specific goods. More importantly, practical reasonableness is not a satisfactory account of practical reasoning, nor can it be assumed without argument as an ideal of practical reasoning. Finally, the idea of transparency does not seem needed for an account of the reason-giving character of the law. All that puts much pressure on Finnis' account of the reason-giving character of the law. Notably, it seems that all the real work is being done by the personal attachments, commitments, cares, and projects of concrete agents. As with Dworkin, my arguments should not be taken as an all-out criticism of Finnis. For instance, it seems to me that the claim that individuals see some sort of good in the law and that this plays a role in its normativity is correct, or at least very plausible. The lesson I want to draw from this chapter is that an account of the reason-giving character of the law that focuses too much on morality is not enough. We need an account that pays attention to the concrete agents as they are, and providing such account was the overall aim of this book.

There is a general lesson that, at first sight, is paradoxical. At the same time that we should, in our philosophical endeavours, be wary of the resources legated to us by much moral philosophy, we should also deepen our understanding of moral psychology if we want to make sense of how law can provide reasons for action. The paradox is only apparent because moral psychology does not need to be moralised. The same holds for our understanding of legal phenomena.

BIBLIOGRAPHY

Aeschylus, 'The Eumenides' in Aeschylus, trans Herbert Weir Smyth (Cambridge, MA, Harvard University Press, 1926).
—— 'The Eumenides' in *The Oresteia*, trans Robert Fagles (New York, Penguin, 1979).
Anscombe, GEM, *Intention*, 2nd edn (Cambridge MA, Harvard University Press, 2000).
Bagg, R, 'Introduction "From what kind of parents was I born?"' in Sophocles, *The Complete Plays of Sophocles – A New Translation*, trans R Bagg and J Scully (London, Harper Perennial, 2011).
Bix, B, 'Natural Law Theory' in D Patterson (ed), *A Companion to Philosophy of Law and Legal Theory* (London, Wiley-Blackwell, 2010).
—— 'The Nature of Law and Reasons for Action' (2012) 5 *Problema* 399.
Bratman, M, 'Reflections on Law, Normativity and Plans' in S Bertea and G Pavlakos (eds), *New Essays on the Normativity of Law* (Oxford, Hart Publishing, 2011).
Chappell, SG, and Smyth, N, 'Bernard Williams' in N Zalta (ed), *The Stanford Encyclopedia of Philosophy* (Fall 2018 Edition), available at plato.stanford.edu/archives/fall2018/entries/williams-bernard/, accessed 3 December 2019.
Coleman, J, *The Practice of Principle* (Oxford, Oxford University Press, 2001).
Darwall, S, 'Two Kinds of Respect' (1977) 88(1) *Ethics* 36.
—— 'Respect and the Second-Person Standpoint' (2004) 78(2) *Proceedings and Addresses of the American Philosophical Association* 43.
Deigh, J, 'Morality and Personal Relations' in J Deigh, *The Sources of Moral Agency – Essays in Moral Psychology and Freudian Theory* (Cambridge, Cambridge University Press, 1996).
—— 'Emotion and the Authority of Law' in J Deigh, *Emotions, Values and the Law* (Oxford, Oxford University Press, 2008).
—— 'Williams on Practical Reason' in J Deigh, *From Psychology to Morality: Essays in Ethical Naturalism* (Oxford, Oxford University Press, 2018).
Delacroix, S, *Legal Norms and Normativity – An Essay in Genealogy* (Oxford, Hart Publishing, 2006).
—— 'Tracing a Genealogy of Legal Normativity: Responsibility, Authorship and Contingency' in S Bertea and G Pavlakos (eds), *New Essays on the Normativity of Law* (Oxford, Hart Publishing, 2011).
Dickson, J, *Evaluation and Legal Theory* (Oxford, Hart Publishing, 2001).
Dworkin, R, *Taking Rights Seriously* (Cambridge, MA, Harvard University Press, 1977).
—— *Law's Empire* (Cambridge, MA, Harvard University Press, 1986).
—— *Justice in Robes* (Cambridge, MA, Harvard University Press, 2006).
—— 'Hart's Postscript and the Point of Political Philosophy' in R Dworkin, *Justice in Robes* (Cambridge, MA, Harvard University Press, 2006).
—— *Justice for Hedgehogs* (Cambridge, MA, Harvard University Press, 2011).
Dyzenhaus, D, 'The Genealogy of Legal Positivism' (2004) 24(1) *Oxford Journal of Legal Studies* 39.
Enoch, D, 'Reason-Giving and the Law' (2011) 1 *Oxford Studies in the Philosophy of Law* 1, available at papers.ssrn.com/sol3/papers.cfm?abstract_id=2607030, accessed 18 January 2021.
Euripides, *Hippolytus*, trans D Greene (Chicago, The University of Chicago Press, 1942).
Finlay, S, and Schroeder, M, 'Reasons for Action: Internal vs. External' in N Zalta (ed), *The Stanford Encyclopedia of Philosophy* (Fall 2017 Edition) available at plato.stanford.edu/archives/fall2017/entries/reasons-internal-external/, accessed 3 December 2019.
Finnis, J, 'Natural Law and Legal Reasoning' in RP George (ed), *Natural Law Theory: Contemporary Essays* (Oxford, Oxford University Press, 1992).
—— 'Law and What I Truly Should Decide' (2003) 48 *American Journal of Jurisprudence* 107.

——*Natural Law and Natural Rights*, 2nd edn (Oxford, Oxford University Press, 2011).
—— 'Natural Law Theories' in N Zalta (ed), *The Stanford Encyclopedia of Philosophy* (Winter 2016 Edition), available at plato.stanford.edu/archives/win2016/entries/natural-law-theories/, accessed 30 April 2020.
Frankfurt, H, *The Importance of What we Care About* (Cambridge, Cambridge University Press, 1988).
——'Identification and Externality' in H Frankfurt, *The Importance of What we Care About* (Cambridge, Cambridge University Press, 1988).
—— 'Identification and wholeheartedness' in H Frankfurt, *The Importance of What we Care About* (Cambridge, Cambridge University Press, 1988).
——'Freedom of the Will and the Concept of a Person' in H Frankfurt, *The Importance of What we Care About* (Cambridge, Cambridge University Press, 1988).
—— 'Rationality and the Unthinkable' in H Frankfurt, *The Importance of What we Care About* (Cambridge, Cambridge University Press, 1988).
——'The Importance of What we Care About' in H Frankfurt, *The Importance of What we Care About* (Cambridge, Cambridge University Press, 1988).
——*Necessity, Volition, and Love* (Cambridge, Cambridge University Press, 1999).
—— 'Autonomy, Necessity, and Love' in H Frankfurt, *Necessity, Volition, and Love* (Cambridge, Cambridge University Press, 1999).
——'On Caring' in H Frankfurt, *Necessity, Volition, and Love* (Cambridge, Cambridge University Press, 1999).
——'On the Necessity of Ideals' in H Frankfurt, *Necessity, Volition, and Love* (Cambridge, Cambridge University Press, 1999).
—— 'On the Usefulness of Final Ends' in H Frankfurt, *Necessity, Volition, and Love* (Cambridge, Cambridge University Press, 1999).
—— 'The Faintest Passion' in H Frankfurt, *Necessity, Volition, and Love* (Cambridge, Cambridge University Press, 1999).
——*The Reasons of Love* (Princeton, Princeton University Press, 2004).
——'Disengaging Reason' in RJ Wallace, P Pettit, S Scheffler and M Smith (eds), *Reason and Value – Themes from the Moral Philosophy of Joseph Raz* (Oxford, Oxford University Press, 2006).
Fricker, M, Keynote Speech 'Postscript: On Having a Reason' in the Conference Agency, Fate and Luck – Themes from Bernard Williams, at Lund University (Sweden), June 2019, available at www.youtube.com/watch?v=kQgh6fjFADw, accessed 25 January 2025.
Gans, C, 'Mandatory Rules and Exclusionary Reasons' (1986) 15 *Philosophia* 373.
Giudice, M, *The Normativity of Law* (Cambridge, Cambridge University Press, 2024).
Greco, L, 'Reflection and the Individual in Williams' Humanistic Philosophy' in A Perry and C Herrera (eds), *The Moral Philosophy of Bernard Williams* (Cambridge, Cambridge Scholars Publishing, 2003).
Green, L, 'Legal Obligation and Authority' in N Zalta (ed), *The Stanford Encyclopedia of Philosophy* (Winter 2012 Edition), available at plato.stanford.edu/archives/win2012/entries/legal-obligation/, accessed 15 July 2020.
Gur, N, 'Legal Directives in the Realm of Practical Reason: A Challenge to the Pre-emption Thesis' (2007) 52 *American Journal of Jurisprudence* 159.
Hart, HLA, *The Concept of Law*, 2nd edn (Oxford, Oxford University Press, 1994).
—— 'Introduction' in HLA Hart, *Essays in Jurisprudence and Philosophy* (Oxford, Clarendon Press, 1983).
Hershovitz, S, 'The End of Jurisprudence' (2015) 124(4) *Yale Law Journal* 1160.
Himma, KE, 'Inclusive Legal Positivism' in J Coleman and S Shapiro (eds), *The Oxford Handbook of Jurisprudence and Legal Philosophy* (Oxford, Oxford University Press, 2001).
Honoré, T, 'Must We Obey? Necessity as a Ground of Obligation' (1981) 67(1) *Virginia Law Review* 39.
Hooker, B, 'Williams' Argument against External Reasons' in E Millgram (ed), *Varieties of Practical Reasoning* (Cambridge, MIT Press, 2001).
Hurd, H, 'Challenging Authority' (1991) 100 *Yale Law Journal* 1611.
Jenkins, M, *Bernard Williams* (Chesham, Acumen Press, 2006).

Kaplan, J, 'Attitude and the Normativity of Law' (2017) 36 *Law and Philosophy* 469.
Katsafanas, P, *Agency and the Foundations of Ethics* (Oxford, Oxford University Press, 2013).
Kelsen, H, *Introduction to the Problems of Legal Theory – A Translation of the First Edition of the Reine Rechtslehre or Pure Theory of Law*, trans B Paulson and S Paulson (Oxford, Clarendon Press, 1992).
Korsgaard, C, 'Skepticism about Practical Reason' in C Korsgaard, *Creating the Kingdom of Ends* (Cambridge, Cambridge University Press, 1996).
—— *The Sources of Normativity* (Oxford, Oxford University Press, 1996).
Manne, K, 'Internalism About Reasons: Sad but True?' (2014) 167 *Philosophical Studies* 89.
Marmor, A, *Philosophy of Law* (Princeton, Princeton University Press, 2011).
—— *Foundations of Institutional Reality* (Oxford, Oxford University Press, 2023).
McDowell, J, 'Might There be External Reasons?' in JEJ Altham and R Harrison (eds), *World, Mind, and Ethics: Essays on the Ethical Philosophy of Bernard Williams* (Cambridge, Cambridge University Press, 1995).
Miam, E, 'The Curious Case of Exclusionary Reasons' (2002) 15 *Canadian Journal of Law and Jurisprudence* 99.
Michelon Jr., C, *Aceitação e objetividade: uma comparação entre as teses de Hart e do positivismo precedente sobre a linguagem e o conhecimento do direito* (São Paulo, Revista dos Tribunais, 2004).
Moran, R, 'Williams, History, and "the Impurity of Philosophy"' (2016) 24(2) *European Journal of Philosophy* 315.
Murata, DP, 'Obligations Beyond Morality: A Critique of Ronald Dworkin's View on Legal Normativity' (2022) 16(2) *Revista Direito Mackenzie* 1.
—— 'Natural Law Archimedianism' (2024) 15(4) *Jurisprudence* 573.
—— 'There are Many Senses to an Emotion – Loss of Power, Diminishment and the Internalised Other' (2024) 43 *Topoi* 435.
—— 'What Does it Take to be Oneself?' [2024] *Res Publica* (DOI: 10.1007/s11158-024-09700-z).
—— 'Justification, Coercion and Political Responsibility: Remarks on Ethical Environmentalism' (2025) 16(2) *Jurisprudence* 352.
Murphy, L, 'The Political Question of the Concept of Law' in J Coleman (ed), *Hart's Postscript: Essays on the Postscript to "The Concept of Law"* (Oxford, Oxford University Press, 2001).
Nagel, T, 'Williams: The Value of Truth' in T Nagel, *Secular Philosophy and the Religious Temperament* (Oxford, Oxford University Press, 2010).
Orrego, C, 'Joseph Raz's Service Conception of Authority and Natural Law Theory' (2005) 50 *American Journal of Jurisprudence* 317.
Patterson, D, 'Explicating the Internal Point of View' (1999) 52 *Southern Methodist University Law Review* 67.
Pavlakos, G, and Bertea, S, 'Introduction' in S Bertea and G Pavlakos (eds), *New Essays on the Normativity of Law* (Oxford, Hart Publishing, 2011).
Perry, S, 'Interpretation and Methodology in Legal Theory' in A Marmor (ed), *Law and Interpretation* (Oxford, Clarendon Press, 1995).
—— 'Hart's Methodological Positivism' in J Coleman (ed), *Hart's Postscript: Essays on the pPstscript to 'The Concept of Law'* (Oxford, Oxford University Press, 2001).
—— 'Hart on Social Rules and the Foundations of Law: Liberating the Internal Point of View' (2006) 75 *Fordham Law Review* 1171.
Postema, G, 'Norms, Reasons, and Law' (1998) 51(1) *Current Legal Problems* 149.
—— *A Treatise of Legal Philosophy and General Jurisprudence*, Vol 11 (Dordrecht, Springer, 2011).
Priel, D, 'Legal Norms and Normativity: An Essay in Genealogy, by Sylvie Delacroix' (book review) (2007) 27(4) *Legal Studies* 750.
Radbruch, G, 'Statutory Lawlessness and Supra-Statutory Law' (2006) 26(1) *Oxford Journal of Legal Studies* 1.
Raz, J, *The Morality of Freedom* (Oxford, Clarendon Press, 1986).
—— 'Facing Up: A Reply' (1989) 62 *Southern California Law Review* 1153.
—— *Practical Reason and Norms* (Oxford, Clarendon Press, 1990).

—— 'Authority, Law, and Morality' in J Raz, *Ethics in the Public Domain: Essays in the Morality of Law and Politics* (Oxford, Clarendon Press, 1995).
—— 'The Obligation to Obey: Revision and Tradition' in J Raz, *Ethics in the Public Domain: Essays in the Morality of Law and Politics* (Oxford, Clarendon Press, 1995).
—— *Engaging Reason* (Oxford, Oxford University Press, 1999).
—— 'Agency, Reason, and the Good' in J Raz, *Engaging Reason* (Oxford, Oxford University Press, 1999).
—— 'When We are Ourselves' in J Raz, *Engaging Reason* (Oxford, Oxford University Press, 1999).
—— 'Kelsen's Theory of the Basic Norm' in J Raz, *The Authority of Law* (Oxford, Oxford University Press, 2009).
—— 'Respect for Law' in J Raz, *The Authority of Law* (Oxford, Oxford University Press, 2009).
—— 'The Claims of Law' in J Raz, *The Authority of Law* (Oxford, Oxford University Press, 2009).
—— 'The Institutional Nature of Law' in J Raz, *The Authority of Law* (Oxford, Oxford University Press, 2009).
—— 'The Obligation to Obey the Law' in J Raz, *The Authority of Law* (Oxford, Oxford University Press, 2009).
—— 'The Problem of Authority: Revisiting the Service Conception' in J Raz, *Between Authority and Interpretation – On the Theory of Law and Practical Reason* (Oxford, Oxford University Press, 2009).
Rodriguez-Blanco, V, 'The Moral Puzzle of Legitimate Authority' in S Bertea and G Pavlakos (eds), *New Essays on the Normativity of Law* (Oxford, Hart Publishing, 2011).
—— *Law and Authority under the Guise of the Good* (Oxford, Hart Publishing, 2014).
—— 'Action in Law's Empire: Judging in the Deliberative Mode' (2016) 29(2) *Canadian Journal of Law & Jurisprudence* 431.
—— 'Tracing Finnis's criticism of Hart's Internal Point of View: Instability and the 'Point' of Human Action in Law' in T Spaak and P Mindus (eds), *The Cambridge Companion to Legal Positivism* (Cambridge, Cambridge University Press, 2021).
Schauer, F, 'Positivism as Pariah' in R George (ed), *The Autonomy of Law* (Oxford, Clarendon Press, 1999).
—— 'The Social Construction of the Concept of Law: A Reply to Julie Dickson' (2005) 25(3) *Oxford Journal of Legal Studies* 493.
Shapiro, SJ, 'What Is the Internal Point of View' (2006) 75 *Fordham Law Review* 1157.
—— *Legality* (Cambridge, Harvard University Press, 2011).
Shiner, R, 'Exclusionary Reasons and the Explanation of Behaviour' (1992) 5(1) *Ratio Juris* 1.
Smyth, N, 'Integration and Authority: Rescuing the 'One Thought Too Many' Problem' (2018) 48(6) *Canadian Journal of Philosophy* 812.
Sophocles, 'Aias' in Sophocles, *The Complete Plays of Sophocles – A New Translation*, trans Robert Bagg and James Scully (London, Harper Perennial, 2011).
—— 'Antigone' in Sophocles, *The Complete Plays of Sophocles – A New Translation*, trans Robert Bagg and James Scully (London, Harper Perennial, 2011).
—— 'Women of Trakhis' in Sophocles, *The Complete Plays of Sophocles – A New Translation*, trans Robert Bagg and James Scully (London, Harper Perennial, 2011).
Strawson, PF, *Freedom and Resentment and Other Essays* (London, Routledge, 2008).
Teichmann, R, 'How Should one Live? Williams on Practical Deliberation and Reasons for Acting' in SG Chappell and MV Ackeren (eds), *Ethics Beyond the Limits* (London, Routledge, 2018).
Tollefsen, C, 'Natural Law, Basic Goods and Practical Reason' in G Duke and RP George (eds), *The Cambridge Companion to Natural Law Jurisprudence* (Cambridge, Cambridge University Press, 2017).
Velleman, JD, 'The Possibility of Practical Reason' (1996) 106(4) *Ethics* 694.
—— 'Love as a Moral Emotion' (1999) 109(2) *Ethics* 338.
—— *The Possibility of Practical Reason*, 2nd edn (Michigan, Michigan Publishing, 2014).
Waldron, J, 'Normative (or Ethical) Positivism' in J Coleman (ed), *Hart's Postscript: Essays on the Postscript to 'The Concept of Law'* (Oxford, Oxford University Press, 2001).

Watson, G, 'Free Agency' in G Watson, *Agency and Answerability – Selected Essays* (Oxford, Oxford University Press, 2004).
Williams, B, 'A Critique of Utilitarianism' in JCC Smart and B Williams, *Utilitarianism – For and Against* (Cambridge, Cambridge University Press, 1973).
—— *Moral Luck* (Cambridge, Cambridge University Press, 1981).
—— 'Internal and External Reasons' in B Williams, *Moral Luck* (Cambridge, Cambridge University Press, 1981).
—— 'Practical Necessity' in B Williams, *Moral Luck* (Cambridge, Cambridge University Press, 1981).
—— 'Persons, Character and Morality' in B Williams, *Moral Luck* (Cambridge, Cambridge University Press, 1981).
—— 'Preface' in B Williams, *Moral Luck* (Cambridge, Cambridge University Press, 1981).
—— 'The Truth in Relativism' in B Williams, *Moral Luck* (Cambridge, Cambridge University Press, 1981).
—— *Morality – An Introduction to Ethics* (Cambridge, Cambridge University Press, 1993).
—— *Shame and Necessity* (Los Angeles, University of California Press, 1993).
—— 'Formal and Substantial Individualism' in B Williams, *Making Sense of Humanity* (Cambridge, Cambridge University Press, 1995).
—— 'Internal Reasons and the Obscurity of Blame' in B Williams, *Making Sense of Humanity* (Cambridge, Cambridge University Press, 1995).
—— 'Formal and Substantial Individualism' in B Williams, *Making Sense of Humanity* (Cambridge, Cambridge University Press, 1995).
—— 'Moral Incapacity' in B Williams, *Making Sense of Humanity* (Cambridge, Cambridge University Press, 1995).
—— 'Saint Just's Illusion' in B Williams, *Making Sense of Humanity* (Cambridge, Cambridge University Press, 1995).
—— 'Replies' in JEJ Altham and R Harrison (eds), *World, Mind, and Ethics: Essays on the Ethical Philosophy of Bernard Williams* (Cambridge, Cambridge University Press, 1995).
—— 'Truth in Ethics' (1995) 8(3) *Ratio* 227.
—— 'Postscript: Some Further Notes on Internal and External Reasons' in E Millgram (ed), *Varieties of Practical Reasoning* (Cambridge, MIT Press, 2001).
—— *Truth and Truthfulness* (Princeton, Princeton University Press, 2002).
—— *In the Beginning was the Deed* (G. Hawthorn ed, Princeton, Princeton University Press, 2005).
—— 'From Freedom to Liberty: The Construction of a Political Value' in B Williams, *In the Beginning was the Deed* (G Hawthorn ed, Princeton, Princeton University Press, 2005).
—— 'In the Beginning was the Deed' in B Williams, *In the Beginning was the Deed* (G Hawthorn ed, Princeton, Princeton University Press, 2005).
—— 'Realism and Moralism in Political Theory' in B Williams, *In the Beginning was the Deed* (G Hawthorn ed, Princeton, Princeton University Press, 2005).
—— *Philosophy as a Humanistic Discipline* (AW Moore ed, Princeton, Princeton University Press, 2006).
—— 'Identity and Identities' in B Williams, *Philosophy as a Humanistic Discipline* (AW Moore ed, Princeton, Princeton University Press, 2006).
—— 'Philosophy as a Humanistic Discipline' in B Williams, *Philosophy as a Humanistic Discipline* (AW Moore ed, Princeton, Princeton University Press, 2006).
—— 'Political Philosophy and the Analytical Tradition' in B Williams, *Philosophy as a Humanistic Discipline* (AW Moore ed, Princeton, Princeton University Press, 2006).
—— 'The Human Prejudice' in B Williams, *Philosophy as a Humanistic Discipline* (AW Moore ed, Princeton, Princeton University Press, 2006).
—— 'Values, Reasons, and the Theory of Persuasion' in B Williams, *Philosophy as a Humanistic Discipline* (AW Moore ed, Princeton, Princeton University Press, 2006).
—— 'What Might Philosophy Become' in B Williams, *Philosophy as a Humanistic Discipline* (AW Moore ed, Princeton, Princeton University Press, 2006).
—— *Ethics and the Limits of Philosophy* (London, Routledge, 2011).

—— *Essays and Reviews 1959-2002* (Princeton, Princeton University Press, 2014).
—— 'The Last Word, by Thomas Nagel' in B Williams, *Essays and Reviews 1959-2002* (Foreword by Michael Wood, Princeton, Princeton University Press, 2014).
—— 'The Moral View of Politics' in B Williams, *Essays and Reviews 1959-2002* (Foreword by Michael Wood, Princeton, Princeton University Press, 2014).
—— 'Why Philosophy needs History' in B Williams, *Essays and Reviews 1959-2002* (Foreword by Michael Wood, Princeton, Princeton University Press, 2014).
Wilson, C, 'Moral Authority and the Limits of Philosophy' in SG Chappell and MV Ackeren (eds), *Ethics Beyond the Limits* (London, Routledge, 2018).
Wittgenstein, L, *Philosophical Investigations*, 4th edn (PMS Hacker and J Schulte eds, London, Willey-Blackwell, 2009).
Wolf, S, 'Moral Saints' (1982) 79(8) *Journal of Philosophy* 419.
Zipursky, B, 'Legal Obligations and the Internal Aspect of Rules' (2006) 75 *Fordham Law Review* 1229.

INDEX

www.ingramcontent.com/pod-product-compliance
Ingram Content Group UK Ltd.
Pitfield, Milton Keynes, MK11 3LW, UK
UKHW020818290926
15470UKWH00003B/1228

9 781509 968855